11/9/12

LISTENING IN

THE SECRET WHITE HOUSE
RECORDINGS OF
JOHN F. KENNEDY

JOHN F. KENNEDY LIBRARY FOUNDATION

SELECTED AND INTRODUCED BY
TED WIDMER

FOREWORD BY
CAROLINE KENNEDY

HYPERION
NEW YORK

OPENING PAGE PHOTOGRAPH: **PRESIDENT KENNEDY SPEAKS INTO HIS DICTAPHONE IN THE OVAL OFFICE, FEBRUARY 12, 1962**

FRONTISPIECE: **PRESIDENT KENNEDY ADDRESSES AMVETS CONVENTION BY PHONE, AUGUST 23, 1962**

The transcripts of conversations contained in this publication represent a best guess at words spoken, and are not meant to be authoritative. The official document is the recording itself. Though sound quality has been enhanced, most of the imperfections have been allowed to stand. In order to make this book as comprehensible for the reader as possible, and in the style of other published oral histories, we have deleted some interjections and broken phrases where they interrupted the flow of the conversation, but only where such changes would not alter the meaning.

CDs edited and sequenced by Tony Goddess at Bang a Song Studios in Gloucester, Massachusetts.

The photographic credits beginning on page 293 constitute an extension of this copyright page.

Library of Congress Cataloging-in-Publication Data
Listening in : the secret White House recordings of John F. Kennedy / Kennedy Library Foundation ; selected and introduced by Ted Widmer ; foreword by Caroline Kennedy. — 1st ed.
    p. cm.
    Includes index.
    ISBN 978-1-4013-2456-8
1. Kennedy, John F. (John Fitzgerald), 1917–1963—Archives. 2. United States—Politics and government—1961–1963—Sources. I. Widmer, Edward L. II. John F. Kennedy Library Foundation.
    E841.L57 2012
    973.922092—dc23
          2012014803

Hyperion books are available for special promotions and premiums. For details contact the HarperCollins Special Markets Department in the New York office at 212-207-7528, fax 212-207-7222, or email spsales@harpercollins.com.

BOOK DESIGN BY SHUBHANI SARKAR

First Edition

10   9   8   7   6   5   4   3   2   1

To explore more about the presidency of John F. Kennedy, go to www.jfklibrary.org

MONDAY, OCTOBER 22, 1962   Page 2

4:03 - 4:45 pm
      Hon. A. Milton Obote
         Prime Minister of Uganda
      Hon. James Simpson
         Minister of Economics of Uganda
      Hon. Grace Ibingira
         Minister of Justice of Uganda
      Hon. Apolo Kironde
         Uganda's Representative-designate to the United Nations
      Mr. John Kakonge
         Secretary General, Uganda People's Congress

      Hon. G. Mennen Williams
      Hon. A. G. Matthews
      Hon. Edmond Hutchinson, AID

4:45 - 5:30 pm
      CABINET MEETING
         The President
         The Vice President
         Hon. Dean Rusk
         Hon. Henry Fowler
         Hon. Robert McNamara
         Hon. Robert Kennedy
         Hon. J. Edward Day
         Hon. Stewart Udall
         Hon. Edward Gudeman
         Hon. W. Willard Wirtz
         Hon. Anthony Celebrezze
         Hon. Orville Freeman
         Hon. T. C. Sorensen
         Hon. Jerome Wiesner
         Hon. David Bell
         Hon. Walter Heller

5:30 - 6:30 pm
      BIPARTISAN LEGISLATIVE LEADERS MEETING
         The President
         The Vice President   Speaker John McCormack
         Sen. Hubert Humphrey   Cong. Carl Albert
         Sen. Richard B. Russell   Cong. Charles A. Halleck
         Sen. J. W. Fulbright   Cong. Carl Vinson
         Sen. Bourke Hickenlooper   Cong. Thomas Morgan
         Sen. Everett M. Dirksen   Cong. Leslie C. Arends
         Sen. Leverett Saltonstall Cong. Robert B. Chiperfie
         Senator Alexander Wiley   Cong. Hale Boggs
         Senator George Smathers
         Senator Thomas Kuchel

MONDAY, JUNE 10, 1963

8:50 am   The President arrived at Andrews Air Force Base
                        following his flight from Honolulu, Hawaii.

9:15 am   Arrived at the White House and went to the Mansion.

9:50 am   The President arrived in the office.

10:20 am   The President departed the White House and motored
                        to American University.

10:25 am   Arrived at American University.   The President
                        was greeted by Dr. Hurst R. Anderson, President of
                        American University.

                        COMMENCEMENT EXERCISES AT AMERICAN
                        UNIVERSITY.
                                                            Policy
10:31 - 10:52 am   ADDRESS BY THE PRESIDENT - Major Foreign/Speech,
                        at the Commencement Exercises of American University.

11:00 am   The President was awarded an honorary degree -
                        Doctor of Civil Laws.

11:10 am   The President departed American University and
                        motored to the White House.

11:20 am   Arrived at the White House and went to the Mansion.

11:40 am   To the office.

11:45 - 11:58 am   SIGNING OF S. 1409 - EQUAL PAY ACT. The following
                        attended the ceremony:
                            The Vice President
                            Senator Hubert Humphrey
                            Senator Lister Hill
                            Senator Wayne Morse
                            Senator Jennings Randolph
                            Senator Winston L. Prouty
                            Senator Maurine Neuberger

(continued on next page)

NOVEMBER 10, 1963 - SUNDAY

ATOKA, VIRGINIA

9:58 am   The President and Mrs. Kennedy left their
                 residence and motored to St. Stephens Martyr
                 Church.

10:00 - 10:50 am MASS at St. Stephens Martyr Church.

10:58 am   Arrived back at the residence.

MONDAY, NOVEMBER 11, 1963   - VETERANS DAY

9:27 am   The President, Caroline and John, Jr., departed
                 the residence by helicopter and flew to the White House.

WASHINGTON, D. C.

9:50 am   Arrived at the White House.

10:52 am   The President and John, Jr., departed the White House
                 and motored to Arlington National Cemetery. They were
                 accompanied by
                      General David M. Shoup
                           Commandant of the Marine Corps
                      Hon. John S. Gleason, Jr.
                           Administrator Veterans Affairs

11:00 am   Arrived at Arlington National Cemetery. The President
                 was greeted by
                      Major General Philip C. Wehle
                           Commanding General, Military District of
                           Washington
                      Mr. John C. Metzler
                           Superintendent of Arlington National Cemetery
                      Mr. Luther Skaggs, Jr.
                           President, Congressional Medal of Honor Winners

                 The President, Mr. Luther Skaggs, Jr., Hon. John S.
                 Gleason and General David M. Shoup walked to the amphi-
                 theater and attended the Veterans Day Ceremony.

CONTENTS

————

ONE

————

HISTORY

POLITICS

CIVIL RIGHTS

FOUR

CUBA

FIVE

THE BOMB

SIX

SPACE

THE BURDEN AND THE GLORY

FOREWORD

BY CAROLINE KENNEDY

All my life people have told me that President Kennedy changed their lives—
they decided to join the Peace Corps, run for office, volunteer in the inner city
or outer space because he asked them to—and convinced them that they could
make a difference.

The generation he inspired changed this country—they fought for Civil
Rights, women's rights, human rights, and nuclear disarmament. They passed
that inspiration down to us—their children and grandchildren. As the first
truly modern president, my father redefined America's timeless values for a
global audience, and asked each individual to take responsibility for making
this a more just and peaceful world.

As we mark the fiftieth anniversary of his presidency, my father's time is
becoming part of history rather than living memory. Yet President Kennedy's
words, his example and his spirit, remain as vital as ever. At a time when young
people are often disillusioned with politics, we need to reach across the generations and recommit ourselves and our country to these ideals.

During times of uncertainty like the present, the future appears threatening
and the challenges to our nation can seem almost insurmountable. Yet history
reminds us that America has faced difficult and dangerous times before—and
that we have triumphed over them.

Listening to these tapes now is a fascinating experience because historical
perspective informs our understanding of events that were unfolding in real
time for the participants. Moreover, many of the issues that defined that tumul-
tuous time—racial justice, economic fairness, and foreign intervention—continue to dominate our national debate today. Studying a legacy of strength in
the face of conflict and examining the leadership of past administrations, we
can identify warning signs, critical turning points, and guiding principles that
can help us deal with current crises.

I was always told that my father installed secret Oval Office recording devices after the Bay of Pigs disaster so that he could have an accurate account of

who said what, in case of any later disputes as to the exact nature of the conversations. And as an avid reader of history, and a Pulitzer Prize–winning author, he intended to draw upon this material in his memoirs. The full 265 and a half hours of tape-recorded conversations that have now been made available by the Kennedy Presidential Library in Boston provide insight into the magnitude, the complexity, and the range of issues confronting a president on a daily basis. They also give a sense of the human side of the presidency—the exhilaration, the frustration, and the sense of purpose that were part of my father's commitment to public service.

The unedited conversations are fascinating but somewhat difficult to decipher and navigate. The sound quality is often poor, and at times it is hard to figure out who is talking. Our family and the Kennedy Library are committed to making the record of my father's presidency widely accessible, so we decided to compile significant excerpts and make them easily available to the public.

We are fortunate to have Ted Widmer as our editor and guide through this material. A historian with a comprehensive knowledge of the historical and the modern presidency, Ted also served as a speechwriter to President Clinton, edited the Library of America's two-volume anthology of American speeches, and has written numerous books and articles on American history. We wanted this collection to include the most significant moments caught on tape, as well as snippets of conversation that give insight into the President's mind at work and the human qualities that made him who he was: serious, purposeful, curious, skeptical, impatient, probing, principled, amused. Ted has done a masterful job of listening, transcribing, selecting, and illuminating this audio record.

As always, I am deeply grateful to the archivists and staff of the John F. Kennedy Presidential Library and Museum and the entire National Archives, who preserve, catalogue, archive, and study the documents, tapes, films, memorabilia, and ephemera that form the stuff of history. Their dedication and their commitment to excellence is something all Americans should find inspiring.

For me, listening to these conversations is a powerful experience. Although at the time, I was too young to understand much of what was happening, I recall spending happy afternoons eating candy and making paper-clip necklaces under my father's desk while men talked in serious voices. The delight in my father's voice when my brother and I appear is something I treasure.

CAROLINE HIDING UNDER THE HMS *RESOLUTE* DESK
IN THE OVAL OFFICE, MAY 16, 1962

I especially hope young listeners will find these selections interesting enough that they will want to further study the Kennedy presidency, and I trust that those who remember these times will gain new perspective. I hope that people will be drawn into the drama and the daily routine of the presidency, that they will feel they have learned something about the kind of person my father was, and most of all, I hope they will be inspired to serve our country as he did.

INTRODUCTION

BY TED WIDMER

"Mythology distracts us everywhere," John F. Kennedy said on June 11, 1962, in a speech at Yale University. Kennedy had spent a good deal of his life debunking the mythologies he encountered. As a senator, he gave important speeches questioning the binary logic of the Cold War in remote theaters like Vietnam and Algeria. As a historian, he was attracted to the lonely few inside Washington's political establishment who possessed the courage to think for themselves. Fresh out of college, he struck closer to home by criticizing the pacifistic idealism of the British leaders who failed to prepare their nation for war in the 1930s. That latter stand included an implicit rebuke of his father, Joseph P. Kennedy, which seems not to have fazed their relationship in the slightest.

A month after the Yale speech, he struck back at mythology yet again. To avoid inaccuracy and possibly worse, Kennedy was determined to have a reliable record of the words that were spoken in the White House. And so in July 1962, Secret Service agents installed a sophisticated taping system in the Oval Office and Cabinet Room of the White House. The reasons for the installation were never explained, by Kennedy or anyone else; in fact, the very existence of the taping system was a closely held secret, communicated to a tiny number of people. The President's secretary, Evelyn Lincoln, knew; her assistance was required to operate the system and maintain the tapes. Robert Kennedy probably knew; it is difficult to believe that he did not, and he used the tapes a few years later to write his memoir of the Cuban Missile Crisis, *Thirteen Days*. But we simply do not know for sure.

The result, however, is not a mystery at all. It is a fact of the highest significance. A vast amount of information was gathered by those recording devices—248 hours of meetings in the Oval Office and Cabinet Room, and 17 and a half hours of telephone conversations and dictated private reflections. They constitute a historical trove of extraordinary consequence. They shed insight into all of the policy decisions of the Kennedy administration, as they were arbitrated at the highest level. And they offer a precious insight into something elusive—how a presidency actually *works*. Minute by minute, we get a sense of what it feels like to occupy the most important office in the world—and likely the loneliest. Earlier presidents had dabbled in taping—Kennedy's three predecessors, Franklin D. Roosevelt, Harry Truman, and Dwight D. Eisenhower, had all put a few meetings on tape. But Kennedy's new initiative was on a vastly different scale.

The agent who installed the taping system, Robert Bouck, recorded an oral history in 1977 that shed some light on the devices, although his memories had already become somewhat hazy. Bouck's responsibilities included the protection of the President from electronic surveillance, so he was a logical person to ask to improvise a new recording system for the private use of the President himself. Accordingly, he placed a microphone in the kneehole of the famous HMS *Resolute* desk and another, disguised, on the coffee table between the two sofas where the President sometimes sat with visitors. Kennedy could activate the device with a push button under his desk. According to Bouck, "It looked just like a button you'd press to signal your secretary—like a buzzer button." Kennedy also had a button on the coffee table, near the chairs where he would sit for more relaxed conversation.

In the Cabinet Room, the microphones were in two spots on the wall where there had once been light fixtures, now covered by draperies. By his place at the table, President Kennedy had another switch to activate recording. The microphones were fed into a Tandberg reel-to-reel tape recorder, whirring in a basement room used by Evelyn Lincoln for storage. Bouck would change the tapes as needed. He believed that Evelyn Lincoln also had the capacity to initiate recording, but he could not remember with certainty. Not long after the installation of the system, Kennedy significantly expanded the operation by creating a separate system that would record his telephone calls. These calls, recorded on Dictaphone belts (also called Dictation Belts or Dictabelts) add real meaning to the record and are generally recorded with higher sound quality. The telephone and Dictabelt recording devices were installed separately, and there is no record of why they were set up. Bouck believed that the President also was able to record inside his private living quarters, but that fact has never been established with authority, and the existing tapes do not corroborate it.

Unfortunately, Bouck was relatively mute on a key question—*why* did President Kennedy suddenly want a record of his conversations in July 1962? Tentatively, Bouck essayed an answer—that "the tensions with the Russians were kind of great during that period, and I think initially his concern was to record understandings that might have been had in those relations." There are grounds for this theory—during the Bay of Pigs episode of April 1961, Kennedy received a great deal of inaccurate information from the planners of the operation, including the CIA and the Joint Chiefs, and it would certainly have been useful for him in the future to have these bland predictions of success on record. During an interview she gave to *Newsweek* in 1982, Evelyn Lincoln speculated that the Bay of Pigs was the reason for the tapes.

But it is hard to explain why Kennedy would have let a year go by before installing the new system. Why not launch the tapes in the summer of 1961? Why, suddenly in July 1962, did the Oval Office turn into a secret recording studio? The solution to that mystery may be irretrievable. Certainly there was a high degree of enthusiasm for recording technology in those years; it was a rare magazine that did not include an advertisement for the latest in stereo equipment, and Tandberg, a Norwegian brand, was well known to audiophiles. It may mean something that on July 23, 1962, the new communications satellite, Telstar 1, beamed its first live television signal across the Atlantic Ocean. The world was quickly becoming wired, and everyone was listening in.

The Bay of Pigs also taught the Kennedy administration that White House communications were inherently balky, and in its immediate aftermath, McGeorge Bundy modernized the West Wing by bringing the latest technological wizardry into the brand-new Situation Room. In that time of expanding capacity, it may have made sense to add audiotapes to the President's arsenal of information. And to use great discretion, since so many others were interested in his conversations. That he asked agents of the Secret Service to carry out the installation suggests that President Kennedy wanted to maintain tight personal control over the tapes. There were certainly military aides available to install recording devices—but that would have exposed the plan to a wider audience. This was a small operation by design.

Surely there were political as well as military reasons for wanting to capture conversations on tape. During the various crises of the Civil Rights Movement, President Kennedy walked a difficult tightrope with the governors of Southern states—Alabama and Mississippi in particular—as they all tried to negotiate face-saving ways to defuse the tensions. In the midst of these highly charged conversations, it would have brought a negotiating edge to reveal to the governors— as Robert Kennedy apparently did—that their private promises to work with the federal government were now an irrevocable part of the record. To have their personal expressions of goodwill exposed would have hurt them at home—which is another way of saying, as Kennedy did to the mayor of Jackson, Mississippi, "I give you full permission to denounce me in public, as long as you don't in private!"

Furthermore, it may have occurred to President Kennedy, an omnivorous consumer of intelligence, that leaving the tapes rolling was an interesting way to hear the conversation when he left the room. There is no evidence that he did this—in fact, Evelyn Lincoln later expressed her opinion that he never listened to any of the tapes at all. But a revealing moment in the middle of the Cuban Missile Crisis occurs when Kennedy leaves and his most shrill critic, Air Force General Curtis LeMay, complains about his leadership. Though it is unlikely Kennedy heard these remarks, definitely *not* intended for the ears of the President, it is fascinating to be able to hear them today, and comforting to know that none of LeMay's reckless suggestions for invading Cuba and launching a nuclear war were heeded. In one of the last tapes declassified, in January 2012, Defense Secretary McNamara reveals to the President that one of his naval commanders was insubordinate at the height of the crisis and wanted to sink a Soviet vessel against his strict orders. If anything, these recordings make the Missile Crisis even more terrifying.

A final reason that Kennedy may have recorded his meetings and calls is simply that he respected the verdict of history and recognized his obligation to record conversations of great consequence for future generations. Mrs. Lincoln voiced her support for this explanation as well, and it makes intuitive sense, judging from his tendency to turn on the machines during important meetings (and not just confrontations with potential adversaries).

It has been a problem since the dawn of the presidency—how do we capture the words and thoughts of the individuals to whom we give so much power? Do they not have a certain obligation to report back to us? The first president, George Washington, kept a diary—a highly imperfect diary, with relatively little of interest and episodic entries. (The first entry, recorded five months after he took office, was "Exercised in my Carriage in the forenoon.") Still, he kept it. And how impoverished our understanding of Lincoln would be without the detailed personal observations written by his secretaries, Nicolay and Hay. But for the most part, we have not known what presidents were saying behind closed doors. For the first 150 years of the United States, there is almost nothing on this subject, though presidents were presumably speaking volubly. We have their letters and their official pronouncements, but not the stuff of daily life. It is a significant loss.

Like Woodrow Wilson and Theodore Roosevelt, John F. Kennedy was himself a historian (his book of senatorial portraits, *Profiles in Courage*, won a Pulitzer for biography in 1957). And personal history must have been on his mind as well. Dating back nearly to the dawn of the presidency, presidents have been expected to write memoirs. In 1821, at the age of seventy-seven, Thomas Jefferson began to write out "some recollection of dates and facts concerning myself," although he stopped before his election in 1800. Lincoln wrote an abbreviated recollection of his life for a campaign sketch in 1860. Grant famously wrote the first presidential memoir that sold well—though he, too, ignored his presidency (for reasons that were all too easy to understand). In 1913, Theodore Roosevelt wrote an account that included the White House years, thereby obligating nearly all of his successors to do the same and launching an armada of autobiographies that may have undone some of his environmental legacy, by wiping out a forest or two. But with most of these laboriously written efforts, there is the feeling of a monument being chiseled.

The Kennedy tapes are different—this is a president being president. There is no chisel in sight; he simply thinks, and talks, and argues, in the heat of the moment. And he reflects on himself, from time to time, almost as if this were a memoir in spoken form—an audiobook before the concept was invented. On a small number of important occasions, he speaks directly into a Dictaphone to record his impressions of a historic day—the first day of the Cuban Missile Crisis, or the day that he hears that South Vietnam's president, Ngo Dinh Diem, has been killed.

After so many words have been written about John F. Kennedy, it feels right to let him speak for himself. This is the closest to an autobiography we will ever get. Kennedy often mentioned his forthcoming memoir in jocular comments, usually at his own expense, on days when things were not going well (he speculated, all too prophetically, that this book might be titled: *Kennedy: The Only Years*). Two of the recordings in this collection predate the presidency and reveal that in early 1960, just after declaring his candidacy, Kennedy was already thinking deeply about the story of his life and the unlikely journey that had brought him so far, so fast. These two recorded documents seem to constitute a first draft of sorts toward a book that was regrettably never written.

Immediately after the assassination, Bouck dismantled the system, and from there, the tapes went on a long journey into warehouses and federal storage facilities before the opening of the Kennedy Presidential Library in 1979. It is impossible to know exactly what happened to them in these years, or if any disappeared. Some recordings found their way into private possession, but over the years many have been tracked down and reunited with the collection.

The existence of the tapes was first revealed in the summer of 1973. Sensationally, the Watergate hearings elicited a remark on July 16 from a Nixon aide, Alexander Butterfield, who told Congress that the president's meetings were routinely recorded. That had immense ramifications for the hearings and Richard Nixon's rapidly plummeting fortunes. But it also resonated with the community of presidential libraries, and that same summer, the Kennedy Library director stepped forward and announced that it, too, had presidential recordings. In fact, we now know that taping was common in the modern presidency. Nearly every president from Franklin D. Roosevelt to Ronald Reagan taped meetings at one point or another.[1] Franklin D. Roosevelt had experimented in the summer of 1940 with a recording system installed by sound engineers from RCA. One microphone was placed in a lamp on the president's desk and another in his telephone, but FDR's interest waned after 1940, and only fifteen hours of tape have survived. Harry Truman briefly experimented with the system, then ordered it dismantled. There are nine and a half hours of his recordings extant, of low sound quality. Dwight D. Eisenhower showed slightly more interest, and records suggest that he made recordings on approximately two dozen occasions, but what survives is of modest importance.

What began in 1962 was a commitment to taping on a very different order. For both quantity and quality, the Kennedy tapes signaled a quantum leap

---

1. Jimmy Carter was the lone exception. After Kennedy, Lyndon Johnson escalated taping even further, recording as many as 9,300 telephone calls and 200 hours of meetings. Following Nixon's resignation, there was a notable reluctance to record. Gerald Ford barely taped anything, and Jimmy Carter nothing at all. Ronald Reagan increased the use of videotaping, and videotaped small segments of meetings, but nothing on the order of Kennedy, Johnson, and Nixon.

PRESIDENT KENNEDY ON THE TELEPHONE DURING A CAMPAIGN STOP IN MCKEESPORT, PENNSYLVANIA, OCTOBER 13, 1962

forward. But if the tapes are part of a long continuum they still came as a shock to Kennedy intimates. Ted Sorensen, the President's speechwriter and one of his closest aides, claimed to be "dumbfounded." Other top staffers—McGeorge Bundy, Robert McNamara, and Arthur Schlesinger, Jr.—confessed that they had no idea. The President's brother, Edward M. Kennedy, did not know at the time. The tapes fit into no known category of presidential information—they were not official documents, they were not classic JFK speeches, and they were not press conference transcripts. They were not rehearsed or prepared for the public in any way. They were simply the raw material of history—and specifically, the hard and not always glamorous work of leading an enormous federal bureaucracy. It can be easy to forget that this unusually photogenic President actually had a day job, and that he spent most of his time in meetings, advancing his domestic and foreign agenda, calming down senators and congressmen, twisting arms here and there, and considering tactics with his hardworking staff. They are the supporting actors in this drama. For every split-second photo op, there were hours and hours of these meetings, driving the business of the nation forward. These were long meetings, in which every point of view was exhausted, and most of the participants as well—but they were effective at lighting a fire when it needed to be lit. The Oval Office is an important ceremonial space, but it is also the boiler room of the ship of state.

What to do with the tapes was a mystery at first. Initially, they were considered the private property of the Kennedy family. But over time, a consensus grew that these irreplaceable sources of information belonged in the public record. The Kennedy family gave the tapes to the National Archives in 1976. Beginning in 1983, the Kennedy Presidential Library began releasing the tapes to the historical community. The process was slow and clunky at first, for many reasons—bits of conversations were made available on cassette audiotapes, and transcripts made, to the best of the ability of librarians. Early releases focused on topical themes like the Civil Rights Movement, and were targeted at relatively small audiences of scholars.

But now we can do vastly better, and this book is designed to celebrate that fact. By the time it is published, the Kennedy Presidential Library will have completed a heroic task, by not only releasing the tapes but putting many of them online in a form that is easily streamed and audible anywhere there is an Internet connection. This is the first publication to draw from the entirety of the tapes. In January 2012 the final forty-five hours of tapes were released, taking the story to the third week of November 1963, and not the first week as previously believed. In effect, the audio archive is now complete.[2]

Of course, nothing fifty years old is perfect, and these tapes are no exception. The sound quality varies widely. Extraordinarily, the most powerful office on earth—an office that could launch a nuclear-tipped intercontinental ballistic missile—encountered some difficulty in recording the human voice. In Evelyn Lincoln's memoir, she recounts an amusing anecdote in which she and President Kennedy tried to install a "squawk box" for interoffice communication but realized that they had no idea how to work it. With the tapes, they fared better, but the results were unpredictable. The sound quality has been notably improved for this publication, but still, there are hisses and crackles and pops. People speak over one another. A voice near a microphone will sound much louder than one farther away. Sometimes the sound drops out for no clear reason, or becomes much too loud. Even the rustling of papers can be deafening. Many of the Dictabelt recordings have skips. These noises offer some verisimilitude and remind us just how simple the recording system was. At other times the tapes continue to roll long after everyone has left the room, including one lilting moment when I could hear the singing of Christmas carols far off in the distance.

Another imperfection is that it is highly difficult to transcribe all of the words with perfect accuracy. It is a slow and painstaking labor to recapture a conversation, especially when several people are talking at once, from different parts of the room. The transcripts here have attempted to eliminate errors, but it is important for readers to remember that even these transcripts represent a best guess at the words spoken. The National Archives considers the official document the tape itself and not any transcript made from it. In this publication, imperfectly heard words will be placed within brackets, or the word "unclear" will be added.

The organizing principle of this collection has been to offer a wide range of Kennedy's meetings and telephone calls. Needless to say, the major episodes are included, and readers will not be surprised to see selections from the Cuban

---

2. Some excisions remain, for reasons relating to national security or deed of gift. In the former category, these reasons include sensitivity relating to ongoing military situations, intelligence matters, or any of the eight topical areas outlined in Executive Order 13526. Deed closures are determined by donors and are typically related to personal privacy. Both forms of restriction are reviewed to determine if the original reasons still hold.

Missile Crisis and the Civil Rights Movement here, including one brief excerpt from the Missile Crisis that has never before been released. But there are other topics included as well, to show the breadth and depth of the Oval Office conversations, and the vaulting ambition of this presidency, which launched a failed invasion of Cuba, then prevailed in the most dramatic nuclear confrontation in history, then succeeded in seriously limiting the testing of nuclear weapons, all while launching the space program, quickening the economy, nurturing a post–Cold War foreign policy for the developing world, and presiding over a dizzying array of social and technological advancements, the most historic of which was the struggle to give all Americans equal access to their rights.

There is laughter in these conversations, and irritation, and disappointment, and exuberance. In a word, they are human. We perhaps expect our presidents to be something greater than that; but these recordings will remind us, healthily, that real people work in the Oval Office. Some of the most evocative phone calls reveal the special relationship that exists between members of the tiny club of fellow presidents. Kennedy and Eisenhower could not have been more different, but the thirty-fourth president's advice was obviously important to the thirty-fifth, especially at times of immense military peril. During the Cuban Missile Crisis, Eisenhower's support was invaluable and helped Kennedy to calm waters that had become dangerously roiled. Further, they seemed to grow fond of each other. One of their crisis calls ends with Kennedy signing off, "Hold on tight!"

Kennedy once said, "I expect my whole time in office to be filled with dangers and difficulties," and his prophecy was soon fulfilled. The most dangerous moment of all, the Cuban Missile Crisis, lends itself well to an audio approach to history; nearly all of the major meetings were recorded in their entirety, and many phone calls, including Kennedy's relieved calls to Presidents Eisenhower, Truman, and Hoover when it was over. To listen to these meetings and calls is to hear that crisis unfold in real time, in a way that no history book can recapture. Likewise, there is a remarkable drama to the story of the Civil Rights struggle in these years, from the Freedom Rides in the spring of 1961 (before the taping began) to the crises in Mississippi and Alabama in 1962 and 1963 (fully captured in arresting detail). The tapes record complex negotiations with recalcitrant governors and reveal some of Kennedy's exasperation at being pulled down a path that he knows will inflict a punishing political cost, including the possibility of a single term. It was a slow and often frustrating path, for all parties involved, including the liberals who longed for Kennedy to become a great champion of their causes (though they had often failed to support him in the past). But the tapes also record his growing conviction over 1963 that the time was right for a great moral crusade and that he was uniquely fit to lead it. In all of these meetings, the vocal inflections say more than the words do; one can hear Kennedy's insistence that Governor Ross Barnett of Mississippi obey the federal writ, and Barnett's grudging acquiescence. We can hear the anger in the voice of Dr. Martin Luther King, Jr., not far below the beatific surface of "I Have a Dream."

One day in particular—August 28, 1963—shows how many of these topics overlapped in that turbulent time. Shortly after King gave his great address during the March on Washington, the leaders of the Civil Rights Movement were ushered into the Oval Office for an extraordinary strategy session. In that meeting, A. Philip Randolph, the aging head of the Brotherhood of Railway Porters, called on Kennedy to assume the mantle of presidential leadership. That moment is all the more evocative for the knowledge that Randolph was captured on tape in one of the earliest recordings ever made in the Oval Office, way back in 1940, as a young man saying more or less the same thing to Franklin D. Roosevelt. This time, as an old man, his message got through, and the President responded with a long discourse on the political path ahead, and the votes that would need to be rounded up—another way of saying that at long last, the plan was going forward.

About six hours earlier, a long noontime meeting about Vietnam tried to salvage U.S. policy in Southeast Asia, with far-reaching consequences. It can be dizzying to realize the range of issues that were pressing upon the Oval Office with hourly urgency. As protected as the White House may seem, it was never that far away from the street, and I thought, by listening hard, that I could hear the sound of the marchers going down the Mall, demanding civil rights, even as the Vietnam meeting was unfolding. Much of the subsequent history of the 1960s was written inside that room, on that single afternoon.

Of course, not all of the topics discussed have the same epic sweep. I tried for topicality with these selections, but they represent only a tiny percentage of the total recorded output. It may surprise students of other presidencies to realize how deeply JFK delved into policy matters that would seem, at first glance, to be sub-presidential. The meetings cover a wide swath of federal governance, from the deeply domestic concerns of local politicians, to the international

11

events that so clearly absorbed Kennedy, to the distant reaches of outer space. Relentlessly, he grilled his advisors on the effects of policies, their vulnerabilities, and the need for follow-up action. Part of his mind was always occupied with the challenge of getting his expansive agenda through Congress, for there was little point in adopting idealistic positions if they had no chance of succeeding. Many of these meetings record that process, winning over senators one vote at a time. But at the same time, there was constant pressure to think beyond Washington and set in motion the enormous engine of the United States government, at home and around the world. Kennedy must have frustrated the State Department nearly as much as it frustrated him, with long meetings about every corner of the earth, often with foreign ministers and ambassadors of other countries who must have been astonished to be speaking directly to the leader of the free world.

Clearly, he loved the job, and loved it precisely for the chance it gave him to translate thought into action. Kennedy called the presidency "the vital center of action in our whole scheme of government." These conversations reveal a man very much inside that center. "The presidency is the place," he says to his dinner party companions in the tape of January 5, 1960, that appears near the beginning of this book—and then over and over again: "it is the seat of all power," "it is the center of the action," and "it's the President who really functions."

These tapes eminently bear out that theory. His vigor—to borrow an overused word of the era—is palpable. There he is, urging his advisors to work harder and think better, impatient with lazy answers. He drives the meeting forward, tapping his fingers, asking clipped questions, shaving away irrelevancies like a carpenter with a lathe. Or when making a phone call, he speeds up the other speaker with staccato "yeahs," until a terminal "righto" ends the call abruptly. Sometimes, when a slower speaker has the floor (Averell Harriman, for example, or Dean Rusk), one can sense Kennedy's impatience.

When asked, during that same 1960 dinner party, why he would urge a young college student to go into politics, he answers that "it provides an opportunity for him to participate in the solution of the problems which interest him." It was an understated way of saying that politics gave him a chance to answer the great challenges of his time, and perhaps to achieve the Greek definition of happiness which he often quoted—"full use of your powers along lines of excellence in a life affording scope." The stakes were big. So were the rewards, but so too were the difficulties. In an age that has become far more cynical about politics and politicians, there is something encouraging about the zeal with which Kennedy and his staff tried to tackle the problems they encountered.

The Kennedy management style can certainly be criticized for unorthodoxy. He favored restless intellects like his own, and those who would argue with him—as James Webb, the head of NASA, does in one of the meetings. It was well known that he disliked the buttoned-down approach of the Eisenhower White House, with carefully groomed meetings and few disagreements. Bluntly, he said, "Cabinet meetings are simply useless. Why should the postmaster general sit there and listen to a discussion of the problems of Laos?" The result is that these Oval Office bull sessions were all the more important for shaping the course of the New Frontier. And they seem, on the face of the evidence, to have generally shaped it well. Not all of these meetings resulted in favorable outcomes. Vietnam presented Kennedy with an array of possible outcomes, all unattractive, in the fall of 1963, and he was deeply troubled by the violent coup of November 2, as a privately recorded dictation in this collection indicates. Another private reflection, from around November 12, indicates that his support for Civil Rights was already raising alarm bells about his reelection prospects. So there were dark clouds on the horizon. But still, the record, as conveyed by these working conversations, is one of a presidency adapting aggressively to the demands of the times and leading the nation forward, exactly as the 1960 campaign had promised to do.

As a student of the past, Kennedy knew well that presidential reputations are variable and depend on a wide range of factors, many of which are beyond the control of the office. In irritation, he once complained to Arthur Schlesinger, Jr., whose father (Sr.) had pioneered the presidential ranking system we now cannot escape, "How the hell can you tell? Only the President himself can know what his real pressures and his real alternatives are."

Kennedy continues to do very well in those rankings, but for reasons that would probably irritate him, or at least touch upon his finely honed sense of irony. He deplored helpless sentimentality, which is exactly what we bring to the memory of our presidents, and to him in particular. He admired unblinking realism, which is in as short supply now as it was then. Critics will point out that he benefited handsomely from well-managed publicity campaigns throughout his career, and after, with a nostalgia for Camelot that has never lost its power, even a startling half century after the fact. But the creation of these tapes in 1962, and their final release in 2012, has done much to sweep away the sentiment and restore the substance that was at the heart of this presidency.

Mythology exists for a reason; we tell ourselves stories to explain complicated subjects, and the presidency of the United States is nothing if not complicated. But in the final analysis, John F. Kennedy preferred history, because its verdicts emanate from facts. The public has a right to as full an accounting from the past as it does from the politics of the present—the mistakes as well as the successes. Thanks to these recordings, and the completion of the fifty-year process that led to their release, a fuller accounting is now possible. We will never know all of the reasons that President Kennedy established this remarkable repository of recorded information. But we can take solace that he did. I hope that readers enjoy this opportunity to listen to these dialogues, from the innermost chamber of the republic, unfiltered and immediate.

The Yale speech that I began with went to the core of the matter:

> For the great enemy of truth is very often not the lie—deliberate, contrived, and dishonest—but the myth—persistent, persuasive, and unrealistic. Too often we hold fast to the clichés of our forebears. We subject all facts to a prefabricated set of interpretations. We enjoy the comfort of opinion without the discomfort of thought.

Now, thanks to these tapes, readers can move past the myth, and judge the essence of a presidency for themselves.

HISTORY

J ohn F. Kennedy may have been the youngest president elected and a supreme modernist in a modernist age, but he also possessed an acute sense of his nearness to the American past. He invited historians to work and speak in the White House, and unlike most presidents, he formally joined the fraternity by enlisting in the American Historical Association, as Theodore Roosevelt and Woodrow Wilson had before him. He read widely in British and American history and wrote with surprising breadth for a hard-charging politician. *Profiles in Courage* explored the great and not-so-great with an impressive disregard for the big names guaranteed to sell a book in 1957—Lincoln or Jefferson or Washington. Instead, Kennedy chronicled the little known (who ever heard of Edmund Ross?) along with the well known but not especially well liked (Daniel Webster) and, surprisingly, made a best-seller and a Pulitzer out of it all.

But *Profiles* was only one point of entry into history. It is a commonplace to lament that Kennedy did not live a longer life, but what is remarkable is how much he saw and achieved in the time that was allotted to him. He witnessed Germany writhing under the madness of Nazism on the eve of the war and attended the anguished debates in Parliament as England wrestled with the vexing question of how to respond to Hitler. He famously served in a distant Pacific outpost of the global conflict that ensued, and in the spring of 1945, as a cub reporter, he covered the San Francisco conference that launched the United Nations and painted a more hopeful vision of the world to come. A month later, he walked through the ruins of Berlin with the secretary of defense and the supreme commander of the Allied Forces in Europe, Dwight D. Eisenhower. All of this took place before he launched his political career in 1946.

Despite the newness so palpably in the air in the 1960s, history colored all of the great events of the Kennedy presidency. Without a doubt, the centennial of the Civil War gave additional urgency to the Civil Rights Movement and even to the geopolitical situation (Kennedy called the Cold War "a global civil war"). The waste and carnage of World War I were not all that far from memory, and in 1962, Kennedy was so taken by Barbara Tuchman's *The Guns of August* that he ordered it sent to military installations around the country. That book, which explored the question of how self-destructive wars are started, could not have been more appropriate on the eve of the Cuban Missile Crisis. And of course, World War II was the experience that unified everyone in the upper reaches of political life, in the United States as well as abroad.

Inevitably, John F. Kennedy's sense of history seeped into the conversations that he recorded. Two remarkable tapes from early 1960 reveal that he was thinking deeply about the circumstances of his life, from primal forces to small accidents of fate, that were leading him to grasp for the great prize in American politics. One of the tapes records him parrying good-natured questions from a group of friends at a Georgetown dinner party, the other dictating more serious reflections on his life. This may have been the natural instinct of a candidate to set the record straight, or to convey a sense of his origins to the American people—much as Lincoln had issued a short autobiographical sketch when he ran a century earlier. But it seems more likely that Kennedy was contemplating a memoir of some kind, a book (to be written later) that he often mentioned in the White House. These conversations take us closer to that book than one might expect.

On October 3, 1961, Kennedy greeted a group of historians who had issued a set of the papers of John Adams, the first occupant of the White House. Revealingly, he told them, "Some of us think it wise to associate as much as possible with historians and cultivate their good will." Then, with typical irreverence, he added that he liked the approach of Winston Churchill, who predicted that history would treat him gently, "because I intend to write it."

That was tongue-in-cheek, of course; Kennedy admired the skepticism of the historical fraternity he had joined, and knew that he would inevitably be judged by them after leaving office, in ways that were beyond his control. He said as much at Amherst College in October 1963, when he praised those who question power, "for they determine whether we use power or power uses us." Clearly, he wanted to tell his part of the story. The tapes offer a beginning.

RADIO INTERVIEW, ROCHESTER, MINNESOTA, 1940

Kennedy published his first book, *Why England Slept*, in 1940, the year that he graduated from Harvard College. A study of England's failure to increase defense spending in response to the rise of Nazism, it showed a serious grasp of international affairs, and its call on the United States to prepare for war flew in the face of many of the pronouncements of his father, former ambassador Joseph P. Kennedy. Nevertheless, Ambassador Kennedy was instrumental in supporting the book's publication, and a range of influential opinion-shapers praised the new work, including the greatest of them all, Henry R. Luce, the force behind *Time* and *Life*. Exactly one radio interview survives from the media blitz, a recording made from a station in Rochester, Minnesota, featuring a very young author not long out of college.

JFK AT HIS HARVARD GRADUATION, 1940

ANNOUNCER: Good evening, ladies and gentlemen. At this time, we are indeed pleased to have with us in our studios Mr. John F. Kennedy, son of Ambassador and Mrs. Joseph P. Kennedy, who is in our city visiting Dr. and Mrs. Paul O'Leary. Mr. Kennedy is the author of the recently published book, *Why England Slept*. . . .

[break]

This young man from Boston has a clear-headed, realistic, unhysterical message for his countrymen, and for his elders. And with that, we want you, too, of the radio audience, to meet Mr. John F. Kennedy, who is known to his friends as Jack Kennedy. But first, before we get into questions about this much-discussed book, I'd like to ask a few questions about how our guest has spent some of his twenty-three years. Tell me, Mr. Kennedy, where did you go to school?

JFK SIGNING A COPY OF HIS BOOK *WHY ENGLAND SLEPT*
FOR ACTOR SPENCER TRACY, NOVEMBER 1940

JFK: Well, I attended Harvard, I just finished there this June.

ANNOUNCER: And what are you studying at the present time?

JFK: Well, I studied international relations there, and I plan to go on to law school the next three years, and study law at Yale University.

ANNOUNCER: And may I ask what are your plans for the future?

JFK: Well, I don't know exactly yet. I'm interested more or less in working sometime in my life for the government, but I haven't really decided as yet.

KENNEDY CAMPAIGN SONG, 1952

In the pre-television age, songs were more essential to campaigns than now, and a small number of recordings preserve music from the early Kennedy campaigns. This selection, from the 1952 Senate race, in which Kennedy defeated the incumbent, Henry Cabot Lodge, offers a robust set of rhyming reasons for a Kennedy vote.

> *When we vote this November,*
> *Let's all remember,*
> *Let's vote for Kennedy!*
> *Make him your selection,*
> *In the Senate election,*
> *He'll do more for you and me!*
> *Look at Kennedy's history,*
> *You'll see it's no mystery,*
> *Why he suits us to a tee.*
> *He's your kind of man,*
> *So do all that you can,*
> *And vote for Kennedy!*

PRESIDENT HARRY TRUMAN HELPS THE KENNEDY SENATE CAMPAIGN,
BOSTON PUBLIC GARDEN, OCTOBER 1952

LETTER TO JACQUELINE KENNEDY, CIRCA 1959

Probably recorded in 1958 or 1959, this dictated letter reveals Kennedy speaking with considerable irony as he records his sharp observations of the summer scene in Newport, Rhode Island, for the benefit of his wife. A previous Newport resident, Edith Wharton, might not have disavowed this tart account of the mores of an elite group of Americans, as the author, both of them and separate from them, prepared his ascent.

JFK: Dearest Jackie, I'm divid[ing] this letter into two parts, one typewritten and the other handwritten, the typewritten part to give you the news of my visit to Newport. I went up there last Friday afternoon, and Caroline looks beautiful. Miss Shaw.[1] She evidently felt rather strange that first three or four days, but since then has spread her charm out, and seemed in great form when I saw her. Yusha[2] had his two twins there, who looked very Slavic and rather green. He drove them up in his open car, with his great Irish nurse holding them both in the back seat of his Buick with the top down for six hours, which may have been responsible for their color. Alice looks as, looks beautiful and as noncommittal as ever. She walks ten yards ahead of Yusha on the beach, and I think will be walking increasingly far ahead of him as time goes on. She's planning to enter the Actors Studio this fall, and I would think that this would produce numerous results. She spent the three days of the weekend in close conversation with [unclear]. Both being artists, they had a good deal in common.

Everyone was up there for the golf weekend. Stanley Mortimer[3] was heard to tell Sarah Russell that they'd had a long discussion the night before and decided that Blenheim[4] was an "inn." The Smiths were there, Leverett Shaw and his wife. I did not, I went over and played with Denny—Governor Roberts[5]—at

---

1. Maude Shaw was the nanny working for then-Senator and Mrs. John F. Kennedy.

2. Hugh D. "Yusha" Auchincloss III (b. 1927), Jacqueline Kennedy's stepbrother.

3. Stanley Grafton Mortimer, Jr. (1913–1999), an heir to the Standard Oil fortune.

4. Blenheim Palace, the magnificent seat of the Dukes of Marlborough, and the birthplace of Winston Churchill and Sarah Russell.

5. Dennis Roberts (1903–1994) was governor of Rhode Island from 1951 to 1959.

PRESIDENT KENNEDY WITH JOHN F. KENNEDY, JR., AT BAILEY'S BEACH,
NEWPORT, RHODE ISLAND, SEPTEMBER 15, 1963

Narragansett on Saturday and stayed only, and went to the Ishams' on Saturday evening. John Isham made several speeches after dinner of the kind that we heard at the wedding. The group was very nice. I was taken into the kitchen and introduced to all the help who were just over from Ireland. I found them more attractive than the guests. I saw Chris Dunphey, who told me Mrs. Fraser's sister, Mrs. Ayres, does not think that I'm serious about politics and therefore cannot support me.

On Sunday I watched the golf tournament, which Bud Palmer and Freddy Cushing won. Bud Palmer and his wife are about to have a baby. Everyone was asking for you, and asking me what I was doing in Newport. I stated that I was up visiting my daughter. She was a great success on the beach and seemed to love the water. Ginny Ryan was there with her rather squinty-eyed children for a five-week period. Miss Shaw is the loveliest figure actually on the beach, and has a beautiful red-brown bathing suit that goes with her hair. She has let herself go, however, slightly, around the middle.

[I flew back Monday with your mother, who was in an excellent humor.] Your mother flew back with me on Monday, and she's in a great humor, and spoke warmly of you and Lee. I hope you and Lee do not get upset at the various stories that Grace and Michael report, they both have sour grapes and their only retort is to indicate how pleasant their life is and how pleasant Stas and Lee's life . . .[6] [sound distorted] I'm sure that Lee when she feels better . . . very satisfactory in England. [distorted] It looks like we will be here until the first part of September, so the African trip is off. I'm enclosing a letter [sound distorted] that I took the liberty of opening as it had news about our prospective visit. It sounds wonderful there, if we only could go. Perhaps we can, if not this year, maybe in December. I shall . . .

---

6. Jacqueline Kennedy's sister, Lee, married three times. Her first husband was Michael Canfield; she then married Prince Stanislas Radziwill. Grace Dudley is Stas Radziwill's former wife.

EXCERPTS FROM DINNER PARTY CONVERSATION, JANUARY 5, 1960

On January 5, 1960, the journalist James M. Cannon recorded a dinner party conversation with a few friends. That was somewhat unusual in an era when tape-recording was still clunky and expensive; what was even more unusual was that the dinner party included a candidate for the presidency of the United States. John F. Kennedy had declared his candidacy three days earlier, on January 2, and on this occasion was relaxing at home with his wife, Jacqueline, and their close friends Ben and Toni Bradlee. Bradlee would later achieve fame as the editor in chief of the *Washington Post* during the Watergate years; in 1960, he was the Washington bureau chief of *Newsweek* and, like Kennedy, a veteran of the navy, the Pacific campaign, and Harvard University. They spoke easily together, as indicated by Bradlee's 1975 book, *Conversations with Kennedy*, and Cannon entered this convivial group without difficulty. Cannon, a *Newsweek* correspondent (and future staffer for President Gerald Ford), was writing a book entitled *Politics USA: A Practical Guide to the Winning of Public Office*. That book, with its tortured title, faded quickly from view, and the tapes as well. But they resurfaced when Cannon sent them to the Kennedy Library in 2007, with the stipulation that they become part of the library's collection upon his death. He died in September 2011, and the entire conversation can now be heard by the public. It includes fascinating and candid revelations about Kennedy's medical problems, his private reasons for wanting to run, and his worry that he was too introverted to be a natural politician.

JFK: This is on? Can it get me from there?

BRADLEE: [unclear] How come? Was it Joe's death that started the . . . ?

CANNON: Why did you get started in politics? Why were you ever interested in it?

JFK: In the thirties, when I was home from school, the conversation was always about politics. Want a cigar?

CANNON: It's all right. Talk loud.

JFK: Not in the sense of sort of being emotionally stirred about great issues, but really, just about the whole interest of my father was [unclear] in politics, in the Roosevelt administration.

[break]

CANNON: . . . When did you take your first step? What year was that?

JFK: January '46, with the election in June.

CANNON: This was for a seat in . . . ?

JFK: Congress.

CANNON: In what district?

JFK: The eleventh congressional district, which my grandfather once represented in Congress. But I didn't know anybody in Boston; I hadn't really lived there much. The war, I'd been away. I'd been at Harvard University. I'd been to Choate School before that, and lived in New York. So I went to live with my grandfather at the Bellevue Hotel, and I began to run, at a much earlier time than anyone else. [To Jacqueline Kennedy and Toni Bradlee: "You might want to go sit in the other room. . . ."]

BRADLEE: No, no, no.

JFK: They don't want to listen to this.

BRADLEE: They do!

TONI BRADLEE: We do, Jack! We love it, Jack!

JFK: Toni doesn't, and I know Jackie doesn't.

TONI: Yes I do, Jack! I'm so interested.

BRADLEE: Bullshit!

TONI: If it makes you uncomfortable, we won't . . .

BRADLEE: It's going to be all stilted unless we can have some of that.

JACQUELINE KENNEDY: Ben said we should interrupt and I should show my views and grasp of issues.

BRADLEE: And provoke! Is that not right?

CANNON: Absolutely.

JFK: You don't think it's working, do you?

CANNON: It's working.

BRADLEE: Don't stare at it.

JFK: OK, now we're in January 1946.

[break]

BRADLEE: Then when was the moment that you absolutely were bitten with it?

JFK: Once I started, I worked damn hard, and I did the same thing in '52 as I

PRESIDENT AND MRS. KENNEDY WITH BEN AND TONI BRADLEE,
ATOKA, VIRGINIA, NOVEMBER 10, 1963

am now doing, which may not be successful nationally. Start early. Try to get the support of nonprofessionals, in a sense, who are much more ready to commit themselves early, and then it's just long, long, long labor. Early.

CANNON: Why?

JFK: Why do it?

CANNON: Why do you do it now? Why do you go to all this effort? Obviously you're a well-to-do guy, who could live off the fat of the land. Why do you go in for politics?

JFK: I think the rewards are, first, infinite.

CANNON: What are they?

JFK: Well, look now, if you went to law school, and I'd gotten out, which I was going to do [unclear] and then I go and become a member of a big firm, and I'm dealing with some dead, deceased man's estate, or I'm perhaps fighting in a divorce case, even a case of one kind or another, or some fellow got in an accident, can you compare that, or let's say more serious work, when you're participating in a case against the DuPont Company in a general antitrust case, which takes two or three years, can you tell me that that compares in interest with being a member of Congress in trying to write a labor bill, or trying to make a speech on foreign policy? I just think that there's no comparison.

[break]

TONI BRADLEE: Can I ask a question?

JFK: Sure.

TONI BRADLEE: Is being president the ultimate of everybody that goes into politics?

JFK: In the sense of being head of whatever organization you're in, I suppose. But most important is the fact that the President today is the seat of all power.

[break]

CANNON: What you are suggesting is that your interest in politics evolved really after you got into it. Is that correct?

JFK: Well, no . . . well, that's partially correct. It wasn't overwhelming. I didn't participate in political activities in college.

CANNON: Not until really you felt the satisfaction of having made a speech come off?

JFK: I hadn't even considered myself, because I'm not a political type.

BRADLEE : Why?

CANNON: Not even now?

JACQUELINE KENNEDY: Why? Ben reminds me of Adlai Stevenson. [laughter]

JFK: Well, I mean the political type. I think it's hard work. My grandfather was a natural political type. Loved to go out to a dinner. Loved to get up and sing with the crowds. Loved to go down and take the train up and talk to eighteen people on the train.

CANNON: What makes you think you aren't, in a different context?

JFK: I just happen to fit the times. My grandfather, his political career was limited partly because he was part of the immigrant group, who would not achieve success, but partly because he did do these things and therefore he never concentrated enough to get what he really wanted, which was either governor or senator. Now it requires far more work, politics is far more serious business. You really aren't so much interested in who's at the . . . really, they try to make, I think the judgment is rather cold in judgment, as to what, the people who have some competence. So the old-type political personality is on his way out. Television is only one manifestation. I think that the problems are so tough, I don't think you have to be this hail-fellow-well-met.

CANNON: Why do you say the problems are tough, what are some of these problems?

JFK: I think, all the problems, war, the destruction of the United States and the world, every problem, urban problems, agricultural, they're all . . . monetary, fiscal, labor-management, inflation. I mean, they're terribly sophisticated. In the nineteenth century you only have about three problems: the development of the West, slavery, tariff and currency.

[break]

BRADLEE: But did you have any remote idea, Jack, that when you ran for Congress, in 1946, that you would run for president?

JFK: No, I didn't.

BRADLEE: Remote? Not even when you went to bed?

JFK: Never. Never. Never. I thought maybe I'd be governor of Massachusetts someday.

[break]

TONI BRADLEE: And yet it's true that there are only some people who have either what it takes, or have . . .

JFK: Desire?

TONI: . . . something in them that makes them go through . . .

JFK: I don't know. Everybody reaches a natural level. It's possible my natural level is in the Senate. I mean, we'll know in the next six months. But there isn't anybody in the House that would not like to advance himself, or anybody who works for anything. My God, if you didn't have that power of desire, the United States and every place else would collapse! That's what moves the country and the world. That's just a part of it. I'm just saying that it's the center of power. I'm not talking about personal, I'm just saying the center of action is the more precise term, is the presidency. Now if you are interested, which many, many people are, not just me, the presidency is the place to be, in the sense of if you want to get anything done.

[break]

CANNON: If you were talking to a college student, why would you tell him that he ought to go into politics?

JFK: Because I think that this opportunity to participate in the solutions of the problems which interest him, I would assume he's interested, I would say the place he could effect some results would be in politics. The second, that your personal sources of satisfactions which come from doing this work is far greater in politics than it will ever be in business. And your financial reward will not be as great, and your insecurity will probably be greater in politics, because you may get defeated in the next election. Those are the disadvantages.

CANNON: Well, should somebody who is contemplating going into politics, should he have some sort of other source of financial security?

JFK: Well, it's desirable for anybody to have financial security, in whatever they do, but quite obviously the mass, the great majority of politicians do not have it, but they seem to survive.

CANNON: Do you feel it's been a help to you?

JFK: Well, I think my biggest help, really was getting started, and my father's having been known. And therefore when you walked up to somebody, you had some entree. That's a far greater advantage to me, I think, than the financial [unclear]. Coming from a politically active family was really the major advantage.

CANNON: You think there's more advantage in having financial backing, so that you didn't have to worry?

JFK: Well, I have to worry, because I could be defeated.

CANNON: But you don't have to worry about your family, about being out of a job, if you should be defeated.

JFK: No, but I worry, I wouldn't like to try to pick up my life at forty-five, -six, or -seven, and start after twenty years of being in politics, and try to pick up my life then. That would be a source of concern to me. Many politicians probably are lawyers and would start in something else. I'm not a lawyer. It would be a problem for me to decide. Maybe need a different degree. I mean, it's like having your leg up to your ankle or to your knee amputated, it's still disturbing.

BRADLEE: Jack, what career might you pick?

JFK: I don't know what I'd do. This just happens to be . . .

BRADLEE: Does that mean that politics is an all-inclusive profession?

JFK: I don't see really what you do out of it. I went in when I was . . . navy, college, politics. Where would you go? What would I do now? I couldn't possibly. I don't know what I'd do.

TONI BRADLEE: Write.

JFK: No, I couldn't, because I've lost the chance. I mean, I'm sure it takes twenty years to learn to be a decent writer. You have to do it every day.

[break]

BRADLEE: Well, what stops a guy, Jack, that hasn't stopped you?

JFK: You mean, where does everybody reach a decision where they'll stay? I think an awful lot is fortune. There is an awful lot of fortune in the thing. As I look ahead now, as I look at these primaries, how they're breaking, bad luck and good luck. Why is it that I have to run in Wisconsin, the one state where I have infinite trouble, when Hubert Humphrey has got nothing anyplace else? That's just a bad break.

BRADLEE: Well, what is there in a man? I mean, why isn't Muskie running for president now, instead of you?

JFK: Muskie may. If I had to pick a vice president, I'd pick Ed Muskie. My judgment is Ed Muskie has the best chance of being vice president of anybody.

BRADLEE: With you?

JFK: Not with me, but if I don't make it. My judgment is, the ticket would be, if I had to pick a long shot, if I don't make it, it would be Stevenson[7] and Muskie.

[break]

BRADLEE: Well, what is the magic? And is the magic that you think exists and is important at forty-three, did you have any idea what it was at twenty-six?

JFK: No, but I did always reasonably well. In the first place I worked harder than my opponents, on at least three occasions, I worked harder, with the exception of Hubert, I think, than anybody else, every time I've run. And then I brought advantages, as I say, I brought advantages in '46, and in '52 I just buried Lodge.

BRADLEE: Advantages . . . well-known family?

---

7. Adlai Stevenson (1900–1965), Democratic candidate for the presidency in 1952 and 1956, former governor of Illinois and ambassador to the United Nations under President Kennedy.

JFK: I don't think he was tough enough, Lodge, because he didn't do the work. He had every advantage in '52. I mean that was really a long shot. Nobody wanted to run against him.

BRADLEE: . . . Eisenhower?[8]

JFK: Well, yeah, he'd won by the biggest majority ever in the history of Massachusetts the previous time he'd run, 560,000, he beat Walsh. After four terms. I mean, Walsh was a soft touch, but it was a hell of a victory, 560,000 votes. Fifty-two, a Republican year coming up, campaign manager.

BRADLEE: But is it true that the magic and the desire changes with the office, because that seems to be true?

JFK: No, I just think that as time moves on, and you move on, your perspective changes. I don't know what makes some politicians succeed and others fail. It's a combination of time and their own quality . . .

BRADLEE: And luck.

JFK: . . . and luck. I mean, the margin is awfully small between, you know, those who succeed and those who don't. Like it is in life.

CANNON: Were you disappointed in '56 when you didn't make it for vice president?

JFK: I was for about a day or so.

CANNON: Is that all, really? What did you do to contain your disappointment?

JFK: I didn't really ever think I was going to run when I went there. I didn't think I had much of a chance ever. When Stevenson asked me to nominate him. I thought I was out, this was a complete surprise to me, I really . . .

BRADLEE: Did you nominate Stevenson in '56?

JFK: Yes.

TONI BRADLEE: Maybe he'll do the same for you now. [laughter]

BRADLEE: You'd ask nothing less.

CANNON: But once it was done, were you disappointed?

JFK: Yeah, I guess we were, the next morning, weren't we, Jackie? I mean, I was tired.

---

8. Henry Cabot Lodge, Jr. (1902–1985) was a Republican U.S. senator, ambassador to the United Nations, and ambassador to South Vietnam during the last few months of the Kennedy administration. JFK defeated him in the 1952 Senate race, and they again ran against each other in 1960, when Lodge was the candidate for vice president with Richard Nixon. His grandfather, Henry Cabot Lodge, defeated John F. Kennedy's grandfather, John F. Fitzgerald, in the Senate campaign of 1916. Lodge also helped persuade General Dwight D. Eisenhower to run for president in 1952.

JACQUELINE KENNEDY: You were so tired. How could you be anything . . .

JFK: It was so damn close, I was disappointed. I was disappointed that night.

CANNON: Did you think that they were going to win?

JFK: Kefauver deserved it. I always thought that [unclear], he'd beaten Stevenson in two or three primaries . . .

BRADLEE: You didn't run in any primaries in that, did you?

JFK: No, but he had, that's why he deserved it.

CANNON: Was there any sense of [unclear]?

JFK: Afterwards? No, it's past [or passed].

CANNON: It was past the next morning. You can honestly say, you could go off the next day to home, or to Hyannisport, or wherever, and say, "Well, nice try."

JFK: Not quite that easy, because I was damn tired, but I have to say, I thought, you know, we did have a close effort, and I had not thought I was going to win, I did much better than I thought I would, I thought Kefauver deserved to win, and therefore I was not desolate. It's a lot different from now. Now it's entirely different. Now I'm [unclear]. It would take me a lot longer to recover.

CANNON: How does a politician get over this sense of loss? Sense of defeat?

JFK: I didn't lose so much. I was still in the Senate, and finally, of course, you know the ticket didn't win.

CANNON: Did you think it was going to?

JFK: Well, in September I thought he might, I thought he had a pretty good chance. At the end of the convention we all got excited. I thought even in September he was doing . . . turned out to be a [unclear].

CANNON: Why did you think he was going to win?

JFK: Well, for a little while there, Stevenson was awfully active and Eisenhower wasn't. I was just talking to Democrats.

CANNON: You're suggesting that you haven't had many disappointments in politics. Have you ever lost a race?

JFK: No. I've run five times.

CANNON: The only thing you've ever lost was the try for the vice presidency.

JFK: That's right.

CANNON: And it really didn't hit you very hard.

JFK: No. At the time. I mean, that day it did.

CANNON: What do you do, what did you say to yourself, when it happened?

JFK: I was disappointed that day, and I was damn tired, and we came awfully close, and then we lost. By twenty-eight votes or something. And I was disappointed.

CANNON: What did you do, go back to the hotel and go to sleep? Or have a drink?

JFK: No, I think we went to have dinner with Eunice, didn't we, Jackie? And then we went back afterwards.

JACQUELINE KENNEDY: You know for five days in Chicago, Jack really hadn't gone to bed. Nobody had. Except for two hours sleep a night. It just was this incredible . . . brutal thing. You don't see how any men are that strong to stay up for five days and talk and talk . . .

BRADLEE: Do you remember wanting to go into politics?

CANNON: Not really, no.

JFK: And here you are, around these history makers, in Washington. Do you ever think you'd rather be a politician than reporting?

BRADLEE: Yup. Yup.

CANNON: I think I can't afford it. I have two children and . . .

JFK: Well, you couldn't, I mean, at this point. Now, after the war? What are you now, about forty-two or -three? Forty-one. Now let's say 1945, you might have been able to.

CANNON: Well, it was not a convenient thing.

JFK: What was it, in '45, were you in the service?

CANNON: Yeah.

JFK: Well, when you came home, you were pretty much [unclear].

CANNON: Yeah, but I was . . . I'm not talking about myself.

JFK: No, but I'm just trying to say, why wasn't it possible, really, in '45?

CANNON: Well, basically, my problem was financial. I recognize that this was something that if you were going to be honest in, you ought to have an independent source of income.

JFK: I don't agree with that. I mean, it may be more difficult for me to talk about it, but I've seen a lot of politicians with money, and I don't find . . . There's so many kinds of being dishonest, the money part is just only one of them. I don't really think you can prove by any test that you have to have money to be successful, politically, or that people with money are more honest than those who aren't.

BRADLEE: Or less honest, you mean.

JFK: I mean more honest. People with money. They may be, not tempted by bribery, but nobody is offering people money in the Senate or the House except on the rarest occasions. There's no idea that anybody attempts to bribe anybody in the United States Senate, with the exception of maybe, possibly . . .

BRADLEE: [unclear]

JFK: Well, here are maybe the rarest influences, but even Ben, who's pretty tough, would have to say, maybe campaign contributors, but we all get campaign contributions, some from labor, and some from business, and I suppose that makes them perhaps somewhat responsive, but you're responsive also to people who vote for you, veterans and other pressure groups. So I don't think that this idea, you can't tell me that, I'll name him, but not for the thing, that Averell Harriman[9] and these people are as political whores as anybody in the United States. Because they are desperately anxious to succeed in this profession which has so many attractions to it. So money is not really a sine qua non.

BRADLEE: There are a thousand objections to running for politics that I . . . Somebody once told me that I ought to run for politics in New Hamsphire. God forbid! There were whole lots of objections, there was one that I couldn't possibly have been elected. [laughter] You know, I mean, a Democrat in New Hampshire? For God's sakes, I mean, I thought very very very seriously about this. Second thing was, there is something in some people's minds that is uncomfortable at constantly being projected in the public eye, that is not uncomfortable to you and to these guys, who not only love it, but transfer it into a good thing. Whereas with somebody else it sort of snarls them up and gets them to eat their own tail. This is something about politics, who has that and why, I think is an important area of why go into politics.

JFK: Let me now just finish this thing, though, and I'm not the best one because I do have some financial resources, so it's rather easier for me, but I do say, looking at it objectively, that money, because you can just go through the House and the Senate, I mean, I know most of my colleagues do not have resources and they have succeeded in politics. The people with money who have succeeded are comparatively few in politics. I mean, it's just most of them don't go into politics, if they have money, and if they do go into politics, they're not any better than their colleagues. I mean, they are just as susceptible to pressure and in many ways more susceptible to pressure because they are desperately anxious, this is their tremendous chance to break through the rather narrow lives they

---

9. W. Averell Harriman (1891–1986) was a senior Democratic statesman from the administration of Franklin D. Roosevelt onward, serving as ambassador to the Soviet Union (1943–1946) and to Great Britain (1946), secretary of commerce (1946–1948), and governor of New York (1955–1958). During the Kennedy administration, he was assistant secretary of state and closely advised President Kennedy on the Nuclear Test Ban Treaty, Vietnam, and the Soviet Union.

may lead. So they're just as anxious to succeed. That's why I say to you, merely getting beaten, the financial problem is an additional one, but not the chief one. The chief one is being cut off from this fascinating life at mid-age, which is what you're suggesting to me. Now, I can survive, but it's still being cut off.

BRADLEE: What about the projection of one's self? The only comparable field I can think of is a movie star.

JFK: No, but I think I personally am the antithesis of a politician as I saw my grandfather who was *the* politician. I mean, every reason that I say, that he was ideal. What he loved to do was what politicians are expected to do. Now I just think that today . . .

CANNON: Don't you?

JFK: No, I don't. I don't enjoy. I'd rather read a book on a plane than talk to the fellow next to me, and my grandfather wanted to talk to everybody else. I'd rather not go out to dinner.

TONI BRADLEE: You look as though you enjoy it. Which helps.

BRADLEE: But Jack, that whole projection that comes with modern times.

JFK: I think I just happen to fit now. I mean, I think people don't like this.

JACQUELINE KENNEDY: I think that's a nineteenth-century politician, don't you, like your grandfather, that you people are suspicious of?

BRADLEE: Now the politicians have to be constantly on the air.

JFK: Bill Fullbright—he's not on the air. He has a particular personality. I have a particular type of personality which, I [don't?] look like a politician, and all the rest, which helps me. Everybody isn't an extrovert in politics. I would say that a lot of the Senate certainly are not extroverts.

BRADLEE: Well, name me one.

JFK: Who's not? Mike Mansfield is not an extrovert. John Cooper is not an extrovert. Richard M. Nixon is not an extrovert. Stuart Symington is a tricky extrovert, if he is one. I don't think he is one. Hubert is. I'm not.[10]

BRADLEE: But Jack, I mean, you are! No?

---

10. Mike Mansfield (1903–2001) was a Democratic senator from Montana from 1953 to 1977, and the longest-serving Senate majority leader (1961–1977). John Sherman Cooper (1901–1991) was a Republican senator from Kentucky who served from 1946 to 1949, 1952 to 1955, and 1956 to 1973. Stuart Symington (1901–1988) was a Democratic senator from Missouri from 1953 to 1976. Hubert Humphrey (1911–1978) was a Democratic senator from Minnesota (1949 to 1964, 1971 to 1978), vice president under Lyndon Johnson, and the Democratic candidate for president in 1968.

JFK: No, I don't think I am, actually.

BRADLEE: But you like it. And you live on it.

JFK: All these things may be true. Listen, I'm just saying, what I would be doing, you know I don't go out to dinner.

BRADLEE: I know, I'm not trying to provoke you.

JFK: I understand. I'd be delighted if I had Hubert Humphrey's disposition. He thrives on this. He loves to go out and campaign for five days. It's a lot of work. I just don't think you have to have that type of personality to be successful today in politics. I think you have to be able to communicate a sense of conviction and intelligence and rather, some integrity. That's what you have to be able to do. This hail-fellow is passé in many ways. Those three qualities are really it. Now, I think that some people can do that. I think I do that well. I mean, I've been really successful, politically. I think I can do that. But it isn't anything to do with being able to go out and just love it. Dancing [unclear], the Fourth of July.

CANNON: Something you naturally do?

JFK: In my first campaign somebody said to me that he thought after I spoke that I would be governor of Massachusetts in ten years. I think I did well from the beginning in this particular key.

BRADLEE: Did that statement create things in you?

JFK: No, but I didn't think it was possible, but I was pleased. Because I had not regarded myself as a political type. My father didn't, he thought I was hopeless.

CANNON: Go into that.

JFK: I mean, Joe was made for it, and I certainly wasn't.

BRADLEE: Why was Joe? I never knew Joe obviously, but why?

JFK: He [Joe] was more a type, an extrovert type.

BRADLEE: Now why did the old boy think you were hopeless?

JFK: At that time I weighed about 120 pounds. [laughter] Where was that picture we saw with Franklin Roosevelt, in the paper?

JACQUELINE KENNEDY: Oh yeah. That's in your old campaign photo?

JFK: No, the one we just saw, in the *Boston Globe*, Sunday.

BRADLEE: Jack, long before I knew you, when I was covering the federal courts in the District of Columbia, you used to, in the contempt cases, you used to come down and testify, "Yes, there was a quorum present. Yes, I was there. Yes, me and one other guy was there, which made up a quorum." And you looked like the wrath of God. I can see you there now. You weighed 120, and you were bright green. You really were.

JFK: There's a picture that the *Boston Globe* ran Sunday, which had the veterans rally in '47, Franklin Roosevelt and I, and I looked like a cadaver.

BRADLEE: But that color was just fantastic. You were really green . . .

JFK: Adrenal deficiency.

BRADLEE: This was 1948, it must have been, '48 or '49.

JFK: Forty-seven or -eight, I guess. Well, the point of the matter is, that's why my father thought that I was not equipped for political life. [unclear]

BRADLEE: And you'd been a congressman for two years. Did you run for Congress with this greenness?

JFK: Oh yeah. Greener.

TONI BRADLEE: What was that? That was atabrine?

JFK: It was atabrine, malaria, and probably some adrenal deficiency,

BRADLEE: Addison's? What is that damn disease?

JFK: Addison's Disease, they said I have. Jack [unclear] asked me today if I have it.

BRADLEE: Who?

JFK: Drew Pearson's man. I said no, God, a guy with Addison's Disease looks sort of brown and everything. [laughter] Christ! See, that's the sun.

TONI BRADLEE: But then your back was later on.

JFK: No, my back was in '45.

TONI BRADLEE: But then you were operated on after.

JFK: I was operated on in '45 too. All these things came together. I was a wreck.

BRADLEE: When was that big slice, just north of your behind there, when was that?

JFK: That was '45, then again in '54, and again in '56.

JACQUELINE KENNEDY: Yeah, he was all better, his crutch broke, and he had to go back again.

CANNON: Does it ever concern you that you have lost your sense of privacy? You obviously can't have . . . since everybody knows you now.

JFK: That's the real pleasure about Jamaica in a way. You really can't go anyplace particularly now without . . . But I don't mind, I think that's part of running, so I'm delighted, really. I used to walk down the streets in '45 and nobody knew me. Now that's fifteen years of effort has gone into getting known. I mean, it isn't pleasant for the person, but as an investment of energy it represents some . . .

CANNON: What's your reaction when someone comes up and says, "I saw you on television"?

JFK: They come from Massachusetts? [laughter] It's all right. I don't mind. I'm asking their support, so, you know.

CANNON: Do you take any special efforts to maintain a sense of privacy? Do you have a private phone? Unlisted?

JFK: I do. But everybody seems to have it.

[break]

JFK: Have we covered everything?

BRADLEE: I just would like two minutes on the magic of politics. [laughter] Because I go back to this guy who told me I ought to run against Styles Bridges.[11] And for about two minutes, I just talked. And there was this whole marvelous sense of mission, that you've been thinking about. Somebody must have said that to you. "You can be . . . ," never mind president, but you can go so high. It's an adrenaline on a man.

JFK: I agree. It's stimulating. Because you're dealing with . . . Life is a struggle and you're struggling in a tremendous sort of arena. It's like playing Yale every Saturday, in a sense.

BRADLEE: But the drama of it. I don't know, somehow . . .

JFK: How could it be more interesting than this sort of checkerboard chess struggle of the next seven months?

BRADLEE: Talk about that, because this is what appeals to me most about you.

JFK: I mean, look at the cold decisions that have to be made that are really life or death. I mean, running in Wisconsin? And what do we do about Mike DiSalle?[12] And how can it be handled?

CANNON: There are 175,999,995 people who aren't interested in it. You say, "What could be more interesting?" Why are you this interested, and the rest of the millions aren't?

JFK: Well, if they were in it. I mean, their lives are interesting to them. I'm having the same struggle that they're having in a different sphere, but in the most sort of dramatic way, for the great effort, the presidency of the United

---

11. Styles Bridges (1898–1961), Republican governor of New Hampshire (1935–1937) and long-term senator (1937–1961).

12. Michael DiSalle (1908–1981) was Democratic governor of Ohio from 1959 to 1963.

States, my checkerboard struggle is going on. As I say, what is sports, spectator sports, the same thing. Johnny Unitas,[13] he might find it interesting to play in a sandlot team, in front of four people, but he's playing for the Colts, the best team in the United States, for the world championship. I mean, I must say, he must find that very absorbing. I'm not comparing the presidency with that, but I'm just saying that, how could it be more fascinating than to run for president under the obstacles and the hurdles that are before me.

_____

13. Johnny Unitas (1933–2002), legendary quarterback of the Baltimore Colts. The team had won the NFL championship in 1958 and 1959.

DICTABELT RECORDING, CIRCA 1960

This recording, probably from early 1960, reveals Kennedy to be thinking deeply about his life and the reasons he went into politics, which he declares, with considerable under-statement, to be "my present profession." It includes a personal confession that he was "at loose ends" following the war and that his entry into politics was somewhat accidental. But as he also knew well, politics was in his DNA, and he accepted his destiny with good cheer and a willingness to work hard. Certain phrases are repeated from the January dinner party conversation, suggesting that it was recorded not long after. But this ver-sion shows him telling the story without interruption, and with a more polished ending. A similar version was submitted to James Cannon for inclusion in his book *Politics U.S.A.* This proto-memoir recounts some of the earliest circumstances of his entry into politics, and his constant desire to get near "the center of action." In 1960, that is precisely where he found himself.

JFK: Mrs. Lincoln, is this tape in? Is this plugged in? Is this plugged in? One, two, three, four, five, six, seven, eight, nine, ten. In a sense, it is important and desirable that people feel this way about politics and politicians in a free society. A politician's power may be great, and with this power goes the necessity of checking it.

But the fact remains that politics has become one of our most abused and neglected professions . . . Yet it is this profession, it is these politicians who make the great decisions of war and peace, prosperity and recession, the deci-sion whether we look to the future or the past. In a large sense everything now depends upon what the government decides.

Therefore, if you are interested, if you want to participate, if you feel strongly about any public question, whether it's labor, what happens in India, the future of American agriculture, whatever it may be, it seems to me that governmental service is the way to translate this interest into action, that the natural place for the concerned citizen is to contribute part of his life to the national inter-est. Like many decisions in life, a combination of factors pressed on me, which directed me into my present profession.

I was at loose ends at the end of the war. I was reluctant to begin law school again. I was not very interested in following a business career. I was vitally interested in national and international life, and I was the descendant of three generations, on both sides of my family, of men who had followed the political profession. In my early life, conversation was nearly always about politics. My father, who had directed much of his energy into business, nevertheless, as the son of a Massachusetts state senator, was himself interested in politics. My mother, also, shared the interest. Her father had been mayor and a United States congressman, and both my great uncles were state senators and my father's first cousin was mayor of Brockton, Massachusetts.[14]

For all the Irish immigrants, the way up in Boston was clearly charted. The doors of business were shut. The way to rise above being a laborer was through politics. So they all went into it, everybody in the Kennedy or the Fitzgerald family. But I never thought at school and college that I would ever run for office myself. One politician was enough in the family and my brother Joe was obviously going to be that politician.[15] I hadn't considered myself a political type and he filled all the requirements for political success. When he was twenty-four he was elected as a delegate to the Democratic convention in 1940, and I think his political success would have been assured. I [unclear] recall that I was a freshman at Harvard when Henry Cabot Lodge[16] was elected to the United States Senate. I don't suppose I ever thought, in those days, that I would someday run against him and defeat him for the Senate. I suppose there's some freshman in college, today, who isn't aware that he's probably going to end up by defeating me sometime.

My brother Joe was killed in Europe as a flyer in August 1944, and that ended our hopes for him. But I didn't even start to think about a political profession until more than a year later. When the war came, I didn't know what I was going to do . . . and I didn't find it oppressive that I didn't know. In '44 and

---

14. JFK's father, Joseph P. Kennedy (1888–1969), received several political appointments; he was the first chairman of the U.S. Securities and Exchange Commission (1934–1935), and ambassador to the Court of Saint James (1938–1940). JFK's paternal grandfather, P. J. Kennedy (1858–1929), was a longtime political boss in Boston Democratic circles, representing the East Boston neighborhood and serving in the upper and lower chambers of the Massachusetts legislature. JFK's maternal grandfather, John F. Fitzgerald (1863–1950), or "Honey Fitz," had a storied political career, serving as a congressman and as mayor of Boston. Joseph P. Kennedy's cousin Charles Hickey was mayor of Brockton, Massachusetts.

15. Joseph P. Kennedy, Jr. (1915–1944).

16. Lodge helped persuade Eisenhower to run in 1952 and served as his campaign manager.

JOHN F. KENNEDY CAMPAIGNS FOR CONGRESS IN THE NORTH END OF BOSTON BY THE OLD NORTH CHURCH AND PAUL REVERE STATUE, 1948

'45 I had been in the hospital for about a year recovering from some injuries I received in the Pacific. Then I worked as a reporter covering the San Francisco conference, the British election, and the Potsdam meeting, all in 1945.[17]

So there never was a moment of truth for me when I saw my whole political career unfold. I came back in the fall of '55 [1945] after Potsdam, at loose ends, and the head of the Boston Community Fund asked me to help him during the drive. That was Mike Kelleher, who later became my finance chairman when I ran for the Senate in 1952.

[unclear] Kelleher or his assistant meant making speeches for the first time in my life, and they seemed to be acceptable. The first speech I ever gave was on "England, Ireland, and Germany: Victor, Neutral, and Vanquished." It took me three weeks to write and was given at an American Legion Post. Now, the speech went rather well. A politician came up to me afterwards and said that I should go into politics, that I might be governor of Massachusetts in ten years. Then I began to think about a political career. I hadn't even considered it up till then. Later in the fall, James M. Curley[18] was elected mayor of Boston and a congressional seat became vacant. This was the seat, this was the eleventh congressional district, which my grandfather had once represented in Congress fifty years before.

Suddenly, the time, the occasion, and I all met. I moved into the Bellevue Hotel with my grandfather and I began to run. I've been running ever since. Fascination began to grip me and I realized how satisfactory a profession the political career could be. I saw how ideally politics filled the Greek definition of happiness: "Full use of your powers along lines of excellence in a life affording scope."[19]

---

17. The conference to create the United Nations was held in San Francisco from April 25 to June 26, 1945; the British election pitted a Labour candidate, Clement Attlee, against the Conservative prime minister and wartime hero Winston Churchill, and resulted in Attlee's surprising victory on July 26, 1945; the Potsdam Conference was held outside Berlin from July 16 to August 2, 1945, and attended by the leaders of the United States, the Soviet Union, and Great Britain. JFK covered all three major episodes as a young newspaper correspondent and observer.

18. James M. Curley (1874–1958) was a legendary four-term mayor of Boston and served as the inspiration for the character of Frank Skeffington in Edwin O'Connor's *The Last Hurrah*. He also served in Congress and as governor of Massachusetts.

19. This quotation, cited frequently enough by JFK to be nearly ascribed to him, was probably borrowed from Dean Acheson, who in turn borrowed it from a 1923 book, Henry W. Nevinson's *Changes*

I might have gone to law school, which so many were doing after the dislocations of war, and become a member of a big firm and [unclear] or a divorce case, or been involved in an accident suit. But how can anyone compare that in interest with being a member of Congress, with trying to write legislation on foreign policy or on the relationship between labor and management. Or I could have worked, or I could have taken part in an antitrust case against a great corporation, a case which might have taken two or three years. How can you compare in interest that job with a life in Congress where you are able to participate to some degree in determining which direction this nation will go?

Even reporting has its disadvantages, and that was the first profession I tried. A reporter is *reporting* what happens; he's not *making* it happen. Even the good reporters, the ones who are really fascinated by what happens and who find real stimulus in putting their noses into the center of action. Even they, in a sense, are in a secondary profession. It's reporting what happened, but it isn't participating.

I had in politics, to begin with, the great advantage of having a well-known name, and that served me in good stead. Beyond that, however, I was a stranger in Boston to begin with, and I still have a notebook, which is filled page after page with the names of all the new people I met back there in that first campaign.

I had several disadvantages as a candidate. I was an outsider, really. I was living in a hotel. I had never lived very much in the district. My family roots were there, but I had lived in New York for ten years, and on top of that I had gone to Harvard, not a particularly popular institution at that time in the eleventh congressional district. But I started early, in my opinion the most important key to political success. In December, for the primary election next June.

My chief opponents, the mayor of Cambridge and Mayor Curley's secretary, followed the old practice of not starting until about two months before the election. By then I was ahead of them. In 1952 I worked a year and a half ahead of the November election, a year and a half before Senator Lodge did. I am following the same practice now. I believe most aspirants for public office start much too late. When you think of the money that Coca-Cola and Lucky

---

and Chances. Acheson gives it as "the exercise of vital powers along lines of excellence, in a life affording them scope." See Acheson, *Present at the Creation: My Years in the State Department,* p. 239. The quotation has also been attributed to Edith Hamilton, who cited it in her 1930 classic, *The Greek Way.*

Strike put into advertising day after day, even though they have well-known brand names, you can realize how difficult it is to become an identifiable political figure. The idea that people can get to know you well enough to support you in two months or three months is wholly wrong. Most of us do not follow politics and politicians. We become interested only around election time. For the politician to make a dent in the consciousness of the great majority of the people is a long and laborious job, particularly in a primary where you don't have the party label to help you.

Once I did start, I worked really hard, trying to get the support of the non-professionals, who are much more ready to commit themselves early than the traditional politicians. In my opinion, the principle for winning a ward fight or congressional fight, really, is the same as winning a presidential fight, and the most important ingredient is a willingness to submit yourself to long, long, long labor.

Halfway through that campaign the mayor of Cambridge offered me the job of his secretary if I withdrew and he won. I refused. Finally, after a tough fight, I won with a generous margin.

And almost immediately, politics lived up to the great expectations I had for it as a profession. The first thing I did in Congress was to become the junior Democrat on the labor committee. At the time we were considering the Taft-Hartley Bill.[20] I was against it, and one day in Harrisburg, Pennsylvania, I debated the bill with a junior Republican on that committee who was for it . . . his name was Richard Nixon. And now, here we are debating again, fourteen years later.

Why does a politician continually raise his sights and leave a job that represented complete satisfaction at one time for a higher position? Part of the reason lies in the normal desire to move ahead, the motivation that helps move the world; perhaps a more important part lies in the recognition that a greater opportunity to determine the direction in which the nation/world will go lies in higher office. The scope and power are bigger.

When I was in the House, I was especially interested in my district, in Boston, in the future, in the navigation, for example, of Boston Harbor. I still am. But in the House you are one of 435 members. You have to be there many,

---

20. The Taft-Hartley Act of 1947 amended the 1935 National Labor Relations Act and monitored the activities of labor unions.

many years before you get to the hub of influence, or have an opportunity to play any role on substantive matters. After I'd been in the House for six years, I made up my mind that there was a greater opportunity to function in the United States Senate. I prepared to move on.

In the same way, during my years in the Senate I have come to understand that the presidency is the ultimate source of action. The Senate is not. It may have been in 1840, but it isn't today. Take the Labor Bill, for instance. In 1958 I had worked for two years on that bill. President Eisenhower made one fifteen-minute speech, which had a decisive effect on the House. Two years versus one fifteen-minute speech. I worked for a year on a proposal to send an economic mission to India. The State Department opposed it. It was defeated in the conference. I worked for a year on a bill to change the Battle Act[21] to allow a greater economic trading with countries behind the Iron Curtain, such as Poland. The president withdrew his support on the day of the vote. We were defeated by one vote. All of the things that you become interested in doing, the president can do and the Senate cannot, particularly in the area of foreign policy.

There is, in fact, much less than meets the eye in the Senate, frequently. The administration controls, in my opinion, today, and in the administration it's the President who controls and who can affect results, while we play in the vital issues of national security, defense, and foreign policy a secondary role in the United States Senate.

The President, all public officials, today face serious and sophisticated problems unheard of in the nineteenth century, where political leaders dealt for several generations with the problems of the development of the West, slavery, tariff, and the currency. Today, politics has become infinitely complicated. One day we deal with labor law, the next with significant matters of foreign policy, the following day with fiscal and monetary policy, the next day with the problems of which new weapons should we put our emphasis on.

With the new complexity and intensity of political problems, I think the politics and politicians have changed. The hail-fellow-well-met extrovert is passing from [the] political scene. A good many of the politicians I know in the Senate are quiet and thoughtful men, certainly not extroverts.

---

21. The Battle Act, or Mutual Defense Assistance Control Act, of 1951 banned U.S. aid to countries doing business with the USSR. Its sponsor was Representative Laurie Battle of Alabama.

A successful politician today must have and communicate a sense of intelligence and integrity, and he must be willing to work. Money helps, of course. It is desirable for anyone to have financial security in whatever they do, but it is certainly not an essential for success. The fact is that people with private resources who have succeeded in politics are comparatively rare. Most of them do not go into politics, and for some who have, money has been a hazard. In any case, this is not the decisive question and I think our history has demonstrated this very clearly. Franklin Roosevelt had some personal resources. Lincoln did not. They were both successful political leaders and great presidents.

In looking back, I would say that I have never regretted my choice of profession, even though I cannot know what the future will bring. I hope all Americans, men and women, regardless of what may be their chosen profession, will consider giving some of their life to the field of politics. Winston Churchill once said: "Democracy is the worst form of government except for all of the other systems that have been tried." It is certainly the most demanding, it requires more from us all than any other system. Particularly in these days when the watch fires of the enemy camp burn bright, I think all of us must be willing to give some of ourselves to the most exacting discipline of self-government. The magic of politics is not the panoply of office. The magic of politics is participating on all levels of national life in an affirmative way, of playing a small role in determining whether, in Mr. Faulkner's words, "freedom will not only endure, but also prevail."[22]

---

22. These words are from William Faulkner's Nobel Prize acceptance speech, delivered on December 10, 1950.

MEETING WITH GENERAL DOUGLAS MACARTHUR, AUGUST 16, 1962

On August 16, 1962, not long after the tapes were installed, General Douglas Mac-Arthur, eighty-two years old, came to Washington to be feted at a lunch ceremony on Capitol Hill. He took advantage of his visit to pay a social call at the White House, where he found a receptive President Kennedy eager to join him in conversation. Kennedy had admired MacArthur for years, for his personal courage as a soldier in the First World War and his strategic vision in the wars that followed. They'd met in New York in April 1961, in the immediate aftermath of the Bay of Pigs disaster, when MacArthur offered valuable public support. A year later, they enjoyed an easy, discursive conversation, ranging over politics, Southeast Asia (where MacArthur advocated caution), and their shared interest in history. At one point, the conversation was interrupted by a phone call from the President's father, who, though eight years younger than General MacArthur, was incapacitated by a stroke. World War I was on JFK's mind, and he described Barbara Tuchman's recent book, *The Guns of August*, to MacArthur; MacArthur recounted some of his adventures in that war, including his memory of a young French tank commander, Charles de Gaulle. In the selection that follows, MacArthur vents his criticism of the media, and the difficulty of living in the public eye.

MACARTHUR: You have inherited difficulties that you probably will just about settle [and] you'll get through and then some other fellow will come in and get all the credit.

JFK: [laughs] That'll be all right.

MACARTHUR: That's the old story of the pioneer.

JFK: [laughs]

MACARTHUR: There isn't a single trouble that you have that isn't a relic of either the—most of them from the Eisenhower administration and some of them from the preceding administration that he drove under the rug and left for you to clean up. But the general situation is undoubtedly on the up curve. You probably place more emphasis on these columnists, who are the damnedest bunch of petty liars the world has ever seen.

JFK: Or second-guessers.

MEETING WITH GENERAL DOUGLAS MACARTHUR, AUGUST 16, 1962

[break]

JFK: [Yeah?]

MACARTHUR: This talk about the Republican Party taking the House is a lot of [hocus bull?]. They've got no more chance of taking the House than I have of flying over this house.

[break]

JFK: Yeah, yeah. Do you know this fellow Romney? Have you met Romney? George Romney?[23]

MACARTHUR: Only casually.

JFK: Yeah, yeah.

MACARTHUR: He doesn't stand a chance.

JFK: What do you think, Rockefeller? You think he has . . .

MACARTHUR: He's a very presentable man, personally, he would fill the bill. He looks it and everything. But he . . . to begin with, Mr. President, he's practically unknown. I tried it out. I talked with one hundred people the other day, just as I happened to meet them. The bellhops. They would be window cleaners [?]. They were the maids. They were the servants. They were my own board of directors, and others. And of those hundred people, with the exception of the board of directors, there were only two that knew who Romney was.

JFK: [Yeah?]

MACARTHUR: You can't pick the president that way. Now I know this piece came out yesterday, according to the *New York Times*, which is not always reliable.

JFK: [laughs]

MACARTHUR: And said he wasn't going to run in '64.

JFK: Yeah, I heard those statements.

MACARTHUR: Well, he [laughs], it was a pretty smart move, because even if he got the nomination, he couldn't win it. And he'd have to build himself up as

---

23. George Romney (1907–1995) was CEO of American Motors Corporation, governor of Michigan (1963–1969), and Republican candidate for president in 1968. His son, Mitt Romney (b. 1947), was governor of Massachusetts (2003–2007) and ran unsuccessfully for the Senate against Edward M. Kennedy in 1994. He became the Republican nominee for president in 2012.

the governor of Michigan and make a campaign from the bottom up. No, don't worry about these smart-aleck columnists that have to write something. It's their bread and butter, you know. And the easiest thing is to get the big figure and damn him. I remember listening to old Mr. Hearst once. William Randolph Hearst.[24] And he was talking to a group of young reporters that he had just assembled. And at that time, he was at the height of his journalistic empire. And he said, "Now," he said, "the best way, the main purpose of my papers," he says, "is to sell them." And he says, "Dry and dull papers," he says, "never make the grade." Now, he says, "When you don't get something sensational," he says, "make it." And some little fellow says, "Well, Mr. Hearst, how do you make it?" Well, he says, pick out the finest, the most honest, the most prominent man in your society, and attack him [physically and—?]

JFK: [laughs]

MACARTHUR: He says, "He'll deny it," he says, "and then you'll have the sensation."

JFK: Yeah. Then you'll have it.

MACARTHUR: And there are a great many of these horrors. They'd rise up and vehemently deny, but a great many of them do that. Their stock in trade is a tirade against the great.

---

24. William Randolph Hearst (1863–1951) was a legendary newspaper publisher, the originator of "yellow journalism," and the inspiration for the lead character in the 1941 film *Citizen Kane*. He was also a Democratic member of Congress (1903–1907).

MEETING WITH PRESIDENT DWIGHT D.
EISENHOWER, SEPTEMBER 10, 1962

John F. Kennedy was an unlikely successor to Dwight D. Eisenhower. The former supreme commander of the Allied Forces in Europe took a while to warm up to the former navy lieutenant, twenty-seven years his junior, whom he called "that young whippersnapper." Kennedy had not met with Eisenhower once during his eight-year presidency, and during the 1960 campaign he freely criticized his complacent leadership. But that surface chilliness concealed a genuine respect that only grew as they began to know each other as fellow presidents. Kennedy drew upon Eisenhower's military and political wisdom on numerous occasions, particularly during the Cuban Missile Crisis. This conversation, in the aftermath of the crisis, included some shared exasperation at the daily price paid for being France's ally; reflections on the Cold War and its flash point, Berlin; and Ike's memories of early tensions with the Russians in the waning days of World War II.

EISENHOWER: Well, of course, on that one, Mr. President, I've personally, I've always thought this from the beginning. If they believe there is no amount of strength you can put in Berlin, they can say that. I would think that you could . . . What's his name, Khrushchev,[25] said to me at Camp David, he was talking about [the United States] needing some more troops [in West Germany], there was somewhat at that time in the public about more, a couple more divisions, and so . . . he says, "What are they talking about?" He says, "For every division they can put in Germany, I can put ten, without any trouble whatsoever."

And I said, "We know that." And I said, "But we're not worrying about that." And I said, "I'll tell you, I don't propose to fight a conventional war." If you declare, if you bring out war, bring on a war of global character, there are going to be no conventional, nothing conventional about it." And I told him flatly. And he said, "Well." He said, "That's a relief. Neither one of us can afford it." "Yes," I said that, and I said, "OK, so I agree to that, too." [laughter]

JFK: Right, right.

---

25. Nikita Sergeyevich Khrushchev (1894–1971), first secretary of the Communist Party and thereby the political leader of the Soviet Union from 1953 to 1964.

EISENHOWER: But you see, what these people are afraid of, I mean the essence of his argument was, if you try to fight this thing conventionally from the beginning, when do you start to go nuclear? And this will never be until you yourselves in other words become in danger and he said, "That means all of Europe is again gone." And that . . .

JFK: But of course, we've got all these nuclear weapons, as you know, stored in West Berlin. All we are . . . what they are really concerned about is that the Russians will seize Hamburg, which is only a few miles from the border, and some other towns, and then they'll say, "We'll negotiate." So then Norstad[26] has come up with this whole strategy. I think the only difficulty is that no one will . . . that if we did not have the problem, as I say, of Berlin and maintaining access through that autobahn authority, then you would say that any attempt to seize any part of West Germany, we would go to nuclear weapons. But of course, they never will. But it's this difficulty of maintaining a position 120 miles behind their lines.

EISENHOWER: Mr. President, I'll tell you, here's something. I can't document everything. But Clay[27] was there. Poor, poor old Smith[28] is gone. We begged our governments not to go into Berlin. We . . . I asked that they build a cantonment capital, a cantonment capital at the junction of the British, American, and Russian zones. I said, "We just don't, we can't do this." Well, it had been a political thing that had been done first in the advisory council, European Advisory Council, in London. And later confirmed and . . . but Mr. Roosevelt said to me this twice—I'm talking about my concern. And he said, "Ike,"—and he was always very, you know, informal—he said, "Ike," he said, "quit worrying about Uncle Joe. I'll take care of Uncle Joe."[29] That's exactly what he told [me]. Once in Tunis and once when I came over here about the first or second or third of January of '44. That's the last time I ever saw him. Now he just wouldn't believe that these guys were these tough and really ruthless so-and-sos they were.

---

26. Lauris Norstad (1907–1988), air force general and commander in chief of the U.S. European Command.

27. Lucius Clay (1897–1978), army general, military governor of the U.S. Zone in Germany (1947–1949), and advisor to President Kennedy on Berlin issues.

28. Walter Bedell Smith (1895–1961), Eisenhower's chief of staff during World War II, ambassador to the Soviet Union (1946–1948), and director of Central Intelligence (1950–1953).

29. A popular nickname for Joseph Stalin.

Ish bin ein Bearleener
    (Ich bin ein Berliner/I am a Berliner),
kiwis Romanus sum
    (civis Romanus sum/I am a Roman citizen),
Lust z nach Bearlin comen
    (Lass' sie nach Berlin kommen/
    Let them come to Berlin)

ABOVE: PRESIDENT KENNEDY'S SPEECH
CARD FROM BERLIN, SPELLED PHONETI-
CALLY TO IMPROVE HIS PRONUNCIATION
OF GERMAN AND LATIN WORDS

LEFT: PRESIDENT KENNEDY ADDRESSES
THE PEOPLE OF WEST BERLIN, RUDOLPH
WILDE PLATZ, JUNE 26, 1963

MEETING WITH VICE ADMIRAL HYMAN RICKOVER, FEBRUARY 11, 1963

Hyman Rickover had one of the most storied military careers of the twentieth century. Born in Poland in 1900, he emigrated with his family in 1905, at the time of anti-Jewish pogroms, and grew up in New York and Chicago, where he graduated from John Marshall High School and won admission to the United States Naval Academy. So began a remarkable naval career encompassing sixty-three years of active duty, marked by administrative ability, tireless work, and extremely independent judgment. Rickover served on submarines in particular and over the course of the 1940s and 1950s became the legendary "Father of the Nuclear Navy," known for his technical expertise, his strategic wisdom, and his personal interest in interviewing thousands of officer candidates. One of them, Jimmy Carter, later claimed that Rickover was the greatest influence on him after his parents. Rickover gave President Kennedy a plaque that he displayed on his desk in the Oval Office, featuring the words of an old Breton fisherman's prayer: "O God, Thy sea is so great and my boat is so small."

Unusually, for a Cold Warrior on the front lines, Rickover was fascinated by education and the role it played in bettering society. In 1960, he published *Education and Freedom,* which announced that "education is the most important problem facing the United States today" and called for a "massive upgrading" of academic standards. Two years later, he published a detailed comparison of American and Swiss schools, arguing that the United States was inferior in nearly every respect. In this conversation with Kennedy, he took advantage of a presidential audience to press his point, dexterously comparing Kennedy's privileged upbringing with his own as a first-generation immigrant.

JFK: I was just reading this rather good article in the *Baltimore Sun* this morning about school dropouts, in Baltimore and some of these other cities, what percentage they are, and why. A rather large percentage is lack of interest and so on. Now, why is it that children seem, particularly on television, and having exposure to the affluent society, why is it that it isn't drilled into them, a sufficient sort of competitive desire . . . [to this rather rich]?

RICKOVER: I'll tell you, you can take two opposite extremes, you can take my case and you can take your case. In your case, you had parents who recognized that money can do you a great deal of harm. And they took care to see, dammit,

MEETING WITH VICE ADMIRAL HYMAN RICKOVER,
FEBRUARY 11, 1963

that it did not. That's because you had intelligent parents. In my case, I was brought up where, a lot times we didn't have enough to eat; you had to go out and fight, and so one recognized the importance of school. I think it's something like that. Now when you get in between, that's where you have your problems.

JFK: What I think of, how drilled into my life was the necessity for participating actively and successfully in the struggle. And yet I was brought up in a luxurious atmosphere, where this was a rather hard lesson. And you, from your own life . . .

RICKOVER: Your parents were exceptional in this respect. The vast majority of parents who have children now [unclear] are just trying to do everything they can to make everything easy. In that way they are really defeating what they are trying to do.

JFK: If you think that it's built into everybody, a survival instinct, which there is, . . .

RICKOVER: You know I do! You know it. You know it. Because everything is made easy for them. Some of them get to expect, your parents will take care of you. So you have youngsters going off and getting married. And fully expecting that the parents, you know, will come to their support. And they do. I can give you any number of cases like that, where the parents would have done much better for their children to throw 'em out. There comes a time in every animal life—and human being is a form of animal life—when you have to fend for yourself. This is where the trouble is. Today you can make these arguments today and society will support you. That never used to be the case before. This is the problem we have to face, and we have to try to get around it. Now excuse me if I'm taking up your time, you're the busiest man in the world.

JFK: Well.

RICKOVER: I don't want to get on all my ideas. But I have thought that if you really wanted to do something for this country, you will [hit on?] education. Because without education, you can't do it.

TWO

POLITICS

A fter losing the nomination for vice president at the 1956 Democratic Convention—the only loss of his career—Kennedy declared, "From now on I'm going to be the total politician." He courted old-school political bosses and new-school television executives; he built relationships around the country and became a formidable presidential candidate in 1960. Despite his earlier claim, in his 1960 dinner-party tape, to be temperamentally challenged, he clearly relished politics, in defiance of a rising 1950s sensibility that disdained backroom deals as a regrettable price to pay for democracy. President Eisenhower once said, "The word 'politics,' I have no great liking for that." Kennedy responded, "I do have a great liking for the word 'politics.' It's the way a president gets things done."

It was in pursuit of politics that Kennedy took to the phones with the zeal that he did. He conducted a great deal of business by telephone; congratulating governors, senators, and representatives when their fortunes were high; comforting them when they were low; and cajoling them for their help when he needed something done. This last he did often, as he drove forward the agenda of the New Frontier, often in the face of fierce headwinds. Even after winning the presidency and a Democratic majority in 1960, he had to deal with an obstructionist Congress that included Republicans and conservative Democrats, among them the "boll weevils" (Southern conservatives), who tied up most of the important committees. Many of these calls reveal democracy in action, as a president does what he can to nudge a bill forward, alternating between charm and political hardball. Despite the obstacles, the Kennedy administration proposed 653 pieces of legislation in its first two years, almost twice Eisenhower's rate, and 304 became law.

If politics was changing because of Kennedy, it was also changing in spite of him; or more specifically, because the change that he represented encouraged many others to alter the status quo, in ways that did not always advance his political fortunes. An enormous number of voters would leave the Democratic Party because of its position on Civil Rights, or simply because they had moved out to the suburbs and had new priorities. But Kennedy's adroit command of the issues, savvy use of television, frequent press conferences, and nimble outreach ensured that his popularity remained high.

MEETING WITH GOVERNOR EDMUND "PAT" BROWN
OF CALIFORNIA, APRIL 20, 1961

CALL TO GOVERNOR EDMUND BROWN, NOVEMBER 7, 1962

The Democrats held their own in the midterm election of 1962, picking up two seats in the Senate and losing four in the House. A notable loss for the Republicans occurred in California, where Richard Nixon, fresh from his presidential defeat in 1960, lost in the gubernatorial race to Edmund "Pat" Brown by nearly 300,000 votes, despite leading in the polls before election day. JFK called in his congratulations to Governor Brown, and midway through the conversation, spoke to the governor's son, Edmund "Jerry" Brown. Jerry Brown succeeded his father as the governor of California, winning election in 1974 and again in 2010.

OPERATOR: Mr. President?

JFK: Yeah.

OPERATOR: He's in a conference room down on the fifth floor. They'll send for him.

JFK: OK. No hurry.

OPERATOR: Thank you.

JFK: [skips] to it in '60. Hell, I'd gotten them all in shape, so that [skips] huh?

PAT BROWN: Well, let me just tell you this . . .

JFK: I'll tell you this, you reduced him to the nuthouse.

PAT BROWN: Listen, but you gave me instructions and I follow your orders . . .

JFK: [chuckling] I understand. But God, that last farewell speech of his . . .[1]

PAT BROWN: Wasn't that terrible?

JFK: Well, no, but it shows [skips] what's going to happen [skips] out there?

PAT BROWN: I don't see how he can ever recover. [skips] the leaders.

---

1. On November 7, 1962, following an unexpected loss in California's gubernatorial election, Richard Nixon held a press conference in the Beverly Hilton Hotel, in which he excoriated the press, "so delighted that I have lost," and announced, "You won't have Nixon to kick around anymore, because, gentlemen, this is my last press conference." Ten years later to the day, he would win reelection to the presidency.

JFK: Yeah.

PAT BROWN: Knight[2] walked out on him, [unclear] told me [skips]. This is a peculiar fellow. [skips] I really think he's psychotic. He's an able man, but he's nuts.

JFK: Yeah.

PAT BROWN: Like a lot of these paranoiacs, they're. . . But [skips] good job.

JFK: What did Kuchel[3] win by?

PAT BROWN: Kuchel won by about [skips] thousand. The Cuban thing really helped him. [skips] flew back, why it really helped him. But we have a legislature [skips] out here now, fifty-three, two-thirds majority and we have two-thirds in the senate. So, California [unclear] [skips] I'll tell you that. We have our responsibilities that I [skips] too.

JFK: Yeah, yeah.

PAT BROWN: But I'd like to make it kind of a model of your [skips] legislative program I'd like to move ahead. Why don't you come out here and spend a couple of days during the—

JFK: Well, I was thinking of coming out in December. I've got to go out to Los Alamos [skips] in December, but I'll give you a call. [skips]

PAT BROWN: [unclear] fine [unclear]. Would you just do one thing for me? Would you say hello to my son Jerry,[4] who came back from Yale Law School and really put me over at San Francisco?

JFK: Oh, good. Fine.

PAT BROWN: [Say] hello to him. This is my son Jerry.

JERRY BROWN: Hello, Mr. President.

JFK: Jerry, how are you?

JERRY BROWN: Fine.

JFK: I was up there campaigning in November [skips] those fellow [unclear]. [laughs]

JERRY BROWN: [unclear] the undergraduates [skips].

---

2. Goodwin Knight (1896–1970) was governor of California (1953–1959).

3. Thomas Kuchel (1910–1994) was a moderate Republican senator from California (1953–1969).

4. Edmund G. "Jerry" Brown, b. 1938, is thirty-ninth governor of California (2011–present), after previously serving as the thirty-fourth (1975–1983). He was a candidate for the presidency in 1976, 1980, and 1992.

JFK: [laughing] I see. Good.

JERRY BROWN: [skips] you sure did.

JFK: I told them that, God, [skips] I could only [skips] by less than the [skips].

JERRY BROWN: Well, you'll take California by ten times as much as you did [skips] before.

JFK: Well, we'll try. Well, listen, good luck [skips]. Take care. Bye, Jerry.

CALL TO ATTORNEY GENERAL ROBERT F. KENNEDY, MARCH 2, 1963

There are a great many tape-recorded conversations between President Kennedy and his brother Attorney General Robert Kennedy, on every imaginable topic. This conversation captures well the intimacy they shared. It is one of the few times anyone used the word "Jack" on the tapes, and it conveys their easy humor, laughing at the idea that their adversaries thought the Kennedys were springing a trap, when they had no idea of its existence. It also reveals an interesting distinction between the two brothers, JFK noting with alarm that his approval rating had declined from 76 to 70 percent, and RFK reminding him that it was still extraordinarily high. JFK's greater caution supports the claim of Arthur M. Schlesinger, Jr.: "John Kennedy was a realist brilliantly disguised as a romantic; Robert Kennedy, a romantic stubbornly disguised as a realist."

RFK: Hello, Jack?

JFK: Yeah.

RFK: The thing, of course, to remember on this, I don't know how much you're gonna get into it, but the thing to remember on this, is this, what you did on that day, Tuesday, for Wednesday, was something that was added to the plan.

JFK: Yeah. Oh, yeah.

RFK: And not something that was taken away or was in a plan that was made inadequate by some deficiency in withdrawal of something . . .

JFK: Yeah, that's right.

RFK: That you added that on Tuesday.

JFK: Yeah.

RFK: Never been planned before and this plan specifically said this wouldn't be done.

JFK: Yeah.

RFK: It was something that you added in order to help.

JFK: You heard about . . .

RFK: But I, you know, if somebody's gonna say something in the Senate about it . . .

JFK: Yeah. Well, you know how they make everything look lousy these days.

You know, Rowland Evans[5] said that he talked to Dirksen.[6] Dirksen said, "I don't quite get this." He said, "What, you know, just say I don't know, they, I think the Kennedys are planning something to trap us into this [laughter] 'cause they're pretty smart down there."

RFK: Well, that's what we have. We haven't figured how to close the trap yet.

JFK: Yeah. That's right. We haven't quite figured out.

RFK: But we'll learn it.

JFK: It just shows you, boy, what that press is, doesn't it?

RFK: But God. Still, the poll.

JFK: What?

RFK: What, you're down to 70 percent?

JFK: When?

RFK: Huh?

JFK: When was this?

RFK: The Gallup Poll.

JFK: When was that?

RFK: Oh, about two days ago?

JFK: No. I didn't see it.

RFK: Yeah. It went 76 percent to 70.

JFK: Yeah?

RFK: But with your popularity 70 percent now . . .

JFK: Yeah.

RFK: You'd break fifty-fifty with a Republican.

JFK: What?

RFK: Jesus. 70 percent, 18 percent are against you.

JFK: Yeah?

RFK: Well, I mean, I don't get what the, the press must be doing you some good.

JFK: Then what, you'd break fifty-fifty?

RFK: Do fifty-fifty with a Republican.

JFK: Oh, you mean on approval and disapproval?

---

5. Rowland Evans (1921–2001) was a conservative Washington-based columnist who worked extensively in both print and TV media. In 1963, he began writing "Inside Report" with his partner, Robert Novak.

6. Everett Dirksen (1896–1969) was a Republican senator from Illinois (1951–1969) and Senate minority leader (1959–1969).

RFK: Yeah. And then the independents.

JFK: I didn't see that poll. Was this in the *Post*?

RFK: I don't know what paper. I read it going up in the plane Wednesday or Thursday.

JFK: I see.

RFK: You think you got troubles, you ought to see what's happening to Nelson Rockefeller.[7]

JFK: Why? What?

RFK: Well, you know, all the bars, they call every drink a Nelson Cocktail, a Rockefeller Cocktail. Everything's the same except it's 15 percent more. [laughter]

JFK: Do they really?

RFK: Oh, and all, you walk along the streets, and out in the front . . .

JFK: Yeah.

RFK: It says, "Come in and buy a Nelson, a Rockefeller Cocktail." Everything costs 15 percent more. In every bar! How would you like that following you around?

JFK: Yeah, but he's lucky those papers aren't publishing . . .

RFK: Well, then, did you see the story about him in . . .

JFK: *Wall Street Journal*?

RFK: *Wall Street Journal*. That's not a complete plus.

JFK: Yeah.

RFK: I think he's really having his problems. Troubles.

JFK: Yeah.

RFK: You're not. I've seen you on television.

JFK: We've dropped 6 percent in a month, have we?

RFK: Since January.

JFK: Oh, since that Congress has been back.

RFK: Yeah, and it gets a little bit more partisan, but imagine 70 percent?

JFK: Yeah.

RFK: Better than you were in '60.

JFK: OK.

RFK: Righto.

---

7. Nelson Rockefeller (1908–1979) was Republican governor of New York (1959–1973), vice president (1974–1977) under Gerald Ford, and a perennial possible candidate for the presidency.

CALL TO ATTORNEY GENERAL ROBERT F. KENNEDY, MARCH 4, 1963

In this typical conversation, RFK and JFK exchange political gossip about friends as well as enemies; they understand each other so well they nearly finish each other's sentences.

JFK: Hello?

RFK: Jack?

JFK: Yeah.

RFK: Oh, Ed Guthman[8] went to a party the other night . . .

JFK: Yeah.

RFK: . . . and was talking to Doris Fleeson[9] . . .

JFK: Yeah.

RFK: . . . who's evidently very bitter.

JFK: Yeah.

RFK: You know as she always, usually is. But I don't know whether there might be some attention paid to her or somebody look at her or something.

JFK: Yeah. What's she bitter about?

RFK: She's just mad, generally.

JFK: Yeah.

RFK: You know the way she gets. [skips]

JFK: Yeah . . . [skips] . . . be Republicans there, and she doesn't like McCone,[10] and she's . . . What is it particularly?

RFK: Well, he didn't . . . she just seemed mad, generally, but I don't know whether . . . she seems always somebody that if somebody gave her a little attention occasionally then maybe she'd come around a bit.

JFK: Well, it's pretty difficult.

---

8. Edwin O. Guthman, RFK's press secretary, and a former Pulitzer Prize–winning reporter for the *Seattle Times*.

9. A reporter who became the first nationally syndicated female columnist in 1945.

10. John A. McCone was appointed director of Central Intelligence on November 29, 1961, succeeding Allen Dulles, who resigned in the wake of the Bay of Pigs disaster.

PRESIDENT KENNEDY CONFERS WITH ATTORNEY GENERAL ROBERT F. KENNEDY
OUTSIDE THE OVAL OFFICE, OCTOBER 3, 1962

RFK: Is it?

JFK: Well, she, you know, is just a waspish woman and she's always mad at something. She's mad at the, because we have the Republicans or we're not fighting hard enough for, I dunno, Civil Rights or some goddamn thing, whatever it may be. She's always sore. I don't have any contact with her.

RFK: Yeah.

JFK: And . . .

RFK: Well, anyway, you might keep it in mind if something comes up.

JFK: You never see her, do you?

RFK: Well, I don't, no. No . . . but she is just a bitter bitch.

JFK: Yeah. She's around yelling all the time. Somebody I . . . Tell me, we hear a rumor that John McCone's gonna quit some time, at a time when it suits him.

RFK: Ah, Marquis Childs.[11]

JFK: You hear that?

RFK: You know what Marquis Childs . . .

JFK: Yeah.

RFK: . . . told Ed Guthman?

JFK: Yeah? He told Ed Guthman what?

RFK: He said that they're really pouring that stuff out of CIA against the administration.

JFK: CIA is?

RFK: Yeah. Did you see his article today?

JFK: Yeah. Well, that was obviously based on what John told him.

RFK: John McCone looked good in that thing.

JFK: Yeah, but I didn't think he looked great. No matter how . . .

RFK: Well, that's what Dave, he said, "I wrote that story in order to make sure that the record was clear on what they're doing."

JFK: What? That they're putting it out?

RFK: Yeah. I tell you . . .

JFK: But, of course, he put it that he was only sending it into the . . .

RFK: Yeah, CIA.

JFK: . . . CIA. But he says that CIA is pouring it out?

RFK: Yeah. And I think he specified on behalf of John McCone.

---

11. Columnist for the *St. Louis Post-Dispatch* and a prominent biographer.

JFK: And McCone was right?

RFK: Well, that John McCone, that they're trying to make themselves look good.

JFK: Yeah.

RFK: And that's what he said. "This is where it's coming from," he said.

JFK: Yeah. Yeah. He's a real bastard, that John McCone.

RFK: Yeah.

JFK: Yeah. We got him. Do you have an . . . ?

RFK: Well, he was useful at a time.

JFK: Yeah, but, boy, it's really evaporated. . . . But he's making such a . . . Of course, everybody's on to him now. That's the trouble. He's stupid himself. Everybody's saying he's a horse's ass. But you mean that fifteen hundred terrorists and guerrillas that are being trained over there isn't quite the way it was. They've got fifteen hundred students, how many of them are being trained as terrorists and guerrillas, how many have been picked up is another good question. They don't, never have anything very precise.

RFK: Yeah.

JFK: The . . .

RFK: Shall I give you another problem?

JFK: Yeah.

RFK: This TFX.[12]

JFK: Yeah.

RFK: Is somebody watching that? The beginning of that whole contract, is that what it is that . . .

JFK: Yeah. Yeah.

RFK: Well, because the newspapermen think that there's something there now.

JFK: Not that we know. Who, what do they think is there?

RFK: Well they think it's, that there's . . .

JFK: What?

RFK: Something funny that went on, but I just think that somebody better . . .

JFK: Well, you know what went on? [laughs] Nobody wanted to go to Topeka, Kansas. [laughs] That's all that went on. [laughs]

---

12. An air force tactical fighter plane program, inherited from the Eisenhower administration, that was plagued by a difficult bid process.

RFK: Yeah. But I want, think we ought to make sure somebody's looking at it. Look at the hearings and everything.

JFK: Well, I don't, you know I think it's a . . . . your friend John McClellan.[13]

RFK: Yeah.

JFK: But, actually, nothing went on, so that's why they're never going to find anything. I know what went on. Nothing. Because of Topeka, Kansas. [laughs] That's where that contract would have gone, you know, that was the alternate.

RFK: Yeah. Well, I remember the discussion.

JFK: Yeah. Well, that was the whole thing.

RFK: Yeah.

JFK: But, let's see, there's that and Doris and what was the other matter?

RFK: Oh, it's just John McCone.

JFK: Yeah, well, I don't know what we can do about old John.

RFK: Except the . . . I suppose if somebody could get the message to him that there . . .

JFK: I thought that you could say that, first that . . .

RFK: They're saying . . .

JFK: . . . all the press are saying that they're pouring out a lot of stuff to try to make, you know, the CIA or McCone look good at the expense of the administration, that there's a lot of talk about it on the Hill and everything. I'd like to have John know about that. So maybe he'd then decide it wasn't so wise.

RFK: Yeah.

JFK: You, you aren't going to be seeing him, are you? Is he coming . . .

RFK: Yeah, I'm going to see him Thursday, Wednesday. He's coming to the house for dinner.

JFK: Uh-huh. Well, he's going up tomorrow to testify. Thought you . . .

---

13. John McClellan (1896–1977) was a long-serving representative of Arkansas as a member of the House of Representatives (1935–1939) and Senate (1943–1977). "Powerful and prickly," in the words of Robert A. Caro, he fiercely defended the interests of his state as chairman of the Senate Appropriations Committee and steered huge quantities of federal largesse toward the construction of dams, navigable rivers, and other improvements. He was also the long-term chairman of the Senate Committee on Government Operations, which Lyndon Johnson once called "the key Democratic post in the whole Senate." McClellan became widely known in the 1950s for his aggressive leadership of the Senate Permanent Subcommittee on Investigations, which looked into the activities of those suspected of subversive activity, organized crime, labor rackets, and defense profiteering. In 1955, he hired Robert F. Kennedy as chief counsel to that committee.

RFK: He's been . . .

JFK: . . . might give it to him Tuesday night.

RFK: . . . better, though, hasn't he, on his testimony?

JFK: I guess he has, though there were . . . Well, that thing of . . . I don't know where Marq Childs got that thing, do you know?

RFK: Yes.

JFK: Did he get it from McCone?

RFK: McCone. That's what he implied to Ed Guthman.

JFK: Yeah, well, I mean that's not, you know, giving the dates when he sent the messages and everything. Christ, he never sent the message to anybody else. [needle skips] Why didn't he come back from his honeymoon?

RFK: Well, I know that . . .

JFK: Huh?

RFK: Well, you know, I understand . . .

JFK: [laughs] I think that's the only thing that, I mean, he isn't going to . . .

RFK: Yeah, I don't think Marquis Childs was too impressed.

JFK: Yeah?

RFK: I mean, the way he talked, he just said that that's where the stuff's coming from and that they're sticking it to you, the administration. So he just wanted to tell us . . .

JFK: Yeah.

RFK: . . . that that's going on.

JFK: Well . . . Well, why don't you tell John that Wednesday night.

RFK: OK.

JFK: Good.

CALL FROM ATTORNEY GENERAL
ROBERT F. KENNEDY, DATE UNKNOWN

In this call, JFK and RFK complain about unfavorable press coverage from Henry R. Luce, the baron of the Time-Life empire. Luce had devoted generous publicity to JFK when he was a rising politician, but as this conversation indicates, the winds could shift course unpredictably. The conversation continues with some reflection on the construction of schools on military bases, and frustrations relating to cost, reception, and the often imperfect relationship between the Kennedy administration and the leaders of the Civil Rights Movement.

RFK: Oh, Jack?

JFK: Yeah. How'd you think *Newsweek* was to you?

RFK: Oh, well, I thought that it was all right. They didn't say anything very new, did they?

JFK: No, but I thought it was fine. I thought it was good.

RFK: Did you?

JFK: Sure. If you read *Time* magazine . . . you read them yet?

RFK: Ye god, that's me?

JFK: Yeah. I saw Harry Luce today.

RFK: Had you seen *Time* at the time you saw him?

JFK: Yup.

RFK: Did you say anything?

JFK: Oh, yeah. I gave it to him for forty-five minutes. He says, "Well, I've been out in Phoenix and it doesn't seem that bad to me." I said, "Well, listen, looks bad to me."

RFK: I thought they were bastards.

JFK: Yeah.

RFK: They really went out of their way on that damn thing, didn't they?

JFK: Yeah. Yeah. But isn't that peculiar? You see, it shows that there's, he's really losing his grip. Here, he's in to see me, to ask me to come up to that dinner, you know . . .

RFK: Yeah.

JFK: . . . and he's coming in, the morning he comes in you'd think that at least he'd have given me a soft soap, that would've been much more difficult.

RFK: Yeah. What'd you say to him?

JFK: Oh, I left it with him in the morning, sort of, let's get a few good ones out of you. But then I decided, you know, and said I'll let you know later if I can come, but I just thought I don't want to leave it in doubt, 'cause you know, he will write a couple of good ones, and then I'd have to go, and I think, the *Newsweek* and Graham and everybody would think that was a, and in addition I think probably for me to be up there for *Time*, after what has obviously been—would we look like a . . .

RFK: Yeah. We wrote out the mistakes they made on the, just on the one thing, which was on the Cuban prisoners and, just incredible! I mean, how many, they just . . .

JFK: Yeah. Yeah.

RFK: . . . they just didn't want to make an effort, do they?

JFK: No. It's you know, it's a real, I mean they're just mean as hell up there. But I don't think it registers on them, or something.

RFK: He doesn't consider it, he doesn't see . . .

JFK: I don't think it registers on him. No, you know, they're awfully fair during, they were good in the campaign, and that was because—[unclear]'s the real . . .

RFK: Yeah.

JFK: He's the son of a bitch up there. And he, you see, he was out in the campaign, and they were pretty good, so I mean I don't think Luce is hostile, I think he just, you know, he hasn't got any sensitivity, he doesn't probably like the thing much anyway, but he hasn't got any sensitivity, he couldn't, he didn't think, seem to think this was bad even though there were five letters to the editor that all stunk. So, anyway, I thought I'd just write and tell him I didn't think I'd go.

RFK: Was he jolly?

JFK: Oh, yeah, he's very agreeable, very pleasant.

RFK: What I called you about is this damn school construction.

JFK: Yeah?

RFK: You know, for the schools down in these bases?

JFK: Yeah.

RFK: Had you wanted the schools to be put up?

JFK: No, I haven't really given this matter any thought at all, I just . . .

RFK: They understood over at HEW, you know, Ribicoff[14] announced it last March.

JFK: Yeah.

RFK: And as I understood that you weren't . . .

JFK: That's right.

RFK: . . . exactly happy about that.

JFK: Well, I didn't know what, that's right.

RFK: And then, they, and it's quite ridiculous actually, but then, and then they announced back in January, because they understood from Ted Sorensen that you wanted an announcement. They were going to put two more schools out, and they've announced six, but, for instance, Fort McClellan, they're gonna erect a school for, well, no, here's one, Fort Rucker. Grades one to six, 892 on-base children, a total of fourteen Negro children, and the estimated cost is $742,000.

JFK: Just because of the fourteen?

RFK: Yeah. Fort Stewart's twenty-three children, that's $297,000. Robbins Air Force Base is eight Negro children, $594,000. Fort Jackson, eighteen children, $234,000.

JFK: Fort Jackson where? Where's Fort Jackson?

RFK: Fort Jackson, South Carolina. Myrtle Beach is . . .

JFK: And what is your suggestion?

RFK: Well, and then they're gonna put two more, so it's eight. It's gonna cost about three million bucks. We got a court case, you see, at the present time.

JFK: Yeah.

RFK: And which probably won't be resolved for another year, or a year and a, maybe two years before it perhaps goes to the Supreme Court which will resolve all of these matters. What they will do by spending for these eight places, they'll spend about $3 million, and they'll get maybe an extra year for about fifty or sixty children . . .

JFK: Yeah.

RFK: . . . Negro children. Well, they've been going all this long period of time, it just seems like a hell of a lot of money. Now . . .

JFK: Well, the problem is a political problem, I suppose, isn't it?

---

14. Abraham Ribicoff (1910–1998), secretary of Health, Education, and Welfare (1961–1962) and senator from Connecticut (1963–1981).

RFK: Yeah. Having made the announcement.

JFK: Yeah. But, you know, was Roy Wilkins criticizing the way HEW did it first?

RFK: Yeah. Well, now, can I, can we see what . . .

JFK: What we should've done is just left with the . . .

RFK: That's right.

JFK: . . . legal case. I don't know how we got beyond that.

RFK: Well that's what was a mistake . . .

JFK: Yeah.

RFK: . . . which was made at the end of January.

JFK: Yeah.

RFK: But I told 'em over there that . . .

JFK: Yeah.

RFK: . . . make sure we have coordination on these damn things.

JFK: Yeah.

RFK: Ah well, can we leave it at that, if you don't have any strong feeling about it?

JFK: I want to talk to Ted Sorensen, 'cause he's been working on it.

RFK: All right.

JFK: Let me find out, 'cause he may know some of the problems that I don't know on it.

RFK: Well, I, what I'd like to do is to see if I could work something out, which would be satisfactory to everybody. Maybe it's not possible, but they are . . .

JFK: Or maybe you can . . .

RFK: Celebrezze[15] thought that you had been personally interested so I want to . . .

JFK: No, I'm not. I don't care. Just a real question of trying to deal with a political problem.

RFK: Well, whatever we do, we'll talk to Ted first.

JFK: OK, fine. I'll talk to him. Right.

---

15. Anthony J. Celebrezze (1910–1998), mayor of Cleveland from 1953 to 1962; in 1962 he would accept appointment from President Kennedy as secretary of Health, Education, and Welfare.

CALL TO SENATOR EDWARD M. KENNEDY,
MARCH 7, 1963

President Kennedy's youngest brother, Edward M. Kennedy, was one of the principal beneficiaries of the 1962 midterm election, and he won the Senate seat that he would hold until his death in 2009. Not yet "the Lion of the Senate," in this call he regales his older brother with humorous stories of Massachusetts politics.

EMK: . . . You know the thing that sort of got this, the one thing like yesterday that they had the big horse laugh about is they said, here's a guy, you know one of the wool people said, here's a guy who's talking about keeping out foreign imports, he says, and what's he do, but pulls up in a Mercedes-Benz!

JFK: Who's that?

EMK: Herter.[16]

JFK: Oh, is that right?

EMK: Yeah, and he evidently drives around here and he's got that Massachusetts governor's license plate on it, or something, so . . .

JFK: [laughs]

EMK: . . . everyone turns around and takes a look . . .

JFK: [laughs]

EMK: . . . he drove up to that wool meeting. He said that really let the balloon, air out of every balloon in there.

JFK: Right.

EMK: But . . .

JFK: But, of course, it's tough, I tell you, boy, we went through that yesterday for two hours . . .

EMK: Yeah.

JFK: . . . about what we could do on wool. You see, those guys don't want to give up that market.

EMK: Yeah.

---

16. Christian Herter (1895–1966), a Republican congressman and governor (1953–1957) of Massachusetts, and secretary of state (1959–1961) under President Eisenhower.

JFK: And, you know, it's just a . . .

EMK: Well, he's got a, you know . . .

JFK: But anyway, Christian, he's a great free-trader, but we're anyway, we're gonna, we're meeting with Pastore[17] tomorrow and we'll discuss it then.

EMK: He's, Mike's got, he's really got a ... awfully good grasp, and he made a hell of a good presentation . . .

JFK: Right.

EMK: . . . of the problem.

JFK: OK, good, fine.

EMK: Good enough.

JFK: See you later.

EMK: Bye.

---

17. John Pastore (1907–2000), Democratic senator from Rhode Island from 1950 to 1976.

CALL TO SENATOR GEORGE SMATHERS, JUNE 4, 1963

As President, Kennedy retained many of his friendships from the Senate. He particularly enjoyed the company of George Smathers, a Florida Democrat who acted as a grooms-man at his wedding, and managed the Southeast for Kennedy's presidential campaign. Smathers did not support much of the Civil Rights agenda, but his personal friendship was meaningful to Kennedy, and as this conversation shows, they laughed easily together.

JFK: [reading a facetious note] ". . . due to your correspondence with various members of the government over the last eighteen months, it appears to me that you are experiencing serious worries that the United States is about to be attacked by the United Nations. This is, indeed, a serious condition. In order to be able to be of assistance to you, I am glad to inform you that the president will fulfill his oath of office and defend the United States from any attack. The President does not believe the United States would be attacked by the United Nations, Iceland, Chad or the Samoan Islands. But he does want you to clearly understand that regardless of the source of the attack he will meet his responsi-bilities under the United States Constitution."

SMATHERS:[18] Right.

JFK: "While we have many other matters before us here, we want you to know that we are always glad to hear from you concerning any matters that are dis-turbing you."

SMATHERS: Fine, now that's very good. [laughter] I think that's good, it's cute.

JFK: Is that all right?

SMATHERS: I think that's fine. And would you have him, yeah, let me have a copy, so . . .

JFK: All right, I'll put on the letter, I'll put "copy to Senator Smathers."

SMATHERS: Yeah, that'd be very helpful.

JFK: OK.

---

18. George Smathers (1913–2007), Florida senator from 1951 to 1969, and a close friend of JFK's.

SMATHERS: I think that's fine.

JFK: OK. Thank you.

SMATHERS: . . . Mr. President, proud of you, [you go and get] . . . [laughter] I got that word, that's good, that'll, just enough, nice, that Samoan Islands. [laughter] But that, just what this damned fool needs to be told, see. He can't show that letter . . .

JFK: No.

SMATHERS: . . . and that'll stop that.

JFK: He can't show this one. OK. We'll get another one then. OK.

SMATHERS: All right. Say, I got, I talked, generally without, you know, about this fellow . . .

JFK: Yeah.

SMATHERS: Negotiating, Southern himself, Southern himself, that, that his crowd and he will do anything. They'll take down their pants and let 'em do anything.

JFK: Yeah.

SMATHERS: But they want to try and get a settlement then and . . .

JFK: Who's Southern?

SMATHERS: Huh?

JFK: Who's . . . Well, you explained to them what I think their problem is?

SMATHERS: Yes.

JFK: And they're conscious of it, are they?

SMATHERS: Yes, sir.

JFK: I see.

SMATHERS: Yes, sir, and they, they really, they all agree that this fellow shouldn't be there. I said, "Why in the hell did you get him there . . ."

JFK: Yeah.

SMATHERS: . . . for Christ's sake.

JFK: Yeah.

SMATHERS: Well, he said, he was the man, I don't know, a couple of big railroad presidents wanted him.

JFK: Yeah.

SMATHERS: But there's, there's some real bright fellows and the one I talked to is bright?

JFK: I'd let him work in the offices preparing the material, but I'd let some real charming fellow . . .

SMATHERS: That's right.

JFK: . . . be their front man.

SMATHERS: Dan Loomis[19] ought to do it, see. He's a . . .

JFK: Well, I don't think, you know, they're not playing for marbles now 'cause we're in it.

SMATHERS: That's right.

JFK: So I don't think they ought to worry about whether Wolfe's feelings are hurt. If he's not the right fellow to accomplish what we want, then . . .

SMATHERS: That's right.

JFK: . . . they ought to get the guy with more charm than anybody else. I mean, let Wolfe mastermind it, but let this guy put it . . .

SMATHERS: You're right.

JFK: . . . in a much more gracious, graceful way. That's my judgment to them.

SMATHERS: Well, I'm not, I'm just making it my own judgment.

JFK: Yeah.

SMATHERS: . . . and at least leaving you out, if it's all right.

JFK: But I'd put it pretty strong.

SMATHERS: Well, I am.

JFK: OK.

SMATHERS: All right, sir.

JFK: Right.

SMATHERS: That *Star* editorial doesn't bother you, does it?

JFK: Which one?

SMATHERS: Last night.

JFK: I didn't read it, fortunately.

SMATHERS: Well, it's . . .

JFK: What was it on? You?

SMATHERS: No, it was on you. [laughter] You know, you know, I . . . If it was on me, I would scream early. [laughter] As I said yesterday, oh, Christ, Drew Pearson[20] is getting ready to write a mean one on me again about some colored property my father owned.

---

19. Daniel P. Loomis, president of the Association of American Railroads.

20. Prominent Washington columnist.

JFK: Oh, well, we don't even think about that crap. We got so many that I don't read all those.

SMATHERS: I know it. I think you're doing fine. I say you're strong. God damn, you're gonna carry Florida.

JFK: OK, OK, see you later.

SMATHERS: OK.

JFK: OK.

SMATHERS: Bye-bye.

CALL TO LOU HARRIS, AUGUST 23, 1963

JFK was a voracious consumer of political information, whether it came from newspapers, friends, or professional pollsters. In the latter category, Lou Harris was a favorite, dispensing quick and sometimes hard information, with efficiency and topicality. Born in 1921, Harris was four years younger than Kennedy, and in his own way was bucking the political establishment, bringing up-to-the-minute information from the American people to the salons and solons of Washington. In 1960, JFK hired him to conduct polls for his campaign, and Harris continued to advise him during his presidency. In 1962, Harris devised the system of computer analysis of key precincts that would allow news organizations to project winners of elections.

JFK: Hello.

HARRIS: Mr. President.

JFK: Lou, how are you?

HARRIS: Just fine, sir. We're going to the field with a study here, and I just wondered on a number of things, what you might want in. We're going to test a lot of these pairings, like Goldwater and Rockefeller, and Romney, and I thought maybe Nixon, what do you think about that?

JFK: Um.

HARRIS: See where he sits.

JFK: Of course, he'll run the strongest, won't he?

HARRIS: I think he might. I also think he'd probably be a pretty good opponent.

JFK: Yeah.

HARRIS: But then, what about [unclear], what do you think about him?

JFK: Yeah, he doesn't have the strength, but, I mean, put him in. You've kept Romney at those same figures, didn't you? I thought that you were going to change them.

HARRIS: No, sir, to be perfectly frank about it, the *Newsweek* fellows got hold of them, and there's nothing I could do about it. I don't think he came out that strong.

JFK: No, as a matter of fact, it was submerged by the Eisenhower story.

HARRIS: Yeah. Which I think was all right, don't you?

JFK: Yeah. It doesn't make any difference.

HARRIS: It's a good way to show where their real strengths lie.

JFK: Of course, Eisenhower's strength is rather special, Nixon would be a better test.

HARRIS: Nixon would, yes. If there's any Republican . . .

JFK: That's right, he's not a party figure, because of that military background.

HARRIS: Now we are going to get a full read on the whites, on this whole Negro thing, that's something people want very strongly and I think especially . . .

JFK: I have the impression this thing's cooled off a bit, but I may be wrong.

HARRIS: Well, I think we will find that out. We're also going to do a before and after on this March on Washington thing. A lot of people say . . . But unless something will take place, I'm not sure it will have that much effect one way or the other.

JFK: Yeah, yeah.

HARRIS: Then on the other issues, I want to get a read to see how much good the test ban has done here.

JFK: Yeah, I'd be interested in that.

HARRIS: And whether they've fallen at all for this idea that all of a sudden we're great pals with Russia. [unclear] We'll have something, it will break at the time of the railroad strike. See if there's much credit on that. There's some indication there is credit from the last one on that.

JFK: Yeah, yeah.

HARRIS: And then the whole area of foreign aid. See how much that has done.

JFK: And the tax cut? Say, that tax cut vote was pretty bad before. What was your question, Lou?

HARRIS: We've got three on tax cut, actually. You know, I'm coming [out?] with something on that, Mr. President, which I think will put it in perspective. The fact is, if you ask people if they're in favor of a tax cut, and you'll get about two to one in favor of a tax cut. But then you ask them, do you think that if we don't have a tax cut, or if we have a tax cut, do you think that will help the economy of the country, and there you get about two and a half to one.

JFK: Yeah.

HARRIS: And [then you ask], would you rather delay the tax cut until the budget is solid, and then you get about a fifty-fifty split.

JFK: Yeah, that's right. I understand that.

HARRIS: So the answer is, I think, is, that as long as the tax cut is justified . . . concern it will help the economy . . . I think it will go . . . some of the people [skip] trying to defend the idea that—of it will. It's never been called that way . . .

JFK: Yeah.

HARRIS: I think you've been absolutely right in the way you've pushed it, the last couple months. That beginning, when [unclear] got up and tried to convince people that spending is a sound idea . . . was just murder on it.

JFK: Well, I thought I'd make a television speech before it came up for a vote.

HARRIS: Well, I think that's good. Do you think it will go through?

JFK: Well, I think so but I'm afraid the Republicans will try to put a limitation on it. God, they are obstructionist! I haven't really talked much about it, but I . . .

HARRIS: The other thing is, if you think it would be helpful to have a whole series on Congress, because I think people are really getting sort of fed up with Congress.

JFK: Yeah.

HARRIS: I don't see why you should be the one to take the rap on it.

JFK: Why don't you . . .

HARRIS: I have this feeling, Mr. President, that people are more and more aware on the issues, and know the congressmen less, than the other way around. In Washington, you get the feeling that it's only the congressmen that count, and the issues don't matter. I think if we can point that out, it would be very helpful.

JFK: I think if you could ask if they approve or disapprove of Congress, a lot of these things . . .

HARRIS: That's right, I could ask a whole series on that.

JFK: When will you be finished?

HARRIS: We'll have this back out, probably at the end of next . . .

JFK: I think you've had good interesting stuff. I think the Eisenhower was an interesting, sort of, new, different thing.

HARRIS: Right.

JFK: Where is Gallup? What's he doing these days? Does he have a new one coming up?

HARRIS: Well, I don't know. He had an awful thing on Negroes the other day, asked whites, "Do you think Negroes in your community really have an equal chance? Or do you think they get a bad break or something?"

JFK: Yeah.

HARRIS: I don't know. I think I'd give him a fifty [unclear] to be perfectly honest, that's what I've heard. We're picking up quite a number of papers now.

JFK: Are you?

HARRIS: Yes, sir. They would syndicate it, we're going to dry run it, right up to

Labor Day. But then the *Detroit Free Press*, the Knight papers picked it up, the [unclear] papers. *Newsday* up here in New York.

JFK: I should think every city that didn't have Gallup, that wasn't a paper that didn't have Gallup, would love to have you.

HARRIS: Well, I think we can get that. Now Mr. President, I do have a couple of ideas on '64 that I think have some merit, one on the whole South thing, and one on this education issue. I'll be down Tuesday, and I'll talk to Evelyn about that.

JFK: OK. OK.

HARRIS: . . . if you'd like to see me.

JFK: I think the problem of the South, of course, those last figures were pretty bad, Gallup had me beat . . .

HARRIS: Well, he's got you so far out in the East, and so low in the South. I'm sure that Eisenhower would be ten points over on the North, I mean the East, and eight points below in the South. So I think . . .

JFK: Is that right? You don't think we're in that bad shape in the South?

HARRIS: No, sir, and I can't believe that 74 percent. That's running as well as you did in Massachusetts. And I can't believe it. And my concern there is, he's going to have you falling ten points in the next three months. Which is bad. I think it's far more leveled out than that. On the South, I feel very strongly now that I think that, maybe you don't do it until after the session, but I think the governors are far better than the senators at this point, they're the guys that really have the political muscle. And I think a great deal can be done there. I have some ideas, should I write something out?

JFK: OK, fine, I'll see you next Tuesday.

CALL TO MAYOR RICHARD DALEY,
OCTOBER 28, 1963

As the Civil Rights Bill moved forward across the summer and fall of 1963, Kennedy needed to muster all of his allies to advance the cause. When an Illinois Democratic congressman named Roland Libonati defected, there was only one recourse, and that was to call the legendary political boss of Chicago, Mayor Richard Daley. Daley was an old friend who still wielded extraordinary influence and had helped Kennedy carry the crucial state of Illinois in 1960. In this call, Mayor Daley minces no words, telling the President that Libonati will "vote for any goddamned thing you want." But Daley's grip was slipping; Libonati did not support the bill. He did, however, pay the expected price, and was not a candidate for renomination in 1964.

JFK: . . . with that Judiciary Committee trying to get this Civil Rights together . . .

DALEY: Yeah.

JFK: Roland Libonati[21] is sticking it right up us.

DALEY: He is?

JFK: Yeah, because he's standing with the extreme liberals who are gonna end up with no bill at all. Then when we put together, he'll, gonna vote for the extreme bill. Then I asked him, If you'll vote for this package which we got together with the Republicans which gives us about everything we wanted, and he says, "No."

DALEY: He'll vote for it. He'll vote for any goddamned thing you want.

JFK: [laughter] Well, can you get him?

DALEY: I surely can. Where is he? Is he there?

JFK: Well, he's in the other room.

DALEY: Well, you have Kenny, tell Kenny to put him on the wire here.

JFK: Or would you rather get him when he gets back up to his office? That's better, otherwise, 'cause he might think . . .

DALEY: That's better. But he'll do it. The last time I told him, "Now look it, I don't give a goddamn what it is, you vote for anything the President wants and

---

21. Roland Libonati (1900–1991) was a Democratic member of Congress from 1957 to 1965. He refused to vote the way Daley urged him to.

this is the way it will be, and this is the way we want it, and that's the way it's gonna be."

JFK: That'd be good.

DALEY: I'll get him as soon as he gets back to the . . .

JFK: [laughs]

DALEY: What are they trying to do, they got you hanging under . . . ?

JFK: Well, we're gonna, we have a chance to pull this out.

DALEY: Yeah, but . . .

JFK: But you see, of course, these guys, they . . .

DALEY: What the hell's the matter with our own fellows?

JFK: That's why, well, it's good. Krol was . . . Philadelphia. Billy got him, and if you can get Libonati.

DALEY: Well, I'll [catch?] Libonati.

JFK: OK, good.

DALEY: Bye now.

JFK: Thanks, Dick.

CIVIL RIGHTS

Attendees included: Medgar Evers, Mississippi NAACP field secretary; Calvin Luper, Oklahoma City NAACP Youth Council president; Edward Turner, president of the Detroit NAACP branch; Jack E. Tanner, Northwest Area Conference NAACP president; Rev. W. J. Hodge; Dr. S. Y. Nixson; C. R. Darden, president of the Mississippi NAACP State Conference branches; Kelly M. Alexander, member of NAACP board of directors; Kivie Kaplan, chairman of NAACP Life Membership Committee; and Bishop Stephen G. Spottswood, chairman of the NAACP board of directors.

On September 27, 1940, in one of the first Oval Office conversations ever recorded, A. Philip Randolph of the Brotherhood of Railway Porters stood before Franklin Roosevelt and asked for better treatment for African-Americans. In the two decades that followed, there had been occasional breakthroughs—the integration of the armed forces, *Brown v. the Board of Education*, the integration of Little Rock—but they came too slowly for African-Americans impatient for full citizenship.

The generational shift signaled by Kennedy's election and the empowerment promised by his speeches only hastened this desire for change, in ways that the Kennedy administration was not at first prepared for. Painfully aware of the thinness of his mandate, JFK liked to quote Thomas Jefferson: "Great innovations should not be forced on slender majorities." His inaugural address, so eloquent on the subject of freedom around the world, was nearly mute on the great question of how the United States would finally live up to its creed at home.

But there was no stopping history. Kennedy had connected with African-American voters who sensed that they too might enjoy a New Frontier; more than 70 percent of them voted for him, nearly double what Adlai Stevenson had received four years earlier, and their support may well have elected him. On January 21, 1961, the day after Kennedy's inaugural address, an air force veteran named James Meredith submitted his application to the University of Mississippi (without noting his racial identity). That spring, an interracial Freedom Riders traveled on integrated buses through the South, challenging the segregated bus terminals as an example of systemic racism that oppressed African-Americans.

By the time the Oval Office tapes began to roll in the summer of 1962, the Kennedy administration had come some distance but still had work to do to catch up to where the leaders of the Civil Rights Movement wanted it to be. These tapes record that work in gripping detail, as President Kennedy uses all of the power of his office to persuade reluctant Southern governors to accede to federal power. The forces of resistance were strong; many American newspapers denounced the Kennedy administration, and a significant majority of American voters disapproved of the rapid pace of change. Ever attentive to public opinion, Kennedy knew that he was losing more voters than he was gaining as he began to lead on Civil Rights. But the moment had arrived, in ways that were increasingly obvious. As JFK worked to build a new foreign policy that included Africa and Asia, it was embarrassing to live in a federal city that was still segregated in most ways. The occasional sting of Soviet insults on the subject added to the pressure to bring American reality in line with American rhetoric. Sometimes it seemed that the fates themselves demanded change. One of the most crucial secret messages of the Cuban Missile Crisis, a private note from Kennedy to Khrushchev, was carried away from the Soviet embassy by a young African-American bicycle messenger.

And history argued for movement in other ways. The centennial of the Civil War spoke urgently to those attuned to nuance, as Kennedy surely was. Sometimes that parallel was overt, as when Dr. Martin Luther King, Jr., stood before the Lincoln Memorial and delivered the speech of his life. At other times, it was muted; when Kennedy signed an executive order commanding federal troops to prepare to enforce the integration of the University of Mississippi, he did so on a table that had belonged to Ulysses Grant, a fact he did not reveal to the media.

As the tapes rolled into the summer and fall of 1963, it was clear that the administration had crossed the Rubicon. Despite polls that indicated he was losing six or seven white voters for every new black voter he gained, Kennedy was determined to deploy the full powers of the presidency to advance the cause. On the great day of the March on Washington, within moments of Martin Luther King's "I Have a Dream" peroration, the leaders of the Movement were in the White House, talking strategy. Appropriately, A. Philip Randolph was there urging a president forward, using nearly the same words he had used in the Oval Office twenty-three years earlier. But this time, history had caught up to him. These conversations indicate a president committed to a meaningful Civil Rights Bill, although that bill did not become law until 1964, in a very different political environment.

PRESIDENT KENNEDY MEETS WITH MRS. MEDGAR EVERS, HER CHILDREN, REENA AND DARRELL EVERS, AND CHARLES EVERS, MEDGAR EVERS'S BROTHER, ON JUNE 21, 1963, TWO WEEKS AFTER MEDGAR EVERS'S ASSASSINATION BY A WHITE SUPREMACIST, OVAL OFFICE, JUNE 21, 1963

CALL TO GOVERNOR ROSS BARNETT, SEPTEMBER 22, 1962

President Kennedy's first call to Governor Ross Barnett of Mississippi during the crisis over the integration of the University of Mississippi revealed the battle lines. Near the end of the call, Governor Barnett, reverting to the ordinary chitchat of politicians, thanked the President for his interest in poultry. Even in that highly charged environment, the incongruity of that remark seemed to cause Kennedy to pause and suppress a laugh.

JFK: Hello? Hello, Governor?

BARNETT: All right. Yes.

JFK: How are you?

BARNETT: Is this . . . ?

JFK: This is the President.

BARNETT: Oh, well, Mr. President . . .

JFK: Well, I'm glad to talk to you, Governor. I am concerned about this situation, down there, as I know . . .

BARNETT: Oh, I should say I am concerned about it, Mr. President. It's a horrible situation.

JFK: Well now, here's my problem, Governor.

BARNETT: Yes.

JFK: Listen, I didn't put him in the university, but on the other hand, under the Constitution, I have to carry out the orders of the . . . carry that order out, and I don't want to do it in any way that causes difficulty to you or to anyone else. But I've got to do it. Now, I'd like to get your help in doing that.

BARNETT: Yes. Well, have you talked with the attorney general this morning?

JFK: Yeah. I talked to him, and in fact, I just met with him for about an hour, and we went over the situation.

BARNETT: Did he and Mr. Watkins[1] have a talk this morning, Tom Watkins, the lawyer from Jackson, or not?

JFK: Yes, he talked to Tom Watkins, he told me.

---

1. Thomas Watkins was a Mississippi attorney and close confidant of Governor Barnett.

JAMES MEREDITH, ESCORTED BY JOHN DOAR,
ASSISTANT ATTORNEY GENERAL FOR CIVIL RIGHTS IN THE
U.S. DEPARTMENT OF JUSTICE, OXFORD, MISSISSIPPI, OCTOBER 1, 1962

BARNETT: Yes, sir. Well, I don't know what . . . I haven't had a chance to talk to him.

JFK: Now, just wait, just one minute, because I've got the attorney general in the outer office, and I'll just speak to him.

BARNETT: All right.

JFK: Hello, Governor?

BARNETT: Yes. Hold on.

JFK: I just talked to the attorney general. Now, he said that he talked to Mr. Watkins.

BARNETT: Yes.

JFK: And the problem is as to whether we can get some help in getting this fellow in this week.

BARNETT: Yes.

JFK: Now, evidently we couldn't; the attorney general didn't feel that he and Mr. Watkins had reached any final agreement on that.

BARNETT: Well, Mr. President, Mr. Watkins is going to fly up there early tomorrow morning.

JFK: Right.

BARNETT: And could you gentlemen talk with him tomorrow? You . . .

JFK: Yes, I will have the attorney general talk to him and then . . .

BARNETT: Yes.

JFK: . . . after they've finished talking I'll talk to the attorney general . . .

BARNETT: All right.

JFK: . . . on the phone and then if he feels it's useful for me to meet with him . . .

BARNETT: I thought . . .

JFK: . . . I'll do that.

BARNETT: I thought they were making some progress. I didn't know.

JFK: Well, now . . .

BARNETT: I couldn't say, you know.

JFK: . . . he and Mr. Watkins, they can meet tomorrow. Now, the difficulty is, we got two or three problems. In the first place, what can we do to, first place, is the court's order to you, which I guess is, you're given until Tuesday. What is your feeling on that?

BARNETT: Well, I want . . .

JFK: What's your position on that?

BARNETT: . . . to think it over, Mr. President.

JFK: Right.

BARNETT: It's a serious matter, now, that I want to think it over a few days. Until Tuesday, anyway.

JFK: All right. Well now, let me, let me say this.

BARNETT: You know what I am up against, Mr. President. I took an oath, you know, to abide by the laws of this state.

JFK: That's right.

BARNETT: And our Constitution here and the Constitution of the United States. I'm on the spot here, you know.

JFK: Well now, you've got . . .

BARNETT: I've taken an oath to do just that, and you know what our laws are with reference to . . .

JFK: Yes, I understand that. Well now, we've got the . . .

BARNETT: . . . and we have a statute that was enacted a couple of weeks ago stating positively that no one who had been convicted of a crime, or whether the criminal action pending against them, would not be eligible for any of the institutions of higher learning. And that's our law, and it seemed like the Court of Appeal didn't pay any attention to that.

JFK: Well, of course the problem is, Governor, that I've got my responsibility, just like you have yours.

BARNETT: Well, that's true.

JFK: And my responsibility, of course, is to the . . .

BARNETT: I realize that, and I appreciate that so much.

JFK: Well now, here's the thing, Governor. I will, the attorney general can talk to Mr. Watkins tomorrow. What I want, would like to do is to try to work this out in an amicable way. We don't want a lot of people down there getting hurt.

BARNETT: Oh, that's right.

JFK: And we don't want to have a, you know, it's very easy to . . .

BARNETT: Mr. President, let me say this. They're calling me and others from all over the state, wanting to bring a thousand, wanting to bring five hundred, and two hundred, and all such as that, you know. We don't want such as that.

JFK: I know. Well, we don't want to have a lot of people getting hurt or killed down there.

BARNETT: Why, that's correct. Mr. President, let me say this. Mr. Watkins is really an A-1 lawyer, an honorable man, has the respect and the confidence of every lawyer in America who knows him. He's of the law firm of Watkins and

Eager. They've had an A rating for many, many years, and I believe this, that he can help solve this problem.

JFK: Well, I will, the attorney general will see Mr. Watkins tomorrow, and then I, after the attorney general and Mr. Watkins are finished then, I will be back in touch with you.

BARNETT: All right. All right. I'll appreciate it so much, now, and there, Watkins will leave here in the morning, and I'll have him to get into touch with the attorney general as to when he can see him tomorrow.

JFK: Yeah, he'll see him and . . .

BARNETT: Yes, sir.

JFK: . . . we will, then you and I'll be back and talk again.

BARNETT: All right.

JFK: Thank you.

BARNETT: All right.

JFK: OK.

BARNETT: I appreciate your interest in our poultry program and all those things.

JFK: Well, we're [suppressed laughter] . . .

BARNETT: Thank you so much.

JFK: OK, Governor. Thank you.

BARNETT: Yes, sir. All right now.

JFK: Bye now.

BARNETT: Thank you. Bye.

CALL TO GOVERNOR ROSS BARNETT, SEPTEMBER 30, 1962

In this follow-up conversation, the stakes have risen, with a death reported during the call, and a breakdown in order seemed imminent. When Kennedy announces, "We'll decide what we're gonna do," and demands that Governor Barnett refrain from giving speeches, it's clear that the tide has shifted.

BARNETT: . . . the commissioner of the highway patrol to order every man he's got.

JFK: Yeah. Well, now, how long's that gonna take? We don't want, uh, somebody . . .

BARNETT: Well, I haven't been able to locate him.

JFK: You can't locate?

BARNETT: The . . . he went to the . . . Here's what happened. He went to the doctor's office with this man that was hurt.

JFK: Yeah.

BARNETT: And he, I finally located him there after you'd told me to get, [have?] him to get more people, don't you see, if . . .

JFK: Yeah.

BARNETT: . . . you needed 'em.

JFK: Yeah.

BARNETT: And he thought then that fifty he had would be sufficient.

JFK: Yeah.

BARNETT: But I told him, by all means, to order out every one he had if he needed it.

JFK: Yeah.

BARNETT: And I'm certainly trying in every way . . .

JFK: Well, we can't consider moving Meredith² as long as, you know, there's a riot outside, 'cause he wouldn't be safe.

BARNETT: Sir?

---

2. James Meredith (b. 1933), an African-American seeking admission to the University of Mississippi, had been inspired to seek change by listening to President Kennedy's inaugural address.

JFK: We couldn't consider moving Meredith, if we haven't been able to restore order outside. That's the problem, Governor.

BARNETT: Well, I'll tell you what I'll do, Mr. President.

JFK: Yeah.

BARNETT: I'll go up there myself . . .

JFK: Well, now, how long will it take you to get there?

BARNETT: . . . and I'll get a microphone and tell 'em that you have agreed to, for him to be removed.

JFK: No. No. Now, wait a minute. How long?

BARNETT: [unclear]

JFK: Wait a minute, Governor.

BARNETT: Yes?

JFK: Now, how long is it going to take you to get up there?

BARNETT: 'Bout an hour.

JFK: Now, I'll tell you what, if you want to go up there and then you call me from up there. Then we'll decide what we're gonna do before you make any speeches about it.

BARNETT: Well, all right. Well . . .

JFK: No sense in . . .

BARNETT: . . . I mean, whatever you, if you'd authorize . . .

JFK: You see, if we don't, we've got an hour to go, and that's not, we may not have an hour.

BARNETT: This, this man . . .

JFK: Won't it take you an hour to get up there?

BARNETT: . . . this man has just died.

JFK: Did he die?

BARNETT: Yes.

JFK: Which one? State police?

BARNETT: A state policeman.

JFK: Yeah, well, you see, we gotta get order up there, and that's what we thought we're going to have.

BARNETT: Mr. President, please. Why don't you, can't you give an order up there to remove Meredith?

JFK: How can I remove him, Governor, when there's a riot in the street, and he may step out of that building and something happen to him? I can't remove him under those conditions. You . . .

PRESIDENT KENNEDY ADDRESSES THE NATION ON THE INTEGRATION OF THE UNIVERSITY OF MISSISSIPPI, SEPTEMBER 30, 1962

BARNETT: But, but . . .

JFK: Let's get order up there, then we can do something about Meredith.

BARNETT: . . . we can surround it with plenty of officials.

JFK: Well, we've gotta get somebody up there now to get order and stop the firing and the shooting. Then when, you and I will talk on the phone about Meredith.

BARNETT: All right.

JFK: But first we gotta get order.

BARNETT: I'll call and tell 'em to get every official they can.

JFK: That's right and then you and I . . .

BARNETT: [unclear]

JFK: . . . will talk when they've got the, when they get order there, then you and I'll talk about what's the best thing to do with Meredith.

BARNETT: All right, then.

JFK: Well, thank you.

BARNETT: All right.

MEETING WITH AMERICANS FOR DEMOCRATIC ACTION LEADERS, MAY 4, 1963

In the spring of 1963, the Civil Rights Movement had shifted its attention to the recalcitrant city of Birmingham, Alabama. An ugly campaign resulted, with growing anger between the advocates for change and the well-organized authorities commanded by Commissioner of Public Safety Theophilus "Bull" Connor. In this meeting, President Kennedy tries to explain his position before a prominent liberal organization, the Americans for Democratic Action, on the day that a now-famous photograph appeared in the *New York Times*, showing police dogs attacking peaceful protesters.

THE PHOTOGRAPH THAT SHOCKED THE NATION: POLICE DOGS ATTACK A PROTESTER IN BIRMINGHAM, ALABAMA, THE *NEW YORK TIMES*, MAY 4, 1963

JFK: There is no federal law that we can pass to do anything about that picture in today's *Times*. Well, there isn't. I mean what law can you pass to do anything about police power in the community of Birmingham? There is nothing we can do. There is no federal law, is no federal statute, no federal law we can pass. Now, the fact of the matter is that Birmingham is in worse shape than any other city in the United States, and it's been that way for a year and a half. We've been working, we've got a new mayor who was elected probably as a result of the efforts of this administration, working with the press, get those papers down there, working with the steel companies to try and get them to change their attitudes, the new mayor who was elected, is coming in on May 18, was elected by the Negroes, got a minority of the white vote. But it's being challenged in the Supreme Court; he doesn't take office until the Supreme Court decision is reached on May 18. And as it is today, Bull Connor's in charge, and this is just what Bull Connor wants.[3] I personally think that if I was in charge down there that I would wait until the new mayor is in. That is the only hope. What we have now is another bad day down there, the prisons are full. I mean, Bull Connor just eats this up. What they want, what the governor wants is to put the National Guard in there.

That's what is going to happen in a day or two. I would have, if I had been in charge of the operation, I think this was [a substantial] view, I would have waited until the new mayor came in. That is the best hope for Birmingham. That's what, all this happened for years [unclear]. I think it's terrible, the picture in the paper. The fact of the matter, that's just what Connor wants. And, as I say, Birmingham is the worst city in the South. They have done nothing for the Negroes in that community, so it is an intolerable situation, that there is no argument about. I am not saying that anybody ought to be patient. This may be the only way these things come to a head. I do think there is a chance which this new mayor represents in about a week. Now, what I think is going to happen, it's going to get much worse, we're going to have the National Guard in there and all sorts of trouble . . .

---

3. Theophilus Eugene "Bull" Connor (1897–1973) was commissioner of public safety in Birmingham, Alabama, and in charge of the city's police and fire departments. A former member of the Ku Klux Klan, he had strong views about segregation and led a walkout of the Alabama delegation when the Democratic convention of 1948 added a civil rights plank to its platform.

[break]

JFK: [pushed for more "moral suasion" on Civil Rights] Well, wait a, let me just say on the Civil Rights business. We have done not enough because the situation is so desperate. But we have shoved and pushed and the Department of Justice has, there is nothing that my brother's given more time to. And I quite agree, if I were a Negro I would be awfully sore, but there's not much. I had some newspaperman in here telling me, "Isn't it outrageous in Birmingham?" and I said, "Why are you over there eating at the Metropolitan Club[4] every day? You talk about Birmingham and you're up there at the Metropolitan Club. Some of our distinguished commentators . . . every day lunch [unclear], they wouldn't even let Negro ambassadors in." So now he said, "Well, we want to work from the inside," and I said, "Well, your one contribution is that now they won't let white ambassadors in." [laughter] Most of your columnists that you read every day, they're all over there at the Metropolitan Club. So I think that we have worked hard on civil rights. I think it is a national crisis.

---

4. The Metropolitan Club is a prominent social organization in Washington, founded in 1863, with the goal of advancing "literary, mutual improvement and social purposes." Its clubhouse is at 17th and H Streets, near the White House. The Metropolitan Club had had a policy of granting honorary membership to all ambassadors posted to Washington. But in the early 1960s when new African nations had been formed and were beginning to send their own ambassadors to Washington, the Metropolitan Club had discontinued the honorary membership policy. Several members of the Kennedy administration, including Robert F. Kennedy, had resigned their memberships in protest of the club's segregation policies.

MEETING ABOUT BIRMINGHAM, MAY 12, 1963

After a night of grim violence in Birmingham, JFK's closest advisors gathered to keep events from spiraling further out of control. With the specter of a full-blown riot coming, they negotiate throughout the day with Martin Luther King, Jr., who is essential to maintaining calm, notwithstanding the fact that he was the target of a bomb the night before. Despite some mutual suspicion, King's team and JFK's work together to defuse the situation, and their official statements, written in collaboration, preserve a modicum of calm.

RFK: Now, have you got what happened last night? You want to hear a few things?

JFK: OK.

RFK: I guess shortly before twelve, maybe eleven-thirty, they had this explosion that took place, I guess first at Martin Luther King's brother's house, Reverend King, and virtually demolished his house, so that he was very fortunate to escape. About thirty minutes later, an explosion took place four miles away at a motel where Martin Luther King stays, and badly damaged it. Immediately, at both places, crowds gathered. And then the crowds got angry, but the police said the sheriff's office were able to have the situation reasonably under control. There was some brick throwing, and the crowd was unfriendly, but by two or so in the morning, they had the situation reasonably under control.

At that time, the governor moved two or three hundred of these special deputies. And the newsmen, Claude Sitton and others, heard the police tell them to put their guns back in the cars, that they didn't need them, but they got out anyway and they started shoving people around, sticking their guns into people, and hitting them with billies, and then the crowd became more [unclear] riots and brickthrowing. All of this lasted for the next three or four hours, and almost got out of hand. A number of the policemen were badly hurt, and I guess a number of the Negroes were badly hurt. And it was very close to becoming complete chaos.

During the course of it, a couple of buildings were set on fire and it appears that a Negro was responsible for that. When the fire department came to put the fire out, a number of Negroes gathered and started throwing rocks and stones and all kinds of things, and wouldn't let them put the fire out. And then another building caught on fire, and the fire department then refused to come back because they said it was so difficult. The result is, I guess, both buildings burned down.

The crowds dispersed as of about daylight this morning, five or six. And all of the police, all of the sheriff's office were up, around, and active. The leaders of the Negroes feel that the sheriff's office and the police handled themselves reasonably well. They do have very bitter complaints about the people who were sent in by the governor. The sheriff said that he didn't think that those who were responsible for the violence as far as the Negroes were concerned were those who were associated with Martin Luther King, but they were the criminal element of Birmingham, and the individuals who never liked the police. Today everybody on both sides, the police department side and to a considerable extent the Negroes, were all worked up about it. The Negro Reverend Walker, whose wife got hit by the butt of a rifle, she had headaches all day, he said that the Negroes, when dark comes tonight, that they're going to start going after the policemen, headhunting, and try to shoot to kill the policemen. He said it's completely out of hand.

Martin Luther King is coming back, I guess he is probably in Birmingham at the present time. He is going to have a rally or meeting at five in which he is going to ask all the Negroes to go back home and stay home tonight and stay off the streets, and that violence has no role to play in this. And that they should pray for what they did last night, causing disorder. He'll have some effect on those that attend, the rest, it's questionable. On the other side, they've got, I suppose, six or seven hundred policemen now, with the ones that they've deputized, the ones the governor sent in, the police that are there anyway in the sheriff's office. So they're going to have the city pretty well patrolled. They're going to be careful, be on top of the situation.

On the other side, the Negroes who are tough and mean and have guns, who have been bitter for a long period of time, who are worked up about this, and figure one of the best services they can perform is to shoot some of them. So if you have an incident, and the incident, another bombing for instance, or something like that, or a fire, and it attracted large numbers of Negroes, the situation might very well get out of hand. The sheriff's office said that he thought that if they had the same kind of situation as last night, that they probably wouldn't be able to control them because of the feeling of the policemen, etc.

Now we have, as far as sending the troops in, we discussed it for a long period of time, and of course there are the obvious drawbacks. We don't have the clear-cut situation that we've had in the other situations where we sent either marshals or troops in. We don't have the situation getting completely out of hand as it did in Montgomery a year ago with the Freedom Riders. In addition to protecting the riders traveling through the state, and then you sent your personal emissary down, John Siegenthaler,[5] and then he was beaten, after the governor had given you assurances he would maintain law and order. We had an excuse, really, sending marshals in at that time. We had certainly as far as Oxford.

We don't have the same kind of situation at the present time. The governor has indicated publicly that he is going to maintain law and order. The group that has gotten out of hand has not been the white people, it's been the Negroes, by and large. So to work up a proclamation, which you'd give us, the basis of which to send troops in, at this time, is far more difficult. The argument for sending troops in and taking some forceful action is what's going to happen in the future. You're going to have these kinds of incidents, the governor has virtually taken over the city. You're going to have his people around sticking bayonets in people, and hitting people with clubs and guns, et cetera. You're going to have rallies all over the country calling upon the President to take some forceful action, and why aren't you protecting the rights of the people in Birmingham? And we feel that based on the success that they had in Birmingham, and the feeling of the Negroes generally, and the reports that we get from other cities, not just in the South, but this could trigger off a good deal of violence around the country now. The Negroes saying that they have been abused for all these years, and they are going to have to start following the ideas of the Black Muslims, not go along with the white people.

If they feel, on the other hand, that the federal government is their friend, and is intervening for them, is going to work for them, this could head some of that off. I think that's the strongest argument for doing something, the fact that we're going to have more difficulties down in Birmingham. It won't perhaps be as clear-cut, as it is at the present time, about sending somebody in, because they're going to be smaller incidents, and perhaps be more difficult to hang our hat as to why we should send it in.

Now, I do want to suggest an alternative or a possibility. What we could

---

5. John Seigenthaler (b. 1927), administrative assistant to Attorney General Robert F. Kennedy.

perhaps do in this case. It's got some disadvantages and some advantages. It's sort of a halfway step, of landing these three or four hundred troops in Birmingham, and just saying that they are going to stand by. Put a statement out by you that you're greatly concerned—maintenance of law and order, the rights of people, et cetera. That these troops will stay in Birmingham and we'll make a determination as time goes by as to whether they should be used, and whether you're going to issue a proclamation to move them into the city. The second alternative to that would be to move them to Fort McClellan.

UNIDENTIFIED: About thirty miles away.

RFK: Thirty miles away. And have it get out that you sent four or five hundred troops in there, and that perhaps that more will go in tomorrow morning.

JFK: The problem really isn't the maintenance of law and order, as you said, is it, because it might be that if we send the troops into Birmingham or McClellan, there would be no disturbances, because there was sort of a repression of the city.

RFK: That's right.

JFK: Then they might tear up that paper agreement they made. Therefore, you'd have the Negroes knocked out again without getting the agreement, and then we wouldn't have any reason to go in there.

RFK: The committee that made the agreement, that backed up the agreement, is meeting right now. And it's going to be suggested to them by one of their leaders that they make their names public. To say that they made this agreement and that they come out publicly for it. Maintenance of law and order, and say that we are going to live up to it. So let it be spread throughout the city. Now these are the people that really control Birmingham—the wealthy, the important.

JFK: They've been able to keep that agreement quiet, I don't know how.

RFK: The names, you mean? Yeah.

JFK: Yeah. What is King? I mean, King has said that we should issue a statement.

RFK: Now as part of sending the troops in to some other place. The preference would be, the first thing we'd do, we'd announce that Burke Marshall[6] is going back. The second thing is probably you would get out that you already have a general in Birmingham. And that's already landed there, and that's making this

---

6. Burke Marshall (1922–2003), assistant attorney general for Civil Rights (1961–1964).

available. And that Burke Marshall is going back, and that you are watching the situation. And the third step is the fact that you are sending these troops in, and they'll be landing in another hour and some more will come in tonight. And then ...

JFK: Let's see, under that strategy, I would issue some sort of statement from here which would be asking the Negroes to stay off the streets, and so on, and then asking the agreement[7] which was made be implemented, and so ... Then Burke Marshall will be going back, then we put the troops in at the airport. How far is the airport?

UNIDENTIFIED: It's five miles from the center of town, Mr. President.

JFK: The general, let's say you began to have trouble during the evening. Once we announce that the troops had arrived, the governor would probably issue a statement saying that he had complete ...

RFK: Well, then, I think you'd probably have to nationalize the Guard, too. So he[8] doesn't take over the Guard.

JFK: He would announce that he has control of the city. So it really is just a question, we have to have two things. First, we have to have law and order, and therefore the Negroes not to be running around the city. And then secondly, we have to get this arrangement working. We can't just have the Negroes not running around the city, and then have the agreement blow up because ... if the agreement blows up, the other remedy we have under that condition then is to send legislation up to the Congress this week as our response to that action happening. Say there's this case, unless there's a means of getting relief, we have to provide legislation. We may have to do that anyways, but at least that would be our public response to the, if that agreement blows up.

BURKE MARSHALL: If that agreement blows up, the Negroes will be ...

JFK: Uncontrollable.

MARSHALL: And I think not only in Birmingham.

JFK: The only thing is, supposing we put our troops in there and then these

---

7. On May 10, after days of turmoil, an agreement was reached between Birmingham authorities and Civil Rights leaders that promised greater hiring and reduced discrimination of African-Americans. The agreement, perceived as a triumph for Dr. Martin Luther King, Jr., was brokered by Burke Marshall and Robert Kennedy.

8. George Corley Wallace (1919–1998) was a Southern populist and segregationist who served four nonconsecutive terms: 1963–1967, 1971–1979, and 1983–1987 as governor of Alabama.

whites then say, "Well, now we are going to withdraw from the agreement." Or do you think they would?

MARSHALL: I can't tell what they'd do. I think, Mr. President, the governor and the outgoing city government are doing everything they can to make that agreement blow up, the basic reason the situation is so difficult. I shouldn't wonder but what these highway patrol are deliberately being awfully tough to provoke incidents, on the theory that the more incidents they can provoke, the more [unclear] in the city and the more scared everyone gets, including the white businessmen.

JFK: Do we have any idea what the white businessmen would think if we put troops in there?

UNIDENTIFIED: They would not like it.

JFK: They wouldn't like it?

MARSHALL: No. I'm quite sure.

JFK: You haven't talked to any of them today, have you?

MARSHALL: No. You see, their whole desire is to prevent that. They want Birmingham to look like Atlanta, and they want it to solve its own problems. So their desire is to prevent that. So they wouldn't like that. And they might rather have that than have a racial war down there, but those are the alternatives, and they understand them clearly as they did last week. They made concessions to the Negroes because they'd rather make concessions than have a great deal of racial disturbances. So again, if the alternatives were clear to them, maybe they wouldn't mind. But the immediate reaction of sending troops in there would be very bad, I'm sure. As the attorney general says, I think in the case of Montgomery, in the case of Oxford, a great many people in the South who are white really thought we had to do what we did. And I don't think a great many white people in the South would think we'd have to send troops into Birmingham.

JFK: One of the reasons is because none of the papers, you have morning and noon, the timing is different. You have morning and afternoon papers. One of the casualties [?] is, this has a lot of Oxford in it, doesn't it?

MARSHALL: Yes, it does, but it's different, because there we had a white mob against a Negro. Here we have a Negro mob.

JFK: Well, except, that's why one of [the] things would be to control the Negro mob. That's one of our purposes. That's the only purpose, what we've got is twofold—to provide an atmosphere in which this agreement can be carried out, and in the meanwhile to prevent the Negroes from rioting, and therefore prevent the whites from reacting against it. That's our purpose. The question really would be, what would be the thing about landing the troops at the airfield, outside, without going in?

GENERAL EARLE WHEELER:[9] Mr. President, there's one other alternative, you could keep the troops in the air for a period of time. As a matter of fact, we could organize to keep troops constantly in the air if we had to. [unclear] They've got about seven hours of flying time, flying from Bragg, they have go, three hours down and three hours up, and they'd have to go and refuel, the turnaround time there is . . . We could organize to have a couple hundred troops in the air, on call in effect, an hour from downtown Birmingham.

MARSHALL: I think the knowledge that the troops were sort of available, or were being moved in order to be available, might have a calming effect on Negroes.

WHEELER: You got a couple of possibilities here. I've got 300 and, about 350 troops. [unclear] Which is an army helicopter . . . we could move to Fort McClellan, which is about thirty miles away, this is in Anniston. Now the airfield there is not very good, but we can get them in, about an hour after we get to work. They would be thirty miles away by road, Mr. President, from Birmingham. The troops that are moving from Fort Bragg in the C123s and the C130s, we could dispose of in two places. We could put Farnham into Maxwell Air Force Base, which is in Alabama. The rest of them we could put into Seward Air Force Base, which is near Fort Campbell, Kentucky. Now the flying time is much shorter, from both Maxwell, and from . . .

JFK: What we want to get out of Martin King is . . . How freely do you talk to King?

MARSHALL: I talk to him freely. I'll tell you what he intends to do, Mr. President. He intends to go to this church and call upon his people to [unclear] the attorney general said. And then tomorrow, he intends to go around the city and visit pool halls and saloons and talk to the Negroes and preach against violence. Those are his intentions.

JFK: Now, what has he, he's issued a statement calling upon me to make a statement. But what our problem is here, we can make this statement, but if there's

---

9. General Earle Wheeler (1908–1975), chief of staff of the army (1962–1964), and chairman of the Joint Chiefs (1964–1970).

going to be violence tonight, that is obviously what Governor Wallace wants. We don't want to, we don't like to put troops in there because then we think it is going to be more difficult for a success to be made of this agreement. But we will if there's going to be violence tonight. Now, what is his judgment about that?

MARSHALL: Well, now, do you want to get into a discussion I had about that?

[several people talking]

RFK: He might say that we are talking to him about it.

MARSHALL: I haven't done that, sir.

JFK: Well, I think you ought to look like you're talking just on your own, without saying we're considering it then. What our problem is, is to try to make a judgment on whether the Negro community is going to be out in the street tonight. If it is, then we are going to have to put troops in there, because they're either going to get beaten up or they're going to beat someone up. Maybe he can't tell us that. The other thing, he wants me to make a statement. I don't know what a statement . . . He said that "he hopes would not jeopardize these bombings, et cetera." Now there's one other thing where he's asked me to make a statement, "said today the new outbursts would make it mandatory to take a forthright stand against the indignities as to . . ."

RFK: I think you can make a statement, because, I mean, you can say about the fact that these two places have been bombed. His brother's house was bombed.

JFK: Yeah.

RFK: And the motel was bombed.

JFK: We'd also urge the Negroes to . . .

RFK: I mean, you can make a pretty strong statement at this time.

MEETING ABOUT BIRMINGHAM,
MAY 21, 1963

Attorney General Robert F. Kennedy had been leading the Kennedy administration's response to the violence in Birmingham, and as this recording makes clear, he felt a rising indignation. He launches the meeting with what is in effect a long soliloquy, including not simply a denunciation of violence against African-Americans, but the larger problem—that decent jobs are unavailable to them, including those they might expect from the federal government. He does not mention Martin Luther King, Jr., for some time, which only increases the perceived influence of this other powerful actor on the stage. Then, near the end of these remarks, King is finally named. He is clearly now seen as an ally, and a much-needed force for restraint. Simultaneously, the Kennedy administration was preparing a Civil Rights Bill. Birmingham was a watershed.

RFK: . . . to come out for some accommodation with the Negroes were as against him[10] coming back, and we were against him coming back. And we tried to prevail upon him to wait until Boutwell[11] had been able to take over the administration of the city, and put in the reforms that he indicated that he would do. So we were not successful. He came back and, as I say, did not have the support of the Negro community, and he sought a license to parade and to put on a demonstration, and Bull Connor refused. So he went out and got eight or ten people, and they were all arrested.

---

10. "Him" refers to Dr. Martin Luther King, Jr. (1929–1968), the legendary leader of the Civil Rights Movement. King had achieved national acclaim in 1955, as the twenty-five-year-old pastor of the Dexter Avenue Baptist Church in Montgomery, Alabama, at the time of the protests against segregation launched by the refusal of Rosa Parks to sit in the back of a public bus. But in the eight years since, he had at times struggled to rediscover his voice. In 1957, he helped to found the Southern Christian Leadership Conference, and in the spring of 1963, he was deeply involved in a campaign of civil disobedience against the racist authorities of Birmingham, Alabama. Known as Project C, this campaign combined sit-ins, marches, and other forms of resistance, including a "children's crusade." Incarcerated for his activities, King wrote his celebrated "Letter from a Birmingham Jail" on April 16, 1963. The first excerpts were published, without his permission, in the *New York Post Sunday Magazine*, on May 19, 1963, two days before this meeting. The full version was published in a variety of formats in the summer of 1963. King's reemergence would culminate in the March on Washington, August 28, 1963.

11. Albert Boutwell (1904–1978), mayor of Birmingham (1963–1967).

And then when they were arrested, that got a little bit more publicity, although the papers had arranged between them that they would never put this on the front page, and that they would play it down. Television played it up, and it got around the Negro community. So then he started to get more and more support as more and more of his people were arrested. Then he got himself arrested on Good Friday, so that he stays in jail over Easter Sunday, and then of course he got everybody around the Negro community, and then he came out. And he started having larger and larger demonstrations, and as more and more people were arrested, the Negro community, the local Negro community, felt that they couldn't let him do all these things by himself, 'cause they didn't have the support. So they started to support him.

And then the NAACP, which had been strongly against him going in there and having these demonstrations, they started to feel that they had to support him, because they were losing everything to him. And so finally you start getting more and more people who come his way. And then he hit upon the idea of having children come out, and that's when the thousands of people started to gather. He got these large groups of people out, Friday or Saturday, about two and a half weeks ago. And there was then, of course, with all those children and all those people, there was great danger.

The problem at that time was that the white people and the Negro people weren't talking to one another. Many in the Negro leadership didn't know what they were demonstrating about. They didn't know whether they were demonstrating to get rid of Bull Connor, or whether they were demonstrating about the stores, or whether they were demonstrating against the city government. Ninety percent of the people who were demonstrating certainly didn't know what they were demonstrating about, and none of the white community knew what they were demonstrating about. None of the white community would get near the Negro community at that juncture, because they felt that they were being disorderly, and so nobody was talking to anybody. And you had all these demonstrations, which were getting larger and larger.

So then the President sent Burke Marshall down . . . [to] Birmingham to see if something could be done about getting people together. First, he went to the Negro community to find out what they wanted. And that was difficult, because a lot of them didn't know what they wanted. And finally, through efforts with Martin Luther King, found out what they wanted, which [unclear] to desegregate the lunch counters, which was to take the signs off the toilets and the drinking fountains, to have a better hiring system in Birmingham in the department stores, and to hire at least one clerk in one of the stores.

So he went back to the white community, to the department store heads, the majority of whom were branch stores and had their main offices outside the city, and told them this. So they started having meetings. Douglas Dillon[12] and some others called the heads of the big chains. I spoke to some of them and expressed our concern. Burke met with the local people in Birmingham, and finally they said that they'd be willing to do some of these things, but that they would want to wait until something else happened in Birmingham. They wanted to have some other desegregation take place before they took the first step.

And what they hit upon was the schools. When the schools were desegregated, they said that they would then do these other things. Well, the earliest the schools would be desegregated was September, so the Negroes were unwilling to wait until that happened. And the department stores said they were unwilling to take the first step, so the result was, this was into Monday, Tuesday. And then the demonstrations got larger and larger, and then, as demonstrations got into the thousands, of course they got out of hand. Then Martin Luther King preaches nonviolence, and if you're hit you kneel down and say your prayers and don't hit back, which is all very good. And those who hear him, they follow him exceptionally well. I mean, there is no violence as far as the Negroes are concerned.

But the Negro community of Birmingham has probably the toughest group of Negroes in the country. And so, when some of them started to turn out, they [unclear] with the police for a long period of time. And they came out with their bricks and their knives and started running through the park and going into the department stores. And so, the situation had gotten completely out of hand.

The white community, then, became, itself, became exercised, concerned as to what they should do. And we felt that if we could get the substantial white citizens who owned the, ran the financial life of Birmingham behind the department store heads, that perhaps we could get the department store heads to move. So they had a meeting down there, and Burke attended it, and said that what you were going to have in Birmingham was complete chaos. You would

---

12. C. Douglas Dillon (1909–2003), ambassador to France (1953–1957); undersecretary of state (1959–1961); and secretary of the treasury (1961–1965).

have bloodshed unless something was done. That the Negro demands were quite reasonable, that they should support the department store heads and urge them to make this agreement. Finally, some of these meetings went to four or five in the morning, and Burke was the only contact between the whites and the Negroes, and finally brought them together, and the white financial, economic leaders agreed to support the department store heads, and then they would go down the line and they also would take steps to improve the lot of the Negroes. When that happened, the department store heads said that they would make this agreement.

Then we got in touch with Martin Luther King and said that they had agreed to make the agreement, and he said, "Well, I've had businessmen tell me in Albany that they'd made an agreement, and then they didn't keep their word, so we are going to go on with the demonstrations." We said to him that you had the demonstrations to accomplish a certain purpose, you've accomplished that purpose, then to go on with the demonstrations doesn't make a great deal of sense. He said, "Well, I've got to get people out of jail. The only way to get my people out of jail," he then had a couple of thousand in jail, "is to have demonstrations so that they have so many people who are in jail and such a crisis in Birmingham that they let everybody out of jail."

This really didn't make a great deal of sense. But if he'd had another day of demonstrations, you would have had great bloodshed in Birmingham, and then the governor, who would then start moving into Birmingham, would have taken over the city. So you would never have anything accomplished. So we were able to prevail upon him to call off his demonstrations, just really in time because I don't think there was any question by that Wednesday night, the governor would have moved into the city, and he would have had complete control of it, and you would never have had any of these gains.

So they called off their demonstrations, and then you had the Saturday night at ten after eleven, you had one stick of dynamite thrown in Martin Luther King's brother's house, and then thirty minutes later, eleven-forty, you had eight sticks of dynamite were thrown in the Gaston Motel where Martin Luther King had stayed. The Negroes gathered, several thousands, when the police came and the fire department came with their fire hoses. They threw rocks and stones, brought out their knives. They got out of hand.

The local police, the sheriff's office, and the police department, by two in the morning had brought them pretty much under control. Then the governor sent his people in, and his people were game wardens with armbands, and alcohol and tax people with armbands, and tough [unclear]. They had carbines and they got out of their cars with clubs with these guns, and the local police asked them to get back, go away, that they had the situation under control, and that they would kill somebody, and they said that's what they were here for. So then they started clubbing people, beating them, and then the situation got completely out of control for the next three hours. And it was finally brought under control about six Sunday morning.

Well, the Negro [unclear] felt that they had been betrayed, and all day Sunday, they indicated quite clearly that that night you were going to have a real war in Birmingham. A number of them were armed. They had knives, they had guns, and that they were going after these people with the armbands. And they felt that the governor had come in, taken over the city, and that there was no solution as far as they were concerned.

The President then made the determination to send the troops into Alabama, and that they would be available to be used in Birmingham if it was felt to be necessary, and he also went on television that night just before Martin Luther King came back and made a speech to the Negroes. That changed the whole complexion of the situation, because Martin Luther King told these people to calm down and stay at home, that the federal government was interested and was going to be active in the situation to protect them. The fact that we moved the troops into Alabama calmed the Negro community down, so there weren't any incidents because I don't think there's any question that if that step hadn't been taken that night, that the Negro community would have gotten out of hand, and you would have had a tough fight between the governor's people and the Negro community.

We think that the agreement will be kept that was made. And there are problems, such as yesterday the school board suspending the thousand students that participated in the demonstrations. The Negro lawyer's going to bring a lawsuit, which we may or may not enter also, to try to enjoin the school board from suspending the students. That will have to be worked out, but at least it would appear that the agreement that was made will be kept at least at the present time. We are optimistic about it. We're not out of the woods as yet, but I think we feel that we have a good chance of having that kept.

The lessons that we've learned from it are, first, the importance of having some biracial committee in a community. Each one of these local communities, and in the state, the Negroes and the whites talking to one another so that they can air their grievances. One of the great problems as far as the Negroes we found in the last two and a half years is, that they feel there is no solution for what they want to accomplish, that nobody will talk to them. And in community after community, we find that to be so, that they don't have, the Negroes feel that they have grievances, that there is no place for them to go. Then they want to demonstrate and they can't get a license to demonstrate. And so that they want to walk down the street, and they're not given a license, and therefore they're put in jail. That exercises the other Negroes, they don't have any place to go, they don't have any place to complain, and they can't picket about it because then they're put in jail. So they feel a sense of frustration, and that's what's growing up in the South and really in the Northern cities.

The second thing that we learned, and which I'd like to take up with you today, is when Burke met with these business leaders in Birmingham and talked to them about hiring Negroes, they looked at the government agencies and said, "Well, why should we hire Negroes? You don't hire Negroes." And we looked at the situation in Birmingham, and found that it's really a disgraceful situation as far as the government departments are concerned, that we really had done a very poor job.

The VA had done well and there were a number of Negroes who were employed by the post office. But by and large, they were of very low grade. There weren't any Negroes that held any positions that anybody could see them, except perhaps somebody to sweep the floor or something like that. Otherwise, they weren't being used as clerks or out front in positions of importance in any of these offices. And so we felt that something needed to be done to remedy that, and that you could do it quickly. I talked to a number of you about the situation in your own department, and John Macy[13] did a great deal about pulling it all together, and I think we helped the situation down there. But sorry, Mr. President, I'd like to have maybe Mr. Macy give a report as to what the situation was in Birmingham, and what it is in some of these other major cities, and what's been done about it in Birmingham.

---

13. John Macy (1917–1986), chairman of the Civil Service Commission.

MEETING WITH CIVIL RIGHTS LEADERS, AUGUST 28, 1963

On what may have been the most historic day of the Civil Rights Movement, in the immediate aftermath of the "I have a dream" speech just delivered by Martin Luther King, Jr., the leaders of the March on Washington were invited to the White House. They were greeted by a president who was obviously moved by the speech he had watched on television and, more to the point, had a detailed political plan for pushing forward the legislation they wanted. The tapes continue from these excerpts to reveal him going through the membership of the entire Congress, with great specificity, to help the leaders of the movement understand how high the mountain was that they were trying to climb. A. Philip Randolph had first called for a march on Washington in the summer of 1940; at last his moment had come, even if a new generation was required to put his vision into law. In these excerpts, the leaders exult in their momentary triumph, and gird for battle in the fall. Vice President Lyndon Johnson, who often felt excluded from the inner councils of the Kennedy administration, here speaks movingly about what can and cannot be achieved by a president working to advance civil rights.

ROY WILKINS:[14] You gave us your blessings. We think it changed the character of the protests. It was one of the prime factors in turning it into an orderly protest to help our government rather than a protest against our government. I think you'll agree that was psychologically important. And the mood and attitude of the people there today pleased all of us, without exception.

[break]

WALTER REUTHER:[15] The other thing that I think will come out of this, as I said today in my speech, after we get the legislation, that only means we've got a set of tools to work with. It doesn't mean that automatically this problem is resolved. What we have to do is to develop a broad coalition of men of goodwill in every

---

14. Roy Wilkins (1901–1981) was the executive secretary of the NAACP.

15. Walter Reuther (1907–1970) was a prominent labor leader who headed the United Automobile Workers and pledged support to the Civil Rights Movement.

community, where we've got to implement this program. And I think that this is what this march has done. It has brought into being an active, functioning coalition around this central question of equality of opportunity and first-class citizenship. And I think if we reflect this by practical work in each community, we can mobilize the community, we can mobilize the men of goodwill, and we can search for answers in the light of reason by rational, responsible action. Because if we fail, then the vacuum that we create, through our failure, is going to be filled by the apostles of hatred. And reason is going to yield to riot. Brotherhood is going to yield to bitterness and bloodshed. So I think that this is really a more significant aspect of what we're doing. We have put together the kind of coalition that can be meaningful at the community level, across this country, after we get the legislation, and it can be effective in mobilizing support for the legislation.

JFK: Very fine, but let me just say a word about the legislation. There's one thing that I, on this question of education. We have this juvenile program, as you know, in New York, and a lot, and the attorney general was out in Chicago on it the other day and was shocked by some of the crowding of the class, the leaving [?] of the school, the fact that the best teachers . . . and there's no visiting by the teachers in their homes. And they won't study, and the children won't study unless [unclear] regardless of what their color or their income level is. Now, isn't it possible for the Negro community to take the lead in committing major emphasis upon the responsibility of these families, even if they're split and all the rest of the problems they have, on educating their children? Now, in my opinion, the Jewish community, which suffered a good deal under discrimination, and what a great effort they made, which I think has made their role influential, was in education, education of their children. And therefore they've been able to establish a pretty strong position for themselves.

[break]

A. PHILIP RANDOLPH:[16] Mr. President, from the description you have made of the state of affairs of the House and Senate, it's obvious that it's going to take nothing less than a crusade to win approval for civil rights measures. And if it is going

---

16. A. Philip Randolph (1889–1979) was an early Civil Rights leader and the head of the Brotherhood of Sleeping Car Porters, which he organized in 1925. He had conceived the idea of a march on Washington as far back as 1940, to protest segregation within the armed forces, and his voice is heard on some of the earliest tape recordings made inside the Oval Office, when he spoke with FDR.

to be a crusade, I think that nobody can lead this crusade but you. I think that the people have got to be appealed to over the heads of the congressmen and senators.

[break]

JFK: Here's the vice president, he would like to say something before we . . .
LBJ: [unclear] . . . this president has issued the strongest executive orders in housing, employment, armed services, that any administration has ever issued. He's made the strongest recommendations to Congress, so far, [unclear]. Now he had more conferences in this room over here, where Medgar Evers[17] used to hang out, [unclear]. He's had [unclear], he's had lawyers, has had business soci-

---

17. Medgar Evers (1925–1963) was the NAACP's first field secretary for Mississippi. He was murdered on June 12, 1963, hours after President Kennedy's speech to the nation on Civil Rights.

PRESIDENT KENNEDY AND VICE PRESIDENT LYNDON B. JOHNSON
MEET WITH ORGANIZERS OF "THE MARCH ON
WASHINGTON FOR JOBS AND FREEDOM" IN THE OVAL OFFICE,
WHITE HOUSE, WASHINGTON, DC, AUGUST 28, 1963

Left to right: Willard Wirtz, secretary of labor; Floyd McKissick, national chairman of Congress of Racial Equality (CORE); Mathew Ahmann, executive director of the National Catholic Conference for Interracial Justice; Whitney M. Young, Jr., president of the National Urban League; Dr. Martin Luther King, Jr.; John Lewis, representative for the Student Nonviolent Coordinating Committee (SNCC); Rabbi Joachim Prinz, president of the American Jewish Congress; Reverend Eugene Carson Blake, president of the National Council of the Churches of Christ in the USA (NCC); A. Philip Randolph, president of the Negro American Labor Council (NALC); President Kennedy; Vice President Johnson; Walter P. Reuther, president of United Auto Workers (UAW); Roy Wilkins, executive secretary of the NAACP.

eties, councils, all others, the attorney general, the vice president, the President, [unclear] with them to get behind this legislation. I think he's demonstrated in his television appearances and other public statements that he's a champion in the cause of human rights, as a moral commitment because that's what's right, regardless of the political effect it may have.

Now there's one thing the President can do, he can plead and lead and persuade and even threaten Congress, but he can't run the Congress. Franklin Roosevelt at the height of his popularity in '37 lost his court plan overwhelmingly, and he only lost two states in the '36 election. I came here during that period. And this President can't get those sixty votes, if he turned this White House upside down, and he preached on the television an hour every day, it will just drive some of those men stronger into [unclear]. Maybe the men at this table can do it. But things are going to be pretty hard, because those men have agreements, working language.

AMBASSADOR ADLAI STEVENSON, THE U.S. DELEGATE TO THE
UNITED NATIONS, SHAKES HANDS WITH MARTIN LUTHER KING, JR.,
PRESIDENT OF THE SOUTHERN CHRISTIAN LEADERSHIP CONFERENCE,
AT THE WHITE HOUSE ON DECEMBER 17, 1962. THE MEETING OCCURRED
AS PRESIDENT KENNEDY MET WITH MEMBERS OF THE
AMERICAN NEGRO LEADERSHIP CONFERENCE ON AFRICA

MEETING WITH DR. MARTIN LUTHER KING, JR., SEPTEMBER 19, 1963

The euphoria of the March on Washington did not last long, as conditions continued to deteriorate in Birmingham. On Sunday, September 15, the 16th Street Baptist Church was bombed by the Ku Klux Klan. The bomb killed four girls and wounded twenty-two others. Anger seethed through many of the leaders of the movement as they came to the Oval Office to vent their frustration and demand justice.

MLK: We come today representing Birmingham in general, and more specifically some two hundred business and professional, religious, labor leaders who assembled the day after the bombing to discuss the implications and to discuss the seriousness of the whole crisis that we face there in Birmingham. And we come to you today because we feel that the Birmingham situation is so serious that it threatens not only the life and stability of Birmingham and Alabama, but of our whole nation. The image of our nation is involved, and the destiny of our nation is involved. We feel that Birmingham has reached a state of civil disorder.

Now, there are many things that you could say that would justify our coming to this conclusion. I'm sure you are aware of the fact that more bombings of churches and homes have taken place in Birmingham than any city in the United States, and not a one of these bombings over the last fifteen to twenty years has been solved. In fact, some twenty-eight have taken place in the last eight to ten years and all of these bombings remain unsolved. There is still a great problem of police brutality, and all of this came out in tragic dimensions Sunday when the bombing took place and four young girls were killed instantly, and then later in the day, two more. I think both were boys, the other two who were killed.

Now, the real problem that we face is this. The Negro community is about to reach a breaking point. There is a great deal of frustration and despair and confusion in the Negro community, and there is a feeling of being alone and not being protected. If you walk the street, you aren't safe. If you stay at home, you are not safe, there is a danger of a bomb. If you're in church now, it isn't safe. So that the Negro feels that everywhere he goes, if he remains stationary, he's in danger of some physical violence.

Now, this presents a real problem for those of us who find ourselves in leadership positions, because we are preaching at every moment the philosophy and the method of nonviolence. And I think that I can say without fear of successful contradiction, that we have been consistent in standing up for nonviolence at every point, and even with Sunday's and Monday's developments, we continue to be firm on this point. But more and more, we are facing a problem of our people saying, "What's the use?" and we find it a little more difficult to get over nonviolence [to them].

And I am convinced that if something is not done to give the Negro a new sense of hope and a sense of protection, there is a danger that we will face, and that will lead to the worst race rioting we've ever seen in this country. I think it's just at that point. I don't think it will happen if we can do something to save the situation, but I do think—and I voiced the sentiment in the evening as well with those that we met with the other day—that something dramatic must be done at this time to give the Negro in Birmingham and Alabama a new sense of hope and a good sense of protection.

FOUR

CUBA

SOVIET SHIP POLTAVA ENROUTE TO CUBA
15 SEPTEMBER 1962

ПОЛТАВА

The Cuban Missile Crisis was, in the words of British Prime Minister Harold Macmillan, a "strange and still scarcely explicable affair." Macmillan added that it represented the greatest period of strain in his many decades of public service, including World War II. It is generally agreed by historians that the crisis, which extended from October 16 to October 28, 1962, represented the high water mark of a Cold War that lasted nearly half a century between the United States and the Soviet Union. Defense Secretary Robert McNamara was more specific and said that these two weeks saw "what many of us felt then, and what since has been generally agreed, was the greatest danger of a catastrophic war since the advent of the nuclear age." In Robert Kennedy's opinion, it threatened nothing less than "the end of mankind." Scientists had previously estimated that an initial exchange of nuclear missiles would rain death upon seventy million people in both the Soviet Union and the United States. Fortunately, that theory remained a hypothesis only.

It began quietly enough, with overhead surveillance photographs that indicated new construction in Cuba. As the evidence was studied, and gradually ascertained to prove new missile installations built by Soviet technicians, it was clear that all of the underlying assumptions of the Cold War had changed. Robert Kennedy records that his brother called him on the morning of October 16, simply telling him that there was "great trouble."

That trouble was political in many ways. President Kennedy had to both conciliate and stand up to the Soviet Union, in the right measure; he had to win over the court of world opinion; and he had to guide forward a measured American response from a government that did not entirely speak with one voice. The Joint Chiefs of Staff demanded immediate retaliation of a kind that almost certainly would have led to a thermonuclear apocalypse. As they encountered resistance from the President, one of their more outspoken leaders, Air Force General Curtis LeMay, accused Kennedy of "appeasement," a word with a rich legacy, tracing back to Neville Chamberlain's futile accommodation of Adolf Hitler in 1938. Few historians had studied that episode more closely than Kennedy himself.

But Kennedy had on his side the fact that the Soviet Union had baldly lied about its intentions. It also became clear, not long into the crisis, that most of the world stood with him. A complex diplomacy ensued, involving official communiqués, back-door messages, speeches to the nation, confrontations in the United Nations, and a crucial decision to accept certain offers and to reject others as if they never existed. As the tapes reveal, the President was also supported by a superb leadership team that functioned effectively as a unit, going with little sleep and working incessantly to improve his options from the unthinkable to the unpalatable, and ultimately to the acceptable. The resulting decision not to go to war was greeted with euphoria around the world and brought many dividends, including a calming of international tensions, and the Nuclear Test Ban Treaty of 1963.

The Cuban Missile Crisis remains noteworthy for another reason—it shows off the taping system to its finest advantage. We will never know all of the reasons that President Kennedy installed his tapes, but if he was worried about the poor advice he was receiving on military matters, the tapes bear that theory out, and bear witness to this day. They, too, performed well—they rolled through the crisis, and the result is a historic record of enormous importance for any student of the presidency and how it functions in a time of near-cataclysm.

MEETING WITH MILITARY ADVISORS, OCTOBER 16, 1962

This meeting, the first in response to the crisis, begins with a brief conversation between a four-year-old Caroline Kennedy and her father, as the meeting was getting under way.

PRESIDENT KENNEDY WITH DAUGHTER CAROLINE IN THE OVAL OFFICE
(PHOTOGRAPH BY JACQUELINE KENNEDY)

CAROLINE: Daddy?
JFK: Oh, excuse me. I'll see you later, Caroline. I'll see you later.
CAROLINE: Know what? [I won't let you do much?] [laughter]
JFK: OK.

ARTHUR LUNDAHL:[1] This is a result of the photography taken Sunday, sir. There's a medium-range ballistic missile launch site and two new military encampments on the southern edge of Sierra del Rosario, in west-central Cuba.

JFK: Where would that be?

LUNDAHL: West-central, sir.

MARSHALL CARTER:[2] That's south of Havana. I think [unclear] represents your three dots we're talking about. Have you got the . . . ?

[UNIDENTIFIED]: Yes, sir.

LUNDAHL: The President would like to see those. One site, on one of the encampments contains a total of at least fourteen canvas-covered missile trailers measuring sixty-seven feet in length, nine feet in width. The overall length of the trailers plus the tow bars is approximately eighty feet. The other encampment contains vehicles and tents, but with no missile trailers.

CARTER: These are the launchers here. These are missile bases up the [unclear]. In this instance the missile trailer is backing up to the launch point. The launch point of this particular vehicle is here. The missile [unclear] feet long.

LUNDAHL: The site that you have there contains at least eight canvas-covered missile trailers. Four deployed probably missile erector-launchers. These are unvetted. The probable launch positions as indicated are approximately 850 feet, 700 feet, 450 feet, for a total distance of about 2000 feet. In area two, there are at least six canvas-covered missile trailers, about seventy-five vehicles, about 18 tents. And in area number three we have thirty-five vehicles, fifteen large tents, eight small tents, seven buildings, and one building under construction. The critical one—do you see what I mean?—is this one.

CARTER: There is, right there, see? The missile trailer is backing up to it at the moment. It's got to be. And the missile trailer is here. Seven more have been enlarged here. Those canvas-covered objects on the trailers were sixty-seven feet long, and there's a small billet between the two of them. The gate on that side of the particular trailer [unclear]. That looks like the most advanced one. Then the other area is about five miles away. There are no launcher-erectors over there, just missiles.

---

1. Arthur Lundahl (1915–1992) was an expert on aerial photography of military installations and a long-time employee of the Central Intelligence Agency.

2. Marshall Carter (1909–1993), deputy director of the Central Intelligence Agency.

JFK: How far advanced is this?

LUNDAHL: Sir, we've never seen this kind of an installation before.

JFK: Not even in the Soviet Union?

LUNDHAHL: No, sir. . . . But from May of '60 we have never had any U-2 coverage of the Soviet Union. So we do not know what kind of a practice they would use in connection with . . .

JFK: How do you know this is a medium-range ballistic missile?

LUNDAHL: The length, sir.

JFK: The what? The length?

LUNDAHL: The length of it, yes.

JFK: The length of the missile? Which part? I mean, which . . .

LUNDAHL: The missile is . . .

JFK: Which one is that?

LUNDAHL: This will show it, sir.

JFK: That?

LUNDAHL: Yes. Mr. Graybeal, our missile man, has some pictures of the equivalent Soviet equipment that has been dragged through the streets of Moscow. That can give you some feel for it, sir.

SIDNEY GRAYBEAL:[3] There are two missiles involved. One of them is our SS-3, which is 630-mile and on up to 700. It's sixty-eight feet long. These missiles measure out to be sixty-seven feet long. The other missile, the 1100 one, is seventy-three feet long. The question we have in the photography is the nose itself. If the nose cone is not on that missile and it measures sixty-seven feet— the nose cone would be four to five feet longer, sir—and with this extra length we could have a missile that would have a range of 1100 miles, sir. The missile that was drawn through the Moscow parade was, from the pictures, but . . .

JFK: Is this ready to be fired?

GRAYBEAL: No, sir.

JFK: How long have we got? We can't tell, can we, how long before it can be fired?

GRAYBEAL: No, sir. That depends on how ready the GSC[4] . . . how . . .

JFK: But what does it have to be fired from?

---

3. Sidney Graybeal, CIA expert on Russian missiles.

4. GSC is an acronym for a guidance system.

MRBM FIELD LAUNCH SITE
SAN CRISTOBAL NO 1
14 OCTOBER 1962

ERECTOR/LAUNCHER EQUIPMENT

ERECTOR/LAUNCHER EQUIPMENT

8 MISSILE TRAILERS

AERIAL PHOTOGRAPH OF SOVIET
MISSILE INSTALLATIONS IN CUBA,
OCTOBER 14, 1962

EQUIPMENT

TENT AREAS

GRAYBEAL: It would have to be fired from a stable, hard surface. This could be packed dirt. It could be concrete, or asphalt. The surface has to be hard. Then you put a flame-deflector plate on there to direct the missile.

ROBERT MCNAMARA: Would you care to comment on the position of nuclear warheads? This is in relation to the question from the President—when can those be fired?

GRAYBEAL: Sir, we've looked very hard. We can find nothing that would spell nuclear warhead in terms of any isolated area of unique security in this particular area. The mating of the nuclear warhead to the missile from some of the other short-range missiles there would take about a couple of hours to do this.

MCNAMARA: This is not fenced, I believe, at the moment?

LUNDAHL: Not yet, sir.

MCNAMARA: This is important, as it relates to whether these, today, are ready to fire, Mr. President. It seems almost impossible to me that they would be ready to fire with nuclear warheads on the site without even a fence around it. It may not take long to place them there, to erect a fence. But at least at the moment there is some reason to believe the warheads aren't present and hence they are not ready to fire.

GRAYBEAL: Yes, sir. We do not believe they are ready to fire.

MAXWELL TAYLOR:[5] However, there is no feeling that they can't fire from this kind of field position very quickly, isn't that true? It's not a question of waiting for extensive concrete pads and that sort of thing.

GRAYBEAL: The unknown factor here, sir, is the degree to which the equipment has been checked out after it's been shipped from the Soviet Union here. It's the readiness of the equipment. If the equipment is checked out, the site has to be accurately surveyed, the position has to be known. Once this is known, then you're talking a matter of hours.

---

5. General Maxwell Taylor (1901–1987), President Kennedy's favorite military advisor, who became chairman of the Joint Chiefs on October 1, 1962, just before the crisis started (he served until 1964).

PRIVATE DICTATION, OCTOBER 18, 1962

On only a handful of occasions, President Kennedy used his tape-recording equipment as a device to record his own observations, presumably for his future use in writing a memoir. October 18 had obviously been a day of great strain, and as it ended, he recorded his memory of the day, and how members of his staff had lined up on the great questions that were arrayed before them.

JFK: Secretary McNamara, Assistant Secretary Gilpatric, General Taylor, the attorney general, George Ball, Alexis Johnson, Ed Martin, McGeorge Bundy, Ted Sorensen.[6] During the course of the day the opinions had obviously switched from the advantages of a first strike on the missile sites and on Cuban aviation, to a blockade. Dean Acheson,[7] with whom I talked this afternoon, stated while he was uncertain about any of the courses, favored the first strike as being less likely to produce, being most likely to achieve our result and less likely to cause an extreme Soviet reaction, that strike to take place just against the missile sites. When I saw Robert Lovett[8] later after talking to Gromyko, he was not convinced that any action was desirable. He felt that the missile . . . the first strike would be very destructive to our alliances. The Soviets would inevitably bring about a reprisal, that we would be blamed for it and that particularly if the reprisal were to seize Berlin, and we would be regarded as having seized, brought about the loss of Berlin with inadequate provocation, they having lived with these intermediate range ballistic missiles for years. Bundy continued to argue against any action on the grounds that there would be inevitably a Soviet reprisal against Berlin and this would divide our alliance and that we would bear that responsibility. He felt it would be better off to merely take note of existence of these

---

6. Robert McNamara was secretary of defense; Roswell Gilpatric, assistant secretary of defense; General Maxwell Taylor, a top military advisor to President Kennedy; George Ball, undersecretary of state; U. Alexis Johnson, deputy undersecretary of state for political affairs; Edwin Martin, assistant secretary of state for inter-American affairs; McGeorge Bundy, the national security advisor; Theodore C. Sorensen, President Kennedy's special counsel and chief speechwriter.

7. Dean Acheson was the former secretary of state, under Harry Truman.

8. Robert Lovett (1895–1986), secretary of defense (1951–1953) under President Truman.

missiles and to wait until the crunch comes from Berlin, and not play what he thought might be the Soviet game. Everyone else felt that for us to fail to respond would throw into question our willingness to respond over Berlin, would divide our allies and our country, and we would be faced with a crunch over Berlin in two or three months, and that by that time the Soviets would have a large missile arsenal in the western hemisphere which would weaken our whole position in the hemisphere and cause us, and face us with the same problem we are going to have in Berlin anyway. The consensus was that we should go ahead with the blockade beginning on Sunday night. Originally we should begin by blockading Soviet—against the shipment of additional offensive capacity, that we could tighten the blockade as the situation requires. I was most anxious that we not have to announce the state of war existing, because it would obviously be bad to have the word go out that we were having a war rather than a limited blockade for a limited purpose. It was determined that I should go ahead with my speeches so that we don't take the cover off this and come back Saturday night.

MEETING WITH JOINT CHIEFS OF STAFF, OCTOBER 19, 1962

President Kennedy's options, somewhat limited to begin with, were constrained further by the fact that his military advisors were urging him to invade Cuba, and were openly dismissive of diplomatic channels. Kennedy, in other words, had to negotiate around adversaries at home as well as abroad. The Air Force chief of staff, General Curtis LeMay, attempted to force the President's hand when he complained that Kennedy's delay in attack was similar to the appeasement of Hitler at Munich. In fact, since the opening of Russian archives, historians have learned that the Russians had far more missiles and troops in Cuba than were known at the time, and it would have been impossible to knock them all out with an air attack.

JFK: Let me just say a little, first, about what the problem is, from my point of view. First, I think we ought to think of why the Russians did this. Well, actually, it was a rather dangerous but rather useful play of theirs. We do nothing, they have a missile base there with all the pressure that brings to bear on the United States and damage to our prestige. If we attack Cuban missiles, or Cuba, in any way, it gives them a clear line to take Berlin, as they were able to do in Hungary under the Anglo war in Egypt. We will have been regarded as— We would be regarded as the trigger-happy Americans who lost Berlin. We would have no support among our allies. We would affect the West Germans' attitude toward us. And that we let Berlin go because we didn't have the guts to endure a situation in Cuba. After all, Cuba is five or six thousand miles from them. They don't give a damn about Cuba. But they do care about Berlin and about their own security. So they would say that we endangered their interests and security. And the implication [would be] that all the rest [happened] because of the end reaction that we took in Cuba. So I think they've got . . . I must say, I think it's a very satisfactory position from their point of view. If you take the view that what really . . . And clearly, if we do nothing then they'll have these missiles and they'll be able to say anytime we ever try to do anything about Cuba, they'll fire these missiles. So that I think it's dangerous, but rather satisfactory, from their point of view.

If you take the view that what's basic to them is Berlin and, there isn't any doubt. In every conversation we've had with the Russians, that's what . . . Even

PRESIDENTIAL DOODLES

(unclear) McCone visit
military mission
over flights
military

last night we [Gromyko and I] talked about Cuba for a while, but Berlin, that's what Khrushchev is committed to personally. So actually, it's quite a desirable position from their point of view.

Now that's what makes our position so difficult. If we go in and take them out on a quick air strike, we neutralize the chance of danger to the United States of these missiles being used, and we prevent a situation from arising, at least within Cuba, where the Cubans themselves have the means of exercising some degree of authority in this hemisphere. On the other hand, we increase the chance greatly, as I think—there's bound to be a reprisal from the Soviet Union, there always is—of their just going in and taking Berlin by force. Which leaves me only one alternative, which is to fire nuclear weapons—which is a hell of an alternative—and begin a nuclear exchange, with all this happening.

On the other hand, if we begin the blockade that we're talking about, the chances are they will begin a blockade and say that we started it. And there'll be some question about the attitude of the Europeans. So that once again they will say that there will be this feeling in Europe that the Berlin blockade has been

PRESIDENTIAL DOODLES

quarantine
quarantine — how to describe
Letters to heads of state
What would have been
     the strategic effects
Announcement of test conclusion
Reexamination of our test agreement
Release of photographs

commenced by our blockade. So I don't think we've got any satisfactory alternatives. Whether we balance off that, our problem is not merely Cuba, but it is also Berlin. And when we recognize the importance of Berlin to Europe, and recognize the importance of our allies to us, that's what has made this thing to be a dilemma for three days. Otherwise, our answer would be quite easy.

On the other hand, we've got to do something. Because if we do nothing, we're going to have the problem of Berlin anyway. That was made clear last night. We're going to have this knife stuck right in our guts, in about two months. And so we've got to do something. Now, the question really is what are we going to do?

It's safe to say two of these missiles are operational now. They can be launched eighteen hours after the decision to fire has been reached. We've even seen— These missiles could be launched within eighteen hours after the decision to fire. [unclear]. They'd be ready in December of '62. It depends on— intermediate range. Communication, targeting, and an integrated air-defense system are now gaining operational status.

MAXWELL TAYLOR: That means that we're hearing electronic emissions now, suggesting that they have sectors for the air defense of Cuba. I believe this is the latest intelligence file.

JFK: I just wanted to say that these were some of the problems that we have been clearing up. Let's hear from . . .

TAYLOR: Well, I would just say one thing and then turn it over to General LeMay. We recognize these things, Mr. President. But I think we'd all be unanimous in saying that really our strength in Berlin, our strength anyplace in the world, is the credibility of our response under certain conditions. And if we don't respond here in Cuba, we think the credibility is sacrificed.

JFK: That's right. That's right. So that's why we've got to respond. Now the question is, what is our response?

GENERAL CURTIS LEMAY: Well, I certainly agree with everything General Taylor has said. I'd emphasize, a little strongly perhaps, that we don't have any choice except direct military action. If we do this blockade that's proposed, a political action, the first thing that's going to happen is your missiles are going to disappear into the woods, particularly your mobile ones. Now we can't find them, regardless of what we do, and then we're going to take some damage if we try to do anything later on.

JFK: Well, can't they [put] some of these undercover new—now that they've been alerted?

LEMAY: There is a possibility of that. But the way they line these others up, I'll have to say it's a small possibility. If they were going to hide any of them, I would think they would have hid them all. I don't think there are any hid. So the only danger is that we haven't picked up some position in plain sight. This is possible. If we do low-altitude photography over them, this is going to be a tip-off, too.

Now, as for the Berlin situation, I don't share your view that if we knock off Cuba, they're going to knock off Berlin. We've got the Berlin problem staring us in the face anyway. If we don't do anything to Cuba, then they're going to push on Berlin and push real hard because they've got us on the run. If we take military action against Cuba, then I think that the . . .

JFK: What do you think their reply would be?

LEMAY: I don't think they're going to make any reply if we tell them that the Berlin situation is just like it's always been. If they make a move, we're going to fight. I don't think it changes the Berlin situation at all, except you've got to make one more statement on it. So I see no other solution. The blockade and political action, I see leading into war. I don't see any other solution. It will lead right into war. This is almost as bad as the appeasement at Munich.

Because if this whole blockade comes along, MiGs are going to fly. The IL-28s are going to fly against them. And we're just going to gradually slip into a war under conditions that are at great disadvantage to us, with missiles staring us in the face, that can knock out our airfields in the southeastern portions. And if they use nuclear weapons, it's the population down there. We just drift into a war under conditions that we don't like. I just don't see any other solution, except direct military intervention right now.

GEORGE ANDERSON:[9] Well, Mr. President, I feel that the course of action recommended to you by the Chiefs from the military point of view is the right one. I think it's the best one from the political point of view. I'll address myself to the alternative of the blockade. If we institute a blockade, from a military point of view, we can carry it out. It is easier for us and requires less force if we institute a complete blockade rather than a partial blockade, because instituting a partial blockade involves visit and search of all of these neutral ships, and taking them in, perhaps, to ports, which will certainly a great deal of [unclear], than if we go ahead and institute a complete blockade.

If we institute a complete blockade, we are immediately having a confrontation with the Soviet Union, because it's the Soviet-bloc ships which are taking the materiel to Cuba. The blockade will not affect the equipment that is already in Cuba, and will provide the Russians in Cuba time to assemble all of these missiles, to assemble the IL-28s, to get the MiGs in a contract-manner control system ready to go. And I feel that, as this goes on, I agree with General LeMay that this will escalate and then we will be required to take other military action at greater disadvantage to the United States, to our military forces, and probably would suffer far greater casualties within the United States if these fanatics do indeed intend to fire any missiles.

We certainly cannot guarantee under those circumstances that we could prevent damage and loss of life in the United States itself. I think we have a good chance of greatly minimizing any loss of life within the United States under the present conditions, if we act fairly soon, although we do not recognize that will

9. Admiral George W. Anderson (1906–1992), chief of naval operations (1961–1963) and in charge of the naval quarantine of Cuba during the crisis.

be very fast. I do not see that, as long as the Soviet Union is supporting Cuba, that there is any solution to the Cuban problem except a military solution.

On the other hand, we recognize fully the relationship to the Berlin situation. The Communists have got in this case a master situation, from their point of view, where every course of action posed to us is characterized by unpleasantries and disadvantages. It's the same thing as Korea all over again, only on a grander scale.

We recognize the great difficulty of a military solution in Berlin. I think, on balance, the taking of positive, prompt, affirmative action in Berlin demonstrated the competence, the ability, the resolution of the United States. On balance, I would judge it, would be to deter the Russians from more aggressive acts in Berlin, and if we didn't take any action, they'd feel that we were weak. So I subscribe fully to the concept that [unclear].

JFK: It seems to me that we have to assume that just in order to, military . . . when we grabbed their two UN people and they threw two of ours out, we've got to assume that's going to be an [unclear]. They may not do it, any more than we can let these go on without doing something. They can't let us just take out, after all their statements, take out their missiles, kill a lot of Russians, and not do anything. It's quite obvious that what they think they can do is try to get Berlin. That may be a risk we have to take, but . . .

LEMAY: Well, history has been, I think the other way, Mr. President. Where we have taken a strong stand, they have backed off. In Lebanon, for instance.[10]

TAYLOR: I would agree, Mr. President. I think from the point of view of face that they'll do something. But I think it will be considerably less, depending on the posture we show here. I can't really see them putting the screws in. The dangers of hitting Berlin are just as great or greater after our action down here, because we have our [unclear].

JFK: They've got to wait for three months until they get these things all ready, and then squeeze us in Berlin. But I think at that point, for what it's worth, it may not be worth much, but at least we'll have the support of Europe.

TAYLOR: That is true.

---

10. In 1958, the Eisenhower administration landed a large contingent of marines in Lebanon, to prevent a suspected coup.

JFK: This way we have to figure this [unclear] in Europe will regard this action, no matter what pictures we show afterwards of [missiles] having been . . .

EARLE WHEELER: Mr. President, in my judgment, from a military point of view, the lowest-risk course of action if you're thinking of protecting the people of the United States against a possible strike is to go ahead with a surprise air strike, the blockade, and an invasion, because these series of actions progressively will give us increasing assurance that we really have gone after the offensive capability of the Cuban-Soviet corner. Now, admittedly, we can never be absolutely sure until and unless we actually occupy the island.

Now, I've also taken into consideration a couple of other things at the present time. To date, Khrushchev has not really confronted us with Soviet power. In other words, he has not declared Cuba a part of the Warsaw Pact. Nor has he made an announcement that this is a Soviet base, although I think that there is a chance that he may do that at any time, particularly later in November, when he comes to the United States. And this course of action would then immediately have us confronting the Soviets and not Cubans. And at that time Soviet prestige, world prestige, would be at stake, which it is not at the present time.

The effect of this base in Cuba, it seems to me, has at least two sizeable advantages from his point of view, and two sizeable disadvantages from our point of view. First, the announcement of a Soviet base in Cuba would immediately have a profound effect in all of Latin America at least, and probably worldwide, because the question would arise, is the United States incapable of doing something about it, or unwilling to do something about it? In other words, it would attack our prestige. Not only that, increasingly, they can achieve a sizeable increase in offensive Soviet strike capabilities against the United States, which they do not now have. They do have ICBMs that are targeted at us, but they are in limited numbers. Their air force is not by any manner of means of the magnitude and capability that they probably would desire. And this short-range missile course gives them a sort of quantum jump in their capability to inflict damage on the United States. And so as I say, from a military point of view, I feel that the lowest risk course of action is the full gamut of military action by us. That's it.

JFK: Thank you, General.

DAVID SHOUP:[11] Mr. President, there's a question in my mind. Under what circumstances would Cuba want to inflict damage on the United States? The placing of the kind of weapons and the bombers that can do that certainly demand a hell of a lot of attention. There's one feature of this that I've been unable to reconcile. And I wonder whether the American people and the other nations of the world can reconcile it, and that is that we are now so anxious or we're discussing the anxiety of eliminating the possibility of damage to America from the Cuban air raid, whereas for a good many months the world has known, and we've known, that we have tremendously greater potential already aimed in on us from Russia, and it has been many months. We didn't attack Russia. I think that's a hard thing to reconcile, at least it is in my mind, and I would think it would be in the American public and other nations of the world. If it's only a matter of distance, that it's closer now, we know they have them in Russia. So if they want to inflict damage, it's a question of whether Khrushchev wants to have them do it, and him keep out of it.

So if there's a requirement to eliminate this threat of damage, then it's going to take some forces, sizeable forces, to do it. And as we wait and wait and wait, then it will take greater forces to do it. And as long as it isn't done, then those forces will increasingly require a greater force. We'll be absolutely tied to that function. That means that they're going to have to stand by and take care of that function. And you will then have a considerable force of troops, ships, aircraft tied to this requirement that someday may happen. I can't conceive that they would attack us just for the fun of it. They might do it at the direction of Khrushchev. But I cannot see why they would attack us, because they couldn't invade to take us. So there's a question in my mind, in the political area, and as I say, the public and the people, what does this mean? Does it mean they're getting ready to attack us, that little pipsqueak of a place? If so, Russia has a hell of a lot better way to attack us than to attack us from Cuba.

Then, in my mind, it all devolves upon the fact that they do matter. They can damage us increasingly every day. And each day that they increase, we have to have a more sizeable force tied to this problem, and then they're not available in case something happens someplace else. And these guys either then have to

---

11. General David Shoup (1904–1983), commandant of the Marine Corps (1961–1963). General Shoup received the Medal of Honor for his valor in World War II. After his retirement he became a prominent critic of the Vietnam War.

take some new action in Berlin, South Vietnam, Korea. You would be degrading. You'd have to degrade your capability against this ever-increasing force in Cuba.

So, in my opinion, if we want to eliminate this threat that is now closer, but it's not clearly the threat we've experienced all these months and months, if we want to eliminate it, then we're going to have to go in there and do it as a full-time job to eliminate the threat against us. Then if you want to take over the place and really put in a new government that is non-Communist, then you'll have to invade the place. And if that decision is made, we must go in with plenty of insurance of a decisive success in as quick [?] as possible.

JFK: Well, it is a fact that the number of missiles there, I would say that no matter what they put in there, we could live today under. If they don't have enough ICBMs today, they're going to have them in a year. They obviously are putting in [unclear] missiles.

LEMAY: Plus increase their accuracy against the fifty targets that we know they could hit now. But the big thing is, if we leave them there, it's a blackmail threat against not only us, but the other South American countries that they may decide to operate against.

There's one other factor that I didn't mention that's not quite our field, [which] is the political factor. But you invited us to comment on this at one time. And that is, if we should talk about Cuba and the SAM sites down there. And we made pretty strong statements about the [unclear] Cuba, that we would take action against offensive weapons. I think that a blockade, and political talk, would be considered by a lot of our friends and neutrals as being a pretty weak response to this. And I'm sure a lot of our own citizens would feel that way, too. In other words, you're in a pretty bad fix, Mr. President.

JFK: What did you say?

LEMAY: You're in a pretty bad fix.

JFK: You're in there with me. [laughter]

EAVESDROPPING ON THE JOINT CHIEFS, OCTOBER 19, 1962

As the tape kept rolling, JFK left the room, and then his closest military advisors, General Maxwell Taylor and Secretary of Defense Robert McNamara, also left. That left several of the Joint Chiefs, unaware that the tape was rolling and recording their conversation. There is no indication that JFK ever listened, but nevertheless, the very fact that their disrespectful conversation was captured constituted a chit for the President, well aware that the military had advised him disastrously during the Bay of Pigs.

DAVID SHOUP: You pulled the rug right out from under him.

CURTIS LEMAY: Jesus Christ. What the hell do you mean?

SHOUP: I agree with that answer, General, I just agree with you, I just agree with you a hundred percent. Just agree with you a hundred percent. That's the only goddamn . . . He finally got around to the word "escalation." I just about [unclear]. That's the only goddamn thing that's in the whole trick. It's been there in Laos, it's been in every goddamn one. When he says escalation, that's it. Somebody's got to keep him from doing the goddamn thing piecemeal. That's our problem. Go in there and frig around with the missiles. You're screwed. You go in there and frig around with anything else, you're screwed.

LEMAY: That's right.

SHOUP: You're screwed, screwed, screwed. And if some goddamn thing, some way, he could say, that they either do the son of a bitch and do it right, and quit frigging around. That was my conclusion. Don't frig around and go take a missile out. [unclear] Goddamn, if he wants to do it, you can't fiddle around with taking out missiles. You can't fiddle around with hitting the missile site and then hitting the SAM sites. You got to go in and take out the goddamn thing that's going to stop you from doing your job.

EARLE WHEELER: It was very apparent to me, though, from his earlier remarks, that the political action of a blind strike is really what he's . . .

SHOUP: His speech about Berlin was the real . . .

WHEELER: He gave his speech about Berlin.

LEMAY: He equates the two.

WHEELER: If we smear Castro, Khrushchev smears Willy Brandt.[12]

---

12. Willy Brandt (1913–1992) was the mayor of West Berlin (1957–1966) and chancellor of West Germany (1969–1974).

CALL TO PRESIDENT DWIGHT D. EISENHOWER,
OCTOBER 22, 1962

As president, Kennedy was of course the ultimate arbiter of American foreign and military policy. But if the buck stopped with him, there were still a small number of former presidents he could consult with, who knew the great burdens of the office and had faced decisions nearly as difficult.

JFK: General, what about if the Soviet Union—Khrushchev—announces tomorrow, which I think he will, that if we attack Cuba that it's going to be nuclear war? And what's your judgment as to the chances they'll fire these things off if we invade Cuba?

EISENHOWER: Oh, I don't believe that they will.

JFK: You don't think they will?

EISENHOWER: No.

JFK: In other words, you would take that risk if the situation seemed desirable?

EISENHOWER: Well, as a matter of fact, what can you do?

JFK: Yeah.

EISENHOWER: If this thing is such a serious thing, here on our flank, that we're going to be uneasy and we know what thing is happening now, all right, you've got to use something.

JFK: Yeah.

EISENHOWER: Something may make these people shoot them off. I just don't believe this will.

JFK: Yeah, right.

EISENHOWER: In any event, of course, I'll say this. I'd want to keep my own people very alert.

JFK: Yeah. Well, hang on tight!

EISENHOWER: Yes, sir.

JFK: Thanks, General.

EISENHOWER: All right. Thank you.

MEETING WITH SENATORS, OCTOBER 22, 1962

The Constitution ordains that the Senate shall give advice and consent to the President on certain matters of foreign policy, including the making of treaties. Pursuant to that mandate, and as a gesture of respect to his old colleagues, JFK invited several Senate leaders to the White House for a private briefing on October 22, 1962. These senators were intimately involved in all of the legislation that JFK was trying to enact. Richard Russell (D-GA) would be a principal opponent of the Civil Rights Act, which would emerge in 1963 and be enacted in 1964. But on this day, they were all Americans, trying to protect their country.

JFK: As I say, this information became available Tuesday morning. Mobile bases can be moved very quickly, so we don't know, [but] we assume we have all the ones that are there now. But the CIA thinks there may be a number of others that are there on the island and have not been set up, which can be set up quite quickly because of the mobility. Intermediate-range ballistic missiles, of course, because of its nature, can take a longer time. We'll be able to spot those. The others might be set up in the space of a very few days.

Beginning Tuesday morning after we saw these first ones, we ordered intensive surveillance of the island, a number of U-2 flights until Wednesday and Thursday. I talked with, I asked Mr. McCone[13] to go up and brief General Eisenhower on Wednesday.

We decided, the vice president and I, to continue our travels around the country in order not to alert this, until we had gotten all the available information we could. The last information came in on Sunday morning, giving us this last site,[14] which we mentioned.

We are presented with a very, very difficult problem because of Berlin as well as other reasons, but mostly because of Berlin, which is rather . . . The advantage is, from Khrushchev's point of view, he takes a great chance, but there are quite some great rewards to it. If we move into Cuba, he sees the difficulty I think we face. If we invade Cuba, we have a chance that these missiles

---

13. John McCone (1902–1991), director of the Central Intelligence Agency (1961–1965).

14. Remedios, a missile site on Cuba.

PRESIDENT KENNEDY ADDRESSES THE NATION ON THE
SOVIET ARMS BUILD-UP IN CUBA, OCTOBER 22, 1962. MORE
THAN 100 MILLION AMERICANS WATCHED THE SPEECH. AS HE
SPOKE, THE NATION ELEVATED ITS READINESS FOR WAR AND
NEARLY 200 AIRCRAFT CARRYING NUCLEAR WEAPONS WERE
AIRBORNE TO AVOID AN ENEMY STRIKE

Good evening, my fellow citizens:

This Government, as promised, has maintained the closest surveillance of the Soviet military build-up on the island of Cuba. Within the past week, unmistakable evidence has established the fact that a series of offensive missile sites is now in preparation on that imprisoned island. The purpose of these bases can be none other than to provide a nuclear strike capability against the Western Hemisphere. Upon receiving the first preliminary hard information of this nature last Tuesday morning at 9 a.m.,

READING COPY OF PRESIDENT KENNEDY'S TELEVISED ADDRESS,
OCTOBER 22, 1962

will be fired on us. In addition, Khrushchev will seize Berlin and that Europe will regard Berlin's loss, which attaches such symbolic importance to Berlin, as having been the fault of the United States, by acting in a precipitous way. After all, they are five or six thousand miles from Cuba, and much closer to the Soviet Union. So these missiles don't bother them, and maybe they should think they should not bother us.

So that whatever we do in regard to Cuba, it gives him the chance to do the same with regard to Berlin. On the other hand, to not do anything but argue that these missile bases really extend only what we had to live under for a number of years, from submarines which are getting more and more intense, from the Soviet intercontinental ballistic missile system, which is in a rapid buildup [and] has a good deal of destruction which it could bring on us, as well as their bombers, that this adds to our hazards but does not create a new military hazard. And that we should keep our eye on the main site, which would be Berlin.

Our feeling, however, is that this would be a mistake. So that, beginning tonight, we're going to blockade Cuba, carrying out the [action] under the Rio Treaty. We called for a meeting of the Rio Pact countries and hope to get a two-thirds vote from them to give the blockade legality. If we don't get it, then we'll have to carry it out illegally or under declaration of war, which is not as advantageous to us.

SENATOR EVERETT DIRKSEN: Now, we don't know if Khrushchev would respond to a complete blockade?

JFK: A blockade as it will be announced will be for the movement of weapons into Cuba. But we don't know what the bloc[15] ships will do. In order not to give Khrushchev the justification for imposing a complete blockade on Berlin, we are going to start with a blockade on the shipment of offensive weapons into Cuba that will stop all ships.

Now, we don't know what the bloc ships will do. We assume that they will probably . . . We don't know what they will do, whether they'll try to send one through, make us fire on it, and use that as a justification on Berlin, or whether he'll have them all turn back. In any case, we're going to start on offensive weapons. We will then consider extending it as the days go on to other, petroleum,

15. Soviet bloc.

oil, lubricants, and other matters, except food and medicine. These are matters we will reach a judgment on as the days go on.

Now, in the meanwhile, we are making the military preparations with regard to Cuba so that if the situation deteriorates further, we will have the flexibility. Though the invasion is, the only way to get rid of these weapons is, the only other way to get rid of them is if they're fired, so that we're going to have to, it seems to me, watch with great care.

I say if we invade Cuba, there's a chance that these weapons will be fired at the United States. If we attempt to strike them from the air, then we will try to get them all, because they're mobile. And we know where the sites are, inasmuch as we can destroy the sites. But they can move them and set them up in another three days someplace else, so that we have not got a very easy situation.

There's a choice between doing nothing if we felt that would compel Berlin rather than help [unclear] Latin America. So after a good deal of searching, we decided this was the place to start. I don't know what their response would be. We've got two, three, four problems. One will be if we continue to surveil them and they shoot down one of our planes. We then have the problem of taking action against part of Cuba. So I think that—I'm going to ask Secretary McNamara to detail what we're doing militarily—if there's any strong disagreement in what at least we set out to do, I want to hear it. Otherwise, I think that what we ought to do is try to keep in very close contact before anything gets done of a major kind differently, and it may have to be done in the next twenty-four hours, because I assume the Soviet response will be very strong and we'll all meet again. Needless to say, the vice president and I have concluded our campaigning.

SENATOR J. WILLIAM FULBRIGHT: Mr. President, do I understand that you have decided, and will announce today, the blockade?

JFK: That's right. The quarantine.

DEAN RUSK: Mr. President, may I add one point to what you just said on these matters? We do think this first step provides a brief pause for the people on the other side to have another thought before we get into an utterly crashing crisis, because the prospects ahead of us at this very moment are so very serious. Now if the Soviets have underestimated what the United States is likely to do here, then they've got to consider whether they revise their judgment quick and fast. The same thing with respect to the Cubans. Quite apart from the OAS and the UN aspects of it, a brief pause here is very important in order to give the Soviets a chance to pull back from the frontier. I do want to say, Mr. President, I think the prospects here for a rapid development of the situation can be a very grave matter indeed.

SENATOR RICHARD RUSSELL: Mr. President, I could not space out under these circumstances and live with myself. I think that our responsibilities are quite immense, and stronger steps than that in view of this buildup there, and I must say that in all honesty to myself.

I don't see how we are going to get any stronger or get in any stronger position to meet this threat. It seems to me that we are at a crossroads. We're either a first-class power or we're not. You have warned these people time and again, in the most eloquent speeches I have read since Woodrow Wilson, that's what would happen if there was an offensive capability created in Cuba. They can't say they're not on notice.

The secretary of state says, "Give them time to pause and think." They'll use that time to pause and think, to get better prepared. And if we temporize with this situation, I don't see how we can ever hope to find a place where . . .

Why, we have a complete justification by law for carrying out the announced foreign policy of the United States that you have announced time . . . That if there was an offensive capability there, that we would take any steps necessary to see that certain things should stop transit. They can stop transit, for example, though, in the Windward Passage and the Leeward Passage, easily with the nuclear missiles and with these ships. They could blow Guantánamo off the map. And you have told them not to do this thing. They've done it. And I think that we should assemble as speedily as possible an adequate force and clean out that situation.

The time is going to come, Mr. President, when we're going to have to take this step in Berlin and Korea and Washington, DC, and Winder, Georgia, for the nuclear war. I don't know whether Khrushchev will launch a nuclear war over Cuba or not. I don't believe he will. But I think that the more that we temporize, the more surely he is to convince himself that we are afraid to make any real movement and to really fight.

JFK: Perhaps, Mr. Senator, if you could just hear Secretary McNamara's words, then we could . . .

RUSSELL: Pardon me. You just said, if anybody disagrees, and I couldn't sit here, feeling as I do.

CALL TO ASSISTANT SECRETARY OF DEFENSE
ROSWELL GILPATRIC, OCTOBER 23, 1962

This telephone call gives as close a view as we are likely to get of how World War III could have started in October 1962. In his call to Assistant Secretary of Defense Roswell Gilpatric, Kennedy envisions the way a U.S. naval vessel will stop a Russian ship attempting to penetrate the American quarantine of Cuba. The confrontation imagined here—and prepared for in detail—never happened, as both sides took care to minimize the risk of confrontation on the high seas.

JFK: But as I understood, there was some report that the Russian ships were not going to stop. That we were going to have to sink them, in order to stop them. I thought that, or we were going to have to fire on them. I was wondering whether the instructions on how that's to be done, or where they're to be shot at, and so on, to cause the minimum of damage. And in addition, if they're boarded, it's very possible the Russians will fire at them as they board, and we'd have to fire back and have quite a slaughter. I would think we'd want two or three things. First, I think we'd want to have some control over cameras aboard these boats, so that we don't have a lot of people shooting a lot of pictures, which in the press might be . . .

GILPATRIC: Yeah, we're gonna control all the picture taking.

JFK: On the boats?

GILPATRIC: Yeah.

JFK: They all turn in their cameras. Secondly, I don't know enough about the ships, but where they ought to fire and whether they ought to go through three or four steps, such as ask them to stop. If they don't stop, asking them to have their crew come above deck so that they won't be damaged, and three, so that we have this record made. Maybe you could talk to somebody about this?

GILPATRIC: Yes. We've got instructions at CINCLANT[16] which start with those steps. Shot across the bow, shot through the rudder.

JFK: Shot through the rudder.

---

16. An acronym for commander in chief, Atlantic Command.

GILPATRIC: Then a boarding party and then order the crews to come on deck. And the minimum amount of force at each stage. Now, maybe we haven't thought of everything, but we'll take another look at it.

JFK: OK, fine. How'd those photographic expeditions go this morning? Do you know?

GILPATRIC: No incidents. They were back a couple of hours ago. We'll see the pictures later.

JFK: I see. You're getting that one from me, aren't you? Of those Florida bases?

GILPATRIC: That's right.

JFK: OK. Have you taken a look at West Palm Beach?

GILPATRIC: Yeah. The air force is doing that. We can look at all of the dispersal possibilities down there.

JFK: OK, good.

GILPATRIC: Did you decide anything about Nelson Rockefeller, or are you going to leave that?

JFK: Wait a minute now. What about, do we know anything more about Nelson Rockefeller?

RFK: [in background] We sent him a telegram.

JFK: We sent him a telegram saying that I'd be in touch with him later. I thought we'd meet at six, but what my thought was that we'd bring down the Civil Defense Committee. If we bring down every governor, then it seems to me we're kind of in the obligation to bring every congressman down to brief.

GILPATRIC: No, he just wanted to have the Civil Defense Committee.

JFK: Well then that's what we'll be in touch with him about, because I'm hoping Pittmann and Ed McDermott[17] will come today anyway.

GILPATRIC: They will.

JFK: Then we'll send a wire from them to him and arrange that meeting.

GILPATRIC: Do it right.

JFK: OK, Ros.

17. Steuart Pittmann was assistant secretary of defense for civil defense, Edward McDermott was director of the Office of Emergency Planning.

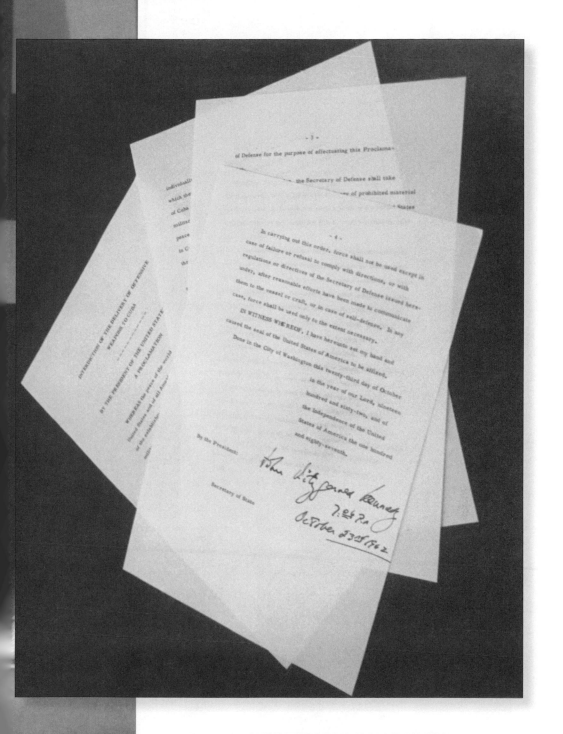

LEFT: **PRESIDENT KENNEDY SIGNS PROCLAMATION 3504 AUTHORIZING A NAVAL QUARANTINE OF CUBA,** OCTOBER 23, 1962

ABOVE: **SIGNED PROCLAMATION 3504**

INTERDICTION OF THE DELIVERY OF OFFENSIVE

WEAPONS TO CUBA

— — — — — — — — — — —

BY THE PRESIDENT OF THE UNITED STATES OF AMERICA

A PROCLAMATION

WHEREAS the peace of the world and the security of the
United States and of all American States are endangered by reason
of the establishment by the Sino-Soviet powers of an offensive
military capability in Cuba, including bases for ballistic missiles
with a potential range covering most of North and South America;

WHEREAS by a Joint Resolution passed by the Congress of
the United States and approved on October 3, 1962, it was declared
that the United States is determined to prevent by whatever means
may be necessary, including the use of arms, the Marxist-Leninist
regime in Cuba from extending, by force or the threat of force, its
aggressive or subversive activities to any part of this hemisphere,
and to prevent in Cuba the creation or use of an externally supported
military capability endangering the security of the United States;
and

WHEREAS the Organ of Consultation of the American Republics
meeting in Washington on October 23, 1962, recommended that the
Member States, in accordance with Articles 6 and 8 of the Inter-
American Treaty of Reciprocal Assistance, take all measures,

individually and collectively, including the use of armed force,
which they may deem necessary to ensure that the Government
of Cuba cannot continue to receive from the Sino-Soviet powers
military material and related supplies which may threaten the
peace and security of the Continent and to prevent the missiles
in Cuba with offensive capability from ever becoming an active
threat to the peace and security of the Continent:

NOW, THEREFORE, I, JOHN F. KENNEDY, President of
the United States of America, acting under and by virtue of the
authority conferred upon me by the Constitution and statutes of the
United States, in accordance with the aforementioned resolutions
of the United States Congress and of the Organ of Consultation of
the American Republics, and to defend the security of the United
States, do hereby proclaim that the forces under my command are
ordered, beginning at 2:00 P.M. Greenwich time October 24, 1962,
to interdict, subject to the instructions herein contained, the delivery
of offensive weapons and associated materiel to Cuba.

For the purposes of this Proclamation, the following are
declared to be prohibited materiel:

Surface-to-surface missiles; bomber aircraft; bombs,
air-to-surface rockets and guided missiles; warheads for
any of the above weapons; mechanical or electronic equipment to support or operate the above items; and any other
classes of materiel hereafter designated by the Secretary

of Defense for the purpose of effectuating this Proclamation.

To enforce this order, the Secretary of Defense shall take appropriate measures to prevent the delivery of prohibited materiel to Cuba, employing the land, sea and air forces of the United States in cooperation with any forces that may be made available by other American States.

The Secretary of Defense may make such regulations and issue such directives as he deems necessary to ensure the effectiveness of this order, including the designation, within a reasonable distance of Cuba, of prohibited or restricted zones and of prescribed routes.

Any vessel or craft which may be proceeding toward Cuba may be intercepted and may be directed to identify itself, its cargo, equipment and stores and its ports of call, to stop, to lie to, to submit to visit and search, or to proceed as directed. Any vessel or craft which fails or refuses to respond to or comply with directions shall be subject to being taken into custody. Any vessel or craft which it is believed is en route to Cuba and may be carrying prohibited materiel or may itself constitute such materiel shall, wherever possible, be directed to proceed to another destination of its own choice and shall be taken into custody if it fails or refuses to obey such directions. All vessels or craft taken into custody shall be sent into a port of the United States for appropriate disposition.

- 4 -

In carrying out this order, force shall not be used except in case of failure or refusal to comply with directions, or with regulations or directives of the Secretary of Defense issued hereunder, after reasonable efforts have been made to communicate them to the vessel or craft, or in case of self-defense. In any case, force shall be used only to the extent necessary.

IN WITNESS WHEREOF, I have hereunto set my hand and caused the seal of the United States of America to be affixed.

Done in the City of Washington this twenty-third day of October in the year of our Lord, nineteen hundred and sixty-two, and of the Independence of the United States of America the one hundred and eighty-seventh.

By the President:

John Fitzgerald Kennedy

7:0⁶ P.M.

October 23ʳᵈ 1962

Dean Rusk

Secretary of State

3504

CONVERSATION WITH ATTORNEY GENERAL
ROBERT F. KENNEDY, OCTOBER 23, 1962

This brief taped excerpt reveals some of the other stresses on President Kennedy during the crisis, from the ordinary pressures of public attendance at events, faced by all presidents, to the particular anxiety noted by Robert Kennedy—that a failure to respond to the Soviet threat would likely have resulted in impeachment proceedings in Congress.

RFK: What was that?

JFK: Oh Christ, about the dinner tonight.

RFK: What?

JFK: About a dinner tonight. She's invited somebody and I invited somebody.

RFK: How does it look?

JFK: Looks like hell. Looks real mean, doesn't it? But on the other hand, there is no other choice. If they get this mean on this one, it's just a question of where they go about it next. No choice. I don't think there was a choice.

RFK: Well, there isn't any choice. I mean, you would have been, you would have been impeached.

JFK: That's what I think. I would have been impeached. I think they would have moved to impeach. I wouldn't be surprised if they didn't move to impeach right after this election, on the grounds that I said, and didn't do it and let . . . I mean, I'd be . . .

RFK: I don't think that's . . . you know, that's a, if we'd gone in and done something else, or taken some other step that wasn't necessary, and then you'd be . . .

JFK: Yeah.

RFK: Yeah. But now, the fact is that you couldn't have done any less. The fact that you got all those South American countries and Central American countries to vote unanimously.[18] When they've been kicking us in the ass for two years, and they vote unanimously for this. And then to get the reaction from the rest of the allies, you, like David Ormsby-Gore[19] and everybody else. Saying that you had to do it. You calculate . . . I mean, if it's going to come at you, it was going to come as something you couldn't have avoided.

---

18. The Organization of American States voted unanimously to endorse the U.S. position in its meeting of October 23, 1962.

19. David Ormsby-Gore (1918–1985) was minister of state for Foreign Affairs under Prime Minister Harold Macmillan from 1957 to 1961 and British ambassador to the United States from 1961 to 1965.

CALL TO BRITISH PRIME MINISTER HAROLD
MACMILLAN, OCTOBER 26, 1962

Despite a twenty-three-year difference in age, President Kennedy and Prime Minister Harold Macmillan shared an easy camaraderie. Throughout the crisis, they talked often, usually at night; Kennedy reported from the epicenter of events, and Macmillan offered calm, resolve, and unstinting support. As this call indicates, he was also willing to offer strategic considerations of high value, including Britain's willingness to give up its Thor missiles. When the crisis was finally resolved, Macmillan took an active part in planning ways to avert any repetition, including his strong recommendation that Kennedy pursue a nuclear test ban treaty with Nikita Khrushchev.

JFK: Hello, Prime Minister.

MACMILLAN: Hello, what's the news now?

JFK: Well, Governor Stevenson[20] saw U Thant[21] this afternoon and made our proposals about the importation of arms ceasing and that work on these bases stopping and leading to eventual dismemberment. There are some reports around, some Russian conversations, but it's rather unofficial and unreliable, about some thought that it's possible they might do something about withdrawing the weapons if they could get a territorial guarantee of Cuba. But that is so unofficial that I'm not in a position now to know whether there's anything to it or not. Khrushchev told U Thant that he would keep his ships out of there for the time being, but he couldn't—he wouldn't do it very long. He isn't giving us very much because actually he's got no ships in the area anyway. But at least he's made that an announcement; he's keeping his ships out of there for the time being. We are continuing the quarantine. The buildup of the sites continues, however. And I put a statement out this afternoon describing how the buildup is going on, so that unless in the next forty-eight hours we get some political suggestions as to dismantling the base we're then going to be faced with a problem of what to do about this buildup.

---

20. Adlai Stevenson was President Kennedy's ambassador to the United Nations.

21. U Thant (1909–1974), secretary general of the United Nations from 1961 to 1971.

PRIME MINISTER HAROLD MACMILLAN OF GREAT BRITAIN AND
PRESIDENT KENNEDY, APRIL 5, 1961

MACMILLAN: There's one idea that you've just mentioned is that Cuba might be made like Belgium was—an international guarantee—an inviolable country which now all of us would guarantee its neutrality and inviolability. Is that a possibility?

JFK: Well, that is a matter which seems to me we ought to be thinking about and we will be talking about that in the next twenty-four hours as to whether there is any room for a settlement on that basis. That would leave Castro in power, it would leave the Russians perhaps free to ship in a good deal more of defensive equipment and they have shipped in a good deal. We now find a good many self-propelled armored vehicles with very sophisticated conventional equipment and so on, but it may be a possibility, but I could probably give you more information about that by tomorrow night, but at least there have been a couple of hints but not enough to go on yet.

MACMILLAN: Yes, now I thought another possibility was that U Thant might himself propose to the United Nations, which I believe they would accept, that he should go with a team and ensure that these missiles were made inoperable during the period of any conference or discussions.

JFK: Yes, that is correct. There would have to be some technical way of determining that these weapons were being made inoperable and that work on the sites was ceasing during these conversations. That is correct.

MACMILLAN: Yes, but do you think that U Thant mightn't . . . I am quite sure that Hammarskjöld[22] would have done such a thing. Mightn't he suggest to the United Nations that he would do this? He would go and do it with a team and see that they were not operable during the period of the talks.

JFK: Yes, there is some suggestion of that. Also they want to inspect some of the refugee camps in Florida and Nicaragua, Guatemala and Swan Island. That came up in the conversation with the governor and I am looking into it. I don't think we have got anything going there that would be difficult to inspect but this is all part of the political proposals which are now being looked at in view of the governor's conversation. So I would sum it up, Prime Minister, by saying that by tomorrow morning or noon we should be in a position of knowing whether there is some political proposal that we could agree to which—and whether the

---

22. Dag Hammarskjöld (1905–1961), secretary general of the United Nations from 1953 until his death in a plane crash on September 18, 1961.

Russians are interested in it or not. We will know a little more I think by tomorrow afternoon. In the meanwhile the quarantine stays, he doesn't send ships in, we let a ship pass this afternoon, but there's no other ships within forty-eight hours or so, so we don't expect any problems on the sea. The problem that concerns us is the continued buildup and I issued a statement on that today. I think I can probably get you a little more precise information on the various political proposals and U Thant's conversation with Stevenson. I'll send you a report on that tonight and then you will have it in the morning.

MACMILLAN: There is just a third point that occurred to us. If we want to help the Russians to save face, would it be worthwhile our undertaking to immobilize our Thor missiles which are here in England during the same period—during the conference.

JFK: Well, let me put that into the machinery and then I'll be in touch with you on that.

MACMILLAN: I think it is just an idea that it might help the Russians to accept.

JFK: Good, Prime Minister, let me send that over to the Department. I think we don't want to have too many dismantlings, but it is possible that that proposal might help; they might also insist on Greece—on Turkey and Italy—but I will keep in mind your suggestion here so that if it gets into that, that may be advantageous.

MACMILLAN: Yes, I don't see why they should ask, because we have got sixty, so that missile for missile you see there wouldn't be as many as that in Cuba.

JFK: Yes that is correct. Let me— I'll let Stevenson know that and he will have that in mind in the conversation.

MACMILLAN: Well now, if there are any other suggestions that we can make, you will probably send me a message tonight and we can get in touch with you tomorrow.

JFK: That is correct, Prime Minister. I think we just have to wait until we've analyzed this conversation. I haven't seen the entire conversation, but I think that there may—and the prospect of a trade of these missiles for some guarantees of Cuba is still so vague that I am not really in a position to say that there is any possibility of it as yet. Maybe by tomorrow evening at this time we'll know better.

MACMILLAN: Yes, because of course at this stage any movement by yours, by you, may produce a result in Berlin which would be very bad for us all. That's the danger now.

JFK: Well, we're not going to have any problem at sea because he is keeping his ships out of there, and as I say we let one ship pass today for the very reason that you've named. On the other hand, if in the end of forty-eight hours we are getting noplace and the missile sites continue to be constructed, then we are going to be faced with some hard decisions.

MACMILLAN: And of course in making those decisions, one has to realize that they will have their effect on Berlin as well as on Cuba.

JFK: That's correct, and that is really why we have not done more than we have done up till now. But of course on the other hand if the missile sites continue and get constructed and we don't do anything about it, then I would suppose that it would have quite an effect on Berlin anyway.

MACMILLAN: Yes, I think that is the difficulty, but anyway there are these political plans which we have now got going, and if I may, I'll send you a message concerning them and you will send me the result of U Thant's conversation.

JFK: Yes, I'll send you a memorandum based on the copy of the conversation that Stevenson had with U Thant. I will also keep in touch with you tomorrow at this time if you're—or otherwise I'll send you a message tomorrow. Maybe I'll send you a message unless we have got something immediate. And number three, we will not take any further action until I have talked to you in any case. I won't bother to call you tomorrow, because I may be down—I may be away from here tomorrow evening and I assume you may be, too. But I will send you a message if there is anything new, and in any case I will talk to you on the phone before we do anything of a drastic nature.

MACMILLAN: Well, thank you. I will be here all day so you can get me any time today, tomorrow, or Sunday.

JFK: Prime Minister, I'm going to send you a note tonight or tomorrow morning about asking if it's agreeable with you if General Norstad stay on until January 1, that there be an overlap with Lemnitzer's[23] tour of duty; that Lemnitzer go over there and take over the American forces and be there and have that sixty-day period to be sort of adjusted to his new responsibilities. You'll be getting a formal letter, and I didn't want to say anything about it because we haven't been in touch with General de Gaulle as yet, who is very sensitive in these NATO

---

23. Lauris Norstad (1907–1988) was an Air Force general and supreme allied commander, Europe; Lyman Lemnitzer (1899–1988) was chairman of the Joint Chiefs from 1960 to 1962.

matters. But I will be in touch with you and I would assume probably that the suggestion would be agreeable to you?

MACMILLAN: It is indeed very sensible.

JFK: Good. Well I'll be in touch in a formal way with you tomorrow on that matter and I'll send you tonight the memorandum on the U Thant conversation—over and I hope all goes well.

MACMILLAN: Well thank you very much and of course Bundy can always ring up de Zulueta[24] here. They can speak to each other so it is quite easy to have a talk.

JFK: Good, fine, Prime Minister, and I'll be in touch with you very shortly. Thank you and good night.

MACMILLAN: Good night.

---

24. Philip de Zulueta, private secretary to Prime Minister Macmillan for foreign affairs.

MEETING IN CABINET ROOM, OCTOBER 27, 1962

On October 27, President Kennedy and his team were weighing different offers from Khrushchev, and the complicated separate issue of dismantling aging Jupiter missiles in Turkey.

RFK: You made an offer, up there now, and you also ask U Thant to find an answer to this. Now if U Thant should come back and say, number one, that they are going to continue the work on the bases, in which case, I suppose we have to move in some way. Or they are going to say that they are going to discontinue the work on the bases. If they say they are going to discontinue the work on the bases, they can either accept our proposal, or they can reject the proposal and say we still want Turkey for Cuba.

If they reject the proposal and say they want Turkey for Cuba, but they are going to discontinue the work on the bases, I would think, would be the time to bring NATO in and say, "This is the proposal, do you want to consider it?" We haven't lost anything, and they have discontinued the work on the bases. If they say they are going to continue the work on the bases, I think then we've got to decide whether, if they have said by tomorrow morning that they are going to continue the work on the bases whether we are going to have a military strike.

I think if you have a meeting of NATO tomorrow morning, I don't see that that is going to, I think it's going to shoot this other possibility which U Thant has suggested, of going forward with this letter, and see if we can trade the non-invasion of Cuba for this, and I think we are keeping the pressure on. We don't look like we're weakening on the whole Turkey complex. I mean, I don't see that you are losing anything by not having the meeting tomorrow morning, except the fact, I admit you are risking something, because some of the allies are going to say that you're out of your mind.

MCGEORGE BUNDY: I would prefer to let Finletter[25] find out for a day what people think.

---

25. Thomas Finletter (1893–1980) was the U.S. permanent representative to NATO's North Atlantic Council.

JFK: It's going to be . . . you see, they haven't had the alternatives presented to them. They'll say, "Well, God, we don't want to trade them off!" They don't realize that in two or three days, we may have a military strike which would bring perhaps the seizure of Berlin or a strike on Turkey. And then they'll say, "My God, we should have taken it!"

CABINET MEETING, OCTOBER 18, 1962

Cabinet meeting attendees included: Clarence Douglas Dillon; Attorney General Robert F. Kennedy; Administrator for the National Aeronautics and Space Administration (NASA) James Webb; Administrator for the Housing and Home Finance Association (HHFA) Robert Weaver; Postmaster General James Edward Day; Secretary of Defense Robert S. McNamara; Secretary of Labor William Willard Wirtz; Secretary of Health, Education, and Welfare (HEW) Anthony Celebrezze; Chairman of the Atomic Energy Commission (AEC) Glenn Seaborg; Special Counsel to the President Theodore C. Sorensen; and Special Assistant to the President Jerome Wiesner.

CONVERSATION WITH SECRETARY OF DEFENSE
ROBERT MCNAMARA, OCTOBER 27, 1962

Even at this late date in the crisis, as pressure for a peaceful solution was mounting on both leaders, there were moments of grave danger. In this conversation, JFK reiterates his desire to call up reserves.

JFK: Let me say, I think we ought to wait till tomorrow, to see whether we get any answers if U Thant goes down there. We're rapidly approaching a real . . . I don't think that firing back at a twenty-millimeter [gun] coming off the ground is good. I think we ought to figure that Monday, if tomorrow they fire at us and we don't have any answers from the Russians. Then Monday, it seems to me, we can, ought to, maybe, consider making a statement tomorrow about the firing and regarding [the fact that] we'll take action now any place in Cuba, on those three areas we can fire. And then go in and take all of the SAM sites out. I'd rather take . . . I don't think that it does any good to take it out, to try to fire at a twenty-millimeter on the ground. You just hazard our planes, and the people on the ground have the advantage.

On the other hand, I don't want, I don't think we do any good to begin to sort of half do it. I think we ought to keep tomorrow clean, do the best we can with the surveillance. If they still fire and haven't got a satisfactory answer back from the Russians, I think we ought to put a statement out tomorrow that we are fired upon. We are therefore considering the island of Cuba as an open territory, and then take out all these SAM sites.

Otherwise, what we're going to do is find this buildup of the protection for the SAM sites low, with guns to fire at low-flying planes, and the SAM sites high, missiles for high-flying aircraft, and we'll find ourselves without . . . Our reply will be so limited that we'll find ourselves with all the disadvantages.

I think we ought to, tomorrow, let's get U Thant our messages. If they fire on us, tell them we'll take them all out. And then if we don't get some satisfaction from the Russians or U Thant or Cuba tomorrow night, figure that Monday we're going to do something about the SAM sites. What do you think?

ROBERT MCNAMARA: I would say only that we ought to keep some type of pressure on tonight and tomorrow night that indicates we're firm. If we call off these air strikes tonight, I think that settles . . .

UNIDENTIFIED: I have a paper here, Mr. President, that we haven't discussed yet.

MCNAMARA: Let me say first, I believe we should issue an order tonight calling up the twenty-four air reserve squadrons, roughly three hundred troop-carrier transports, which are required for an invasion. And this would both be a preparatory move, and also a strong indication of what lies ahead.

JFK: I think we ought to do it.

AERIAL PHOTOGRAPH OF SOVIET MISSILE LAUNCH SITE, SAN CRISTOBAL, CUBA, OCTOBER 27, 1962

CALL TO PRESIDENT DWIGHT D. EISENHOWER, OCTOBER 28, 1962

With the crisis unwinding, President Kennedy placed a round of relieved calls to all three living former presidents: Eisenhower, Truman, and Hoover. The calls with Truman and Hoover are relatively brief, but with Eisenhower (whom Kennedy addressed as both "Mr. President" and "General"), there was more time spent on strategy, including a surprising detour into the "goddamned mountainous country" of Tibet.

JFK: Hello?

OPERATOR: Yes, please.

JFK: Oh, is the general on there?

OPERATOR: I'll put him on, yes, sir. Ready.

JFK: Hello?

EISENHOWER: General Eisenhower, Mr. President.

JFK: General, how are you?

EISENHOWER: Pretty good, thanks.

JFK: Oh, fine. General, I just wanted to bring you up-to-date on this matter, because I know of your concern about it. We got, Friday night, got a message from Khrushchev, which said that he would withdraw these missiles and technicians and so on, providing we did not plan to invade Cuba. We then got a message, that public one the next morning, in which he said he would do that if we withdrew our missiles from Turkey. We then, as you know, issued a statement that we couldn't get into that deal. So we then got this message this morning. So we now have to wait to see how it unfolds, and there's a good deal of complexities to it. If the withdrawal of these missiles, technicians, and the cessation of subversive activity by them . . .

EISENHOWER: Yeah.

JFK: Well, we just have to set up satisfactory procedures to determine whether these actions will be carried out. So I would think that, if we can do that, we'll be, find our interests advanced, even though it may be only one more chapter in a rather long story, as far as Cuba is concerned.

EISENHOWER: Of course, but Mr. President, did he put any conditions in whatsoever, in there?

JFK: No, except that we're not going to invade Cuba.

EISENHOWER: Yes.

JFK: That's the only one we've got now. But we don't plan to invade Cuba under these conditions anyway.

EISENHOWER: No.

JFK: So if we can get 'em out, we're better off by far.

EISENHOWER: That's correct. I quite agree. I just wondered whether he was trying to, knowing we would keep our word, whether he would try to engage us in any kind of statement or commitment that would finally, one day, could be very embarrassing. Listen, suppose they got in, suppose they start to bombard Guantánamo?[26]

JFK: Right.

EISENHOWER: That's what I'm getting at. I quite agree, this is a very, I think, conciliatory move he's made.

JFK: Right.

EISENHOWER: Provided that he doesn't say that . . .

JFK: Oh, well, I agree. Oh yes, that's right. I think what we've got to do is keep . . . That's why I don't think the Cuban story can be over yet. I think we will retain sufficient freedom to protect our interests if he . . .

EISENHOWER: That's all I was saying.

JFK: . . . if he, if they engage in subversion. If they attempt to do any aggressive acts, and so on, then all bets are off. In addition, my guess is that, by the end of next month, we're going to be toe-to-toe on Berlin, anyway. So that I think this is important for the time being, because it requires quite a step down, really, for Khrushchev. On the other hand, I think that, as we all know, they just probe, and their word's unreliable, so we just have to stay busy on it.

EISENHOWER: As I've averred before, Mr. President, there's one thing about . . . They, these people, do not equate, and I think it's been a mistake to equate Berlin with Cuba or anything else.

JFK: Right.

EISENHOWER: They take any spot in the world. They don't care where it is.

JFK: That's right.

---

26. The use of the U.S. naval base on the southeast coast of Cuba was negotiated in the aftermath of the Spanish-American War and has continued through many different political regimes in Cuba.

Уважаемый г-н Президент,

Получил Ваше письмо от 25 октября. Из Вашего письма я почувствовал, что у Вас есть некоторое понимание сложившейся ситуации и сознание ответственности. Это я ценю.

Сейчас мы уже публично обменялись своими оценками событий вокруг Кубы и каждый из нас изложил свое об'яснение и свое понимание этих событий. Поэтому я считал бы, что, видимо, продолжение обмена мнениями на таком расстоянии, пусть даже в виде закрытых писем, вряд ли что-либо добавит к тому, что одна сторона уже сказала другой.

Думаю, Вы правильно поймете меня, если Вы действительно заботитесь о благе мира. Мир нужен всем: и капиталистам, если они не потеряли рассудка, и тем более коммунистам, людям, которые умеют ценить не только свою собственную жизнь, но больше всего - жизнь народов. Мы, коммунисты, вообще против всяких войн между государствами и отстаиваем дело мира с тех пор, как появились на свет. Мы всегда рассматривали войну как бедствие, а не как игру и не как средство для достижения определенных целей и тем более - не как самоцель. Наши цели ясны, а средство их достижения - труд. Война является нашим врагом и бедствием для всех народов.

Так понимаем вопросы войны и мира мы, советские люди, а вместе с нами и другие народы. Это я во всяком случае твердо могу сказать за народы социалистических стран и также за всех прогрессивных людей, которые хотят мира, счастья и дружбы между народами.

Его Превосходительству
Джону КЕННЕДИ,
Президенту Соединенных Штатов
Америки

LETTER FROM SOVIET PREMIER NIKITA KHRUSHCHEV TO PRESIDENT KENNEDY,
OCTOBER 26, 1962

DEPARTMENT OF STATE
DIVISION OF LANGUAGE SERVICES

(TRANSLATION)

LS NO. 46118
T-85/T-94
Russian

[Embossed Seal of the USSR]

Dear Mr. President:

I have received your letter of October 25. From your letter I got the feeling that you have some understanding of the situation which has developed and a sense of responsibility. I appreciate this.

By now we have already publicly exchanged our assessments of the events around Cuba and each of us has set forth his explanation and his interpretation of these events. Therefore, I would think that, evidently, continuing to exchange opinions at such a distance, even in the form of secret letters, would probably not add anything to what one side has already said to the other.

I think you will understand me correctly if you are really concerned for the welfare of the world. Everyone needs peace: both capitalists, if they have not lost their reason, and all the more, communists--people who know how to value not only their own lives but, above all else, the life of nations. We communists are against any wars between states at all, and have been defending the cause of peace ever since we came into the world. We have always regarded war as a calamity, not as a game or a means for achieving particular purposes, much less as a goal in itself. Our goals are clear, and the means of achieving them is work. War is our enemy and a calamity for all nations.

This is how we Soviet people, and together with us, other peoples as well, interpret questions of war and peace. I can say this with assurance at least for the peoples of the Socialist countries, as well as for all progressive people who want peace, happiness, and friendship among nations.

His Excellency
    John Kennedy,
        President of the United States of America

GPO-918984

THE OFFICIAL TRANSLATION OF SOVIET PREMIER KHRUSHCHEV'S LETTER OF
OCTOBER 26, 1962

Эти соображения продиктованы искренним стремлением разрядить обстановку, устранить угрозу войны.

С уважением

Н.ХРУЩЕВ

26 октября 1962 года

5c.

need not explain to you, because you yourself understand perfectly what
dread forces our two countries possess.

Therefore, if there is no intention of tightening this knot, thereby
dooming the world to the catastrophe of thermonuclear war, let us not only
relax the forces straining on the ends of the rope, let us take measures
for untying this knot. We are agreeable to this.

We welcome all forces which take the position of peace. Therefore, I
both expressed gratitude to Mr. Bertrand Russell, who shows alarm and concern
for the fate of the world, and readily responded to the appeal of the Acting
Secretary General of the U.N., U Thant.

These, Mr. President, are my thoughts, which, if you should agree
with them, could put an end to the tense situation which is disturbing all
peoples.

These thoughts are governed by a sincere desire to alleviate the
situation and remove the threat of war.

> Respectfully,
>
> [s] N. Khrushchev
>
> N. Khrushchev

October 26, 1962

EISENHOWER: And it's just the question is, are you in such a place you either can't or won't resist?

JFK: That's right. Yeah.

EISENHOWER: Now, when we got into Tibet. What is it with Tibet? Goddamned mountainous country over there, we couldn't even reach it.

JFK: Right.

EISENHOWER: And so, well, what could we do then was to reverse itself, that's all.

JFK: Right, right.

EISENHOWER: Now, so they get you, and they probe about when you can't do anything. Then if they get another place where they think that you just won't for some reason or other . . .

JFK: Yeah.

EISENHOWER: Why, then they go ahead.

JFK: That's right.

EISENHOWER: So I think you're doing exactly right on this one. Go ahead. But just let them know that you won't be the aggressor. But on the other hand, then you've always got the right to . . .

JFK: That's right.

EISENHOWER: . . . determine whether the other guy is the aggressor.

JFK: Well, we'll stay right at it, and I'll keep in touch with you, General.

EISENHOWER: Thank you very much, Mr. President.

JFK: OK. Thank you.

CALL TO PRESIDENT HARRY TRUMAN, OCTOBER 28, 1962

OPERATOR: Yes, sir.

JFK: President Truman, please.

OPERATOR: Thank you. Hello?

TRUMAN: Yes, hello.

OPERATOR: He'll be with you in just one minute, Mr. President.

TRUMAN: All right. All right.

JFK: Hello.

TRUMAN: Hello, this is Harry Truman.

JFK: Hello. How are you, Mr. President?

TRUMAN: Well, I'm all right, and I'm just pleased to death the way these things came out.

PRESIDENT TRUMAN WAS PRESIDENT KENNEDY'S FIRST OFFICIAL VISITOR TO THE OVAL OFFICE ON HIS FIRST FULL DAY AS PRESIDENT, JANUARY 21, 1961

JFK: Well, we'll just stay at it, and I just wanted to bring you up-to-date on it. We got a letter from him on Friday night which was rather conciliatory on these withdrawals. Then on Saturday morning, twelve hours after the other letter was received, we got this entirely different letter about the missile bases in Turkey.

TRUMAN: That's the way they do things.

JFK: Then, well, we rejected that. Then they came back with and accepted the earlier proposal. So I think we're going to have a lot of difficulties. But at least we're making some progress about getting these missiles out of there. In addition, I think that Khrushchev's had some difficulties in maintaining his position. My judgment is that it's going to make things tougher in Berlin because the fact he's had something of a setback in Cuba is going to make him . . .

TRUMAN: That's right.

JFK: . . . rougher in Berlin. But at least it's a little better than it was a couple of days ago.

TRUMAN: Well, you're on the right track. Now you just keep after them. That's the language that they understand, just what you gave them.

JFK: Right. Good.

TRUMAN: They've been asking me for comments, and I've said the President of the United States is the only man who can comment on it.

JFK: [laughs] All right. OK. Good. Take care, I'll be in touch with you.

TRUMAN: All right.

JFK: Thank you, Mr. President.

TRUMAN: I certainly appreciate your call.

JFK: Well, thank you, Mr. President. Bye-bye.

CALL TO PRESIDENT HERBERT HOOVER, OCTOBER 28, 1962

HOOVER: . . . it seems to me these recent events are rather incredible.

JFK: They are incredible. I just, we got a message on Friday night which was rather forthcoming from them. And then on Saturday we got the one on Turkey. Then this morning we got the one going back to their more reasonable position. So we're going to stay right on it and see if we can work up satisfactory verification procedures, but I just wanted to bring you up-to-date on it. We got a lot of problems still to go, but I think we've made some progress.

HOOVER: This represents a good triumph for you.

JFK: Well, I think we just have to, the rhythm of these things, we'll see what happens this week. But I just wanted you to know. I'll keep in touch with you and keep you up-to-date.

HOOVER: Thank you.

JFK: Thank you, Mr. President. Bye-bye.

PRESIDENT KENNEDY WITH PRESIDENT HERBERT HOOVER,
NEW YORK, NEW YORK, APRIL 28, 1961

THE BOMB

n his inaugural address, President Kennedy pledged that the United States would "bear any burden" to assure the success of liberty and in so doing that we would never "fear to negotiate." In the aftermath of the Missile Crisis, he acted on the second impulse. In these tapes, it is clear that he was willing to invest political capital to make sure the world would never come as close to the brink again.

No one would ever accuse President Kennedy of naïve pacifism. In 1961, he went to Congress three times to ask for military funding, and the result was an extraordinary increase in production—from ten Polaris submarines a year to twenty, a 50 percent increase in Strategic Air Command bombers on alert, a thousand new intercontinental ballistic missiles, nuclear-tipped, with bombs eighty times more lethal than the one dropped on Hiroshima. All told, he increased U.S. defense spending 14 percent in 1961 alone, and that was after President Eisenhower warned of a military-industrial complex. To an extent, this was the fulfillment of a campaign promise to close the so-called missile gap, and to increase the security of the United States.

But Kennedy also felt an instinctive abhorrence of nuclear weapons and the complacent strategic thinking they encouraged. He was concerned by the quickness with which his military advisors went to the final option in their scenarios, dropping a nuclear weapon on a large Communist army they could not defeat by other means. On September 13, 1961, he was presented with the defense plan of last resort, "a massive, total, comprehensive obliterating strategic attack . . . on everything Red." Within fifteen minutes of his command, missiles and bombers would be flying toward 3,729 targets in Russia and China.

On October 28, 1962, the day the crisis ended, Khrushchev had written, "We should like to continue the exchange of views on the prohibition of atomic and thermonuclear weapons, general disarmament, and other problems relating to the relaxation of international tension." Kennedy now took steps to return to their earlier, better aspirations. If it was not possible to rid the world of nuclear weapons, then they could at least prevent the testing of weapons in the earth's atmosphere, underwater, and in space.

Khrushchev had actually proposed a test ban years earlier, in 1955, as scientists began to discover the lethal effects of radioactive fallout. Kennedy had also voiced support in the 1950s, as a young senator frustrated by the Eisenhower administration's rigid dependence on its nuclear arsenal. But the volatility of Cold War tensions had led to continued testing, including by the United States, which resumed tests, in response to Soviet testing, in April 1962. With the solidarity of Prime Minister Macmillan, a new dialogue began that began to pay dividends over the spring of 1963. In March, Kennedy said, "I am haunted by the feeling that by 1970, unless we are successful, there may be ten nuclear powers instead of four, and by 1975, fifteen or twenty." In June, Kennedy gave a speech at American University that revealed how profoundly his thinking had evolved from the brinksmanship of October 1962, and invited the Russians to join him in a renewed quest for a test ban. Khrushchev, who had evolved in his own way, did not miss the opportunity. The three powers met under improved conditions in July 1963, and signed the Limited Nuclear Test Ban Treaty on August 5, which was then ratified by the U.S. Senate on September 24. On October 10, it went into effect. Within a year, much had changed. Nine days later, reflecting on the first anniversary of the crisis, Kennedy spoke at the University of Maine and urged his listeners, "Let us resolve to be the masters, not the victims, of our history."

MEETING ABOUT DEFENSE BUDGET, DECEMBER 5, 1962

This short excerpt reveals Kennedy thinking expansively about the logic of a nuclear attack on an adversary certain to retaliate, or, in the parlance of the day, Mutually Assured Destruction. Clearly, he is tending toward a new strategic vision.

JFK: The other question is, the, we didn't talk about our strategic so much, whether we're, if our purpose of our strategic buildup is to deter the Russians, number one, and number two, to attack them if it looks like they are about to attack us, or to make, be able to, lessen the impact they would have on us, in an attack. I think, they concentrate on our cities, we can't be sure enough of their targets, or they may be hard, or they may have submarines, or we can't acceptably carry out a first strike without taking, as I understood the secretary's position, an inordinate amount of damage.

If our point really then is to deter them, it seems to me that we're getting an awful lot of the Polaris submarines and planes that we have, and the navy's strategic force, and the ballistic missiles we have, an awful lot of megatonnage put on the Soviets sufficient to deter them from ever using nuclear weapons.

However, unless we accept . . . otherwise, what good are they? I don't know, you can't use them as a first weapon yourself. They're only good for deterring, and if they attack us, if we fail to deter them, and they attack us, then it's just, just destroy them, out of, fulfill your part of the contract, just drop it on their cities, and destroy them . . . Russians. I don't quite see why we're building as many as we're building.

PRESIDENT KENNEDY ABOARD THE USS *OBSERVATION ISLAND*,
AUTHORIZING THE LAUNCH OF A POLARIS MISSILE, NOVEMBER 16, 1963

MEETING WITH NORMAN COUSINS,
APRIL 22, 1963

The Kennedy tapes reveal a surprising diversity of conversationalists, and now and then President Kennedy would welcome in iconoclastic thinkers to offer viewpoints from beyond the Beltway. The journalist Norman Cousins (1915–1990) fit that description well; as the editor of the widely read *Saturday Review*, he dispensed opinions on a broad range of topics. But one was paramount: since the dropping of the atomic bomb on Hiroshima he had been a leading advocate for nuclear disarmament, and in the early 1960s, his advocacy climbed to a higher level as he brought personal messages between the Kremlin and the White House. He also consulted the Vatican extensively, a fact of consequence in the spring of 1963, as Pope John XXIII drew up his final encyclical, *Pacem in Terris,* calling for peace, human rights, and the calming of the nuclear terror. In a long meeting on April 22, 1963, he told President Kennedy in great detail about his recent visit to see Nikita Khrushchev at his dacha, including gossipy stories of badminton and badinage with the Soviet leader. They also spoke about the world picture, and the deepening involvement of the United States in Southeast Asia. Kennedy indicated a desire to extricate, and a refusal to become trapped in a protracted war ("we're not going to do that"), but also signaled a desire to adhere to the Geneva Accords, and to maintain some form of support for South Vietnam.

JFK: What about . . . it's really sort of ironical to go through these experiences, talking to both of us. [unclear] Especially when I'm sure when he's dealing with the Chinese, who are hopeless, and I'm dealing with [unclear] and Nixon, and the rest of these people, who are almost hopeless.

COUSINS: The political situation is somewhat the same, it's interesting.

JFK: Agreed. He does seem to feel he has a complaint; I don't think he has one, but he thinks he does, and that's the important thing, not whether I do. But it seems to me when we came down, the Senate had indicated that we might even go down to six,[1] perhaps even five, it wasn't, wouldn't have been a hell of

---

1. The United States hoped for a high number of annual inspections of Soviet nuclear facilities; the Soviets regarded this as spying and pushed for a lower figure.

a concession for him to go up to. Unless he's in very much more trouble than I am. I don't think probably it would get by the Senate anyway, even with six, but at least I wouldn't mind making the struggle, as I said to you before. But his control must be very limited if he can't go from three to five.

COUSINS: As I say, on a personal level, having had the men on the council say, well, Nikita, you made a fool of yourself again. Again, it personalizes the situation.

JFK: That's what happens. Well we have been subjected to the last few months, to the charge that we are constantly lowering our, I mean Nixon said it most recently, but it happens every week, that we are appeasing the Soviets. I know he must dismiss all that, but it's of some importance over here.

CALL TO PRESIDENT HARRY TRUMAN, JULY 26, 1963

On July 26, the day that President Kennedy addressed the nation on national television about the Nuclear Test Ban Treaty, just concluded in principle the day before, this friendly call between two presidents reveals the close camaraderie that Kennedy and Truman now shared in the summer of 1963. Truman felt sufficient closeness to his successor (who had gone to some lengths to cultivate his goodwill, inviting him to the White House for ceremonial occasions) that he offers to support Kennedy with public statements in favor of the test ban.

JFK: Hello.

TRUMAN: Mr. President.

JFK: How are you?

TRUMAN: Well, I'm all right, and I want to congratulate you on that treaty.

JFK: Well, I think Averell Harriman did a good job and I think it protects our interests without, but on the other hand, maybe it's going to help.

TRUMAN: I do, too, and I'm writing you a personal confidential letter about certain paragraphs in it, which I know you're familiar with, but I thought that's what you'd want me to do.

JFK: Right. Right.

TRUMAN: But I'm in complete agreement with what it provides. My goodness, maybe we can save a total war with it.

JFK: Well, I think that's the whole, I think that's just to see where we go, and see what happens with China. I think that's our . . .

TRUMAN: Well, and I'm congratulating you on getting that thing done. I think it's a wonderful thing.

JFK: Well, I appreciate that very much, Mr. President, that's very generous and I'm going to make a . . .

TRUMAN: I will send a special airmail letter from me, confirming what I'm saying to you now.

JFK: Good, fine. Well, I think that anything you say about it will be very helpful.

TRUMAN: Well, I'm not going to say anything publicly until you give me permission to do it.

JFK: Yeah, well, I think . . .

TRUMAN: I don't like these fellows who quote the President on [unclear] occasions . . .

JFK: Well, no, but I tell you what. I'm going to make a speech tonight, then anytime you could say anything would be very helpful.

TRUMAN: I'll be glad to do it.

JFK: Fine.

TRUMAN: I'm going to St. Louis tomorrow . . .

JFK: Yeah.

TRUMAN: . . . to the American Legion convention.

JFK: Yeah.

TRUMAN: Do you think that's a good time?

JFK: I can't imagine a better.

TRUMAN: I'll make some statements on the subject, if it's satisfactory with you, in connection with the letter which I'm sending you. You'll get it in the morning.

JFK: That'd be very helpful.

TRUMAN: Well, I want to do it the way you want it.

JFK: Well, fine. Well, if you could say something tomorrow, I think that would really give us a lift.

TRUMAN: I'll be glad to say it. I thought maybe, Sunday morning's papers might be a good place to say it.

JFK: Oh, good. That's fine, Mr. President. Well, you sound in good shape.

TRUMAN: All right. All right. The only trouble with me is that, the main difficulty I have is keeping the wife satisfied. [laughs]

JFK: [laughs] Well, that's all right.

TRUMAN: Well, you know how that is. She's very much afraid I'm going to hurt myself! Even though I'm not. She's a tough bird. But I want to do whatever will be helpful to you.

JFK: Well, that's fine, I think anything you can say tomorrow would be very good.

TRUMAN: All right.

JFK: Thank you very much, Mr. President.

MEETING WITH SCIENTISTS ABOUT
NUCLEAR TEST BAN TREATY, JULY 31, 1963

This short but revealing excerpt came from a meeting between President Kennedy and four scientists that took place in the Cabinet Room on July 31, 1963. Kennedy expresses optimism that the Nuclear Test Ban Treaty could lead to a larger détente with the Soviet Union. He also conveys some concern that other nations who are not parties to the treaty (such as China) will conduct their own tests, forcing the United States to respond.[2]

JFK: Well I want to, just want to, say a word or two about this treaty and about how we ought to function under it and what we expect from it and what we don't expect from it. There are a good many theories as to why the Soviet Union is willing to try this.

I don't think anybody can say with any precision, but there isn't any doubt that the dispute with China is certainly a factor, I think their domestic, internal economic problems are a factor. I think that they may feel that [events?] in the world are moving in their direction and over a period of time they . . . there are enough contradictions in the free world that they would be successful and they don't want to . . . they want to avoid a nuclear struggle or that they want to lessen the chances of conflict with us.

[Whatever?] the arguments are, we have felt that we ought to try to, if it does represent a possibility of avoiding the kind of collision that we had last fall in Cuba, which was quite close, and Berlin in 1961, we should seize the chance. We felt that we've minimized the risks, our detection system is pretty good, and in addition to doing underground testing, which we will continue, therefore, and we have a withdrawal clause.

And it may be that the Chinese test in the next year, eighteen months, two years, and we would then make the judgment to see if we should go back to testing. As I understood it, we're not going to test till 1964 anyway, in the atmo-

---

2. At the July 31, 1963, meeting, President Kennedy met with Dr. John Foster, director of Livermore Laboratories; Dr. Norris Bradbury, director of Los Alamos Laboratory; Dr. Glenn Seaborg, chairman of the Atomic Energy Commission; and John Palfrey, commissioner of the Atomic Energy Commission.

sphere, so this gives us a year to, at least a year and a half, to explore the possibility of a détente with the Soviet Union—which may not come to anything but which quite possibly could come to something.

Obviously if we could understand the Soviet Union and the Chinese to a degree, it would be in our interest. But I don't think we, I don't think that we, knowing all the concern that a good many scientists have felt with the comprehensive test ban, that the detection system is not good enough and that we, which would make our laboratories sterile, it seems to me that we've avoided most of that. I know there's some problem about outer space, maybe some problem about other detection, but I think generally we can keep the laboratories, I would think, growing at a pretty good force, underground testing which we will pursue as scheduled. And we will see what our situation looks like as the Chinese come close to developing a bomb.

In addition, our detection systems will make it possible for us to determine if the Soviet Union has made any particular breakthroughs which result in their

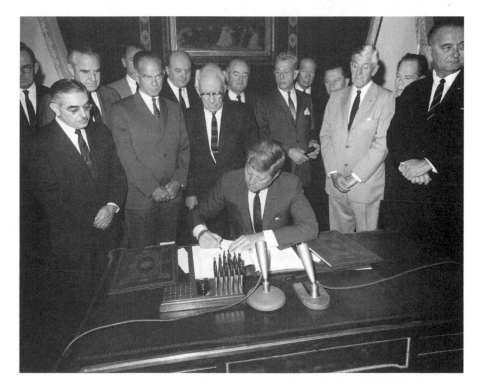

PRESIDENT KENNEDY SIGNS THE LIMITED
NUCLEAR TEST BAN TREATY, OCTOBER 7, 1963

deploying anti-missile systems—which we've got to expect we can or will do and there's no evidence that they [have?], which might change the strategic balance, and therefore might cause us to test again. We can prepare Johnston Island[3] so that we can move ahead in a relatively short time. So I don't think, I'm not sure we're taking, I think we're, the risks are well in hand and I would think in the next twelve months, eighteen months, two years a lot of things may happen in the world and we may decide to start to test again, but if we do, at least we made this effort.

That's the reason, those are the reasons I want to do this. I know Dr. Teller[4] and others are concerned and feel we ought to be going ahead, and [that said?], time may prove that's the wisest course, but I don't think in the summer of 1963, given the kind of agreement we've got, given the withdrawal features we have, given the underground testing program we're going to carry out, it seems to me that this is the thing for us to do.

---

3. Johnston Island is part of an atoll in the Pacific where the United States conducted atmospheric and underground nuclear tests. "Safeguard C" of the Limited Test Ban Treaty gave the United States the right to continue to test nuclear weapons at Johnston Island should the need arise.

4. Edward Teller (1908–2003), nuclear physicist known as "the father of the hydrogen bomb" and a prominent advocate of defense spending, nuclear development, and non-military use of nuclear power. In the 1980s he was a leading supporter of President Reagan's Strategic Defense Initiative.

MEETING WITH SENATOR HENRY "SCOOP" JACKSON, SEPTEMBER 9, 1963

The Nuclear Test Ban Treaty was signed with fanfare on August 5, 1963, in Moscow. But President Kennedy still faced a battle at home as he sought Senate confirmation. From August until late September, he reached out to the essential senators. Early in the day on September 9, 1963, he met with the majority and minority leaders, Mike Mansfield (D-Montana) and Everett Dirksen (R-Illinois), both supporters, to discuss the opposition they still confronted. Later the same day, he sat down with Senator Henry "Scoop" Jackson (D-Washington) for a long conversation that, like so many, took on the world. Jackson, a leading military thinker in the Senate, conveyed with great precision his anxieties about the advantages and disadvantages the treaty would bring. Kennedy countered with eloquent statements of the calming effect that a work-ing treaty would have on a Cold War that had become dangerously hot during the Cuban Missile Crisis. Their extended conversation also touched on Vietnam, where Jackson already had strong reservations, despite his generally hawkish stance. Ken-nedy confessed the delicacy of his position as a Democratic president trying to launch peaceful initiatives when critics like Richard Nixon and others on the right were at-tacking most of his positions ("you'll find there's a hell of a vested interest in proving any Democratic president to be wrong or soft on Communism"). This long and lucid conversation spoke well for the consultative relationship between the Senate and the presidency, designed by the founding fathers.

JFK: The other thing is, I don't think we should apologize to anybody . . .

JACKSON: I'm not apologizing to anyone.

JFK: But it seems to me we do have a story to tell about what we've done in the field of defense. The fact is the B-47 would have been out, it might as well have burned under the previous administration, there wouldn't have been any B-47, we're the ones who continued, after the Berlin Crisis . . .

JACKSON: I agree, that's why I want to see, if [unclear]. This is what I'm con-cerned about. I think anyone who is honest with you will tell you that we've taken unjustified criticism. Here we've had this big buildup, yet the big issue continues to be, I think in this coming campaign, outside of the problem of Civil Rights and so on, the international and national security.

JFK: We came in here and we had two problems, on January 19, when we had a meeting in there, and Eisenhower and Levinson and everybody recommended that we intervene militarily in Laos. And in the summer, we had a . . .

JACKSON: And Berlin was under maximum threat.

JFK: The fact of the matter is Berlin has never been more secure than it now is, we still kept Laos, we are, if—would improve their public relations, we're really doing well in that war there, I've been reading a report from Hartkinson [?] and Krulak, who have just been out there. So I think we're good [?] for all the problems in the world, we're good for the economy, Cuba remains a tough one, but I mean, Christ, we were given that.

JACKSON: Well, I think the criticism we're going to be up against is whether we have the will to use our power, and how far we will do it.

JFK: We made that very clear in two ways. First, in 1961, over Berlin, when we got an ultimatum from Khrushchev, which he had to eat. And the second was last October, in the case of Cuba, when I think we can make the argument, that we're prepared to, on those occasions . . . The fact of the matter is that Khrushchev said in June, in Vienna, that by December he was going to sign a peace treaty, and that any American forces that moved across East Germany would be guilty of an act of war. Well, he had to eat it, after we increased our defense budget.

JACKSON: He can eat an awful lot of crap.

JFK: I know. They're going to make that charge, we've made that charge against them. But I mean, I think we have an answer.

JACKSON: But we still might have to intervene in Laos. I went out there for ten days in Vietnam, went on a couple of missions, watched that operation, and if they play at all smart, all they have to do is take Laos, and completely outflank South Vietnam. I think, you have to, from a strategic point of view, hold that area along the Mekong, that's about two-thirds of Laos . . .

JFK: That's a hell of a place to intervene.

JACKSON: I know, but if they play it smart, where the hell are we? We just keep pouring a million bucks a day into South Vietnam.

JFK: I agree, I think that's why we've always felt we would have to indicate to them that we would intervene along the Mekong, we can't get anybody else to intervene.

JACKSON: No, I say, it's a rough one, but I don't think it's over with.

JFK: I think it is.

JACKSON: The Chinese and Russians.

JFK: But I'd think twice about Laos, even though we've both threatened to, and I think it's been the reason they haven't taken all of Laos, because they think we might.

JACKSON: Well, do it after election.

JFK: Well, all I want to say, Scoop, was that I think it'd make a hell of a difference in this debate, and I think that having gone this far, having signed this, if we get beaten on it I think we'd find ourselves in a much worse position than we would've been if we hadn't brought it up. Now my guess is, the Chinese Communists may explode a bomb in three years, and we may then decide we do the testing. But at least . . .

JACKSON: Sooner than that.

JFK: Maybe a year, eighteen months. I'm not saying, I've never thought this treaty was for good or for long, but I think that as a political effort at this time, we wouldn't be testing anyway until '64, and I think that over the next eighteen months it could be of some significance to us.

JACKSON: Well, again, I think it depends on our will. What we're really doing is reinstituting the moratorium, we hope with our eyes wide open this time.

JFK: Except we have underground testing.

JACKSON: Well, I say, it's one addition.

JFK: [unclear]

JACKSON: Yeah. I think actually they could do more by extrapolation and by various simulated types of tests in addition to actual fairly high-yield underground tests. The great problem, as you know, is the question of what they have found beyond the obvious black capabilities of high-yield nuclear tests. There's a whole field of new scientific phenomena that no one seems to know the answer, and I'll be honest with you, if I go along on the treaty, if I do on it, I hope I can, I'm going to try to decide tomorrow, on it, it seems to me we're going to spend more on delivery systems, because we're going to have to offset the qualitative advantage that they have in high-yield with more delivery systems, to compensate for the advantage we have quantitatively in weapons, I mean in warheads. And I think it's going to cost more to test underground, it's going to run into more money, so this isn't going to cost less, it's going to cost more, that's my own analysis.

JFK: Yeah, I think there will be some great cost.

JACKSON: We're going to have to pay a price for secrecy. That's a hell of a weapon in their arsenal.

JFK: We can watch pretty well what they do.

JACKSON: Well, the only thing, I agree, but the question is, what have they learned, that we really don't know about.

SIX

SPACE

The Cold War was fought in all of the theaters of the world, including one that was extraterrestrial. Outer space was clearly of the utmost importance to a presidency that embraced the future, technology, and the imperative of responding to all foreign challenges. The first Soviet cosmonaut, Yuri Gagarin, had flown into space early in the Kennedy administration, on April 12, 1961. That impressive achievement only deepened the resolve of the new administration to forge an achievement of its own in this very new frontier. Accordingly, Kennedy put enormous pressure on government scientists to equal and exceed the Russians. The lead administrator of NASA, James Webb, was an outspoken public servant who often chafed under this pressure, but who also reciprocated Kennedy's enthusiasm and driving interest. In these two excerpts, President Kennedy and Webb enjoy a spirited exchange about the possibilities opened up by space exploration.

MEETING WITH JAMES WEBB, JEROME WIESNER, AND ROBERT SEAMANS, NOVEMBER 21, 1962

JFK: Do you put this program . . . Do you think this program is the top priority program of the agency?

WEBB:[1] No sir, I do not. I think it is one of the top priority programs, but I think it's very important to recognize here that as you have found what you could do with the rocket, as you found how you could get out beyond the Earth's atmosphere and into space and make measurements, several scientific disciplines that are very powerful have begun to converge on this area.

JFK: Jim, I think it is a top priority. I think we ought to have that very clear. You, some of these other programs can slip six months or nine months and nothing particularly is going to happen that's going to make it. But this is important for political reasons, international political reasons, and for, this is, whether we like it or not, a race. If we get second to the moon, it's nice, but it's like being second anytime. So that, if you're second by six months because you didn't give it the kind of priority, then, of course, that would be very serious. So I think we have to take the view this is the top priority.

WEBB: But the environment of space is where you are going to operate the Apollo and where you are going to do the landing.

JFK: Look, I know all these other things and the satellite and the communications and weather and all, they're desirable, but they can wait.

WEBB: I'm not putting those . . . I am talking now about the scientific program to understand the space environment within which you got to fly Apollo and make a landing on the moon.

JFK: Wait a minute—is that saying that the lunar program to land the man on the moon is the top priority of the Agency, is it?

UNKNOWN SPEAKER: And the science that goes with it . . .

ROBERT SEAMANS:[2] Well, yes, if you add that, the science that is necessary . . .

---

1. James Webb (1906–1992) was the administrator of the National Aeronautics and Space Administration, serving from 1961 to 1968.

2. Robert Seamans (1918–2008) was deputy administrator of NASA.

PRESIDENT KENNEDY WITH NASA ADMINISTRATOR
JAMES WEBB, JANUARY 30, 1961

JFK: The science . . . Going to the moon is the top priority project. Now, there are a lot of related scientific information and developments that will come from that which are important. But the whole thrust of the Agency, in my opinion, is the lunar program. The rest of it can wait six or nine months.

WEBB: Well, the trouble . . . Jerry is holding up his hand . . . Let me say one thing, then maybe you want to [unclear]. The thing that troubles me here about making such a flat statement as that is, number one, there are real unknowns as to whether man can live under the weightless condition and you'd ever make the lunar landing. This is one kind of political vulnerability I'd like to avoid such a flat commitment to. If you say you failed on your number-one priority, this is something to think about. Now, the second point is that as we can go out and make measurements in space by being physically able to get there, the scientific work feeds the technology and the engineers begin to make better spacecraft. That gives you better instruments and a better chance to go out to

MEMORANDUM FOR

VICE PRESIDENT

In accordance with our conversation I would like
for you as Chairman of the Space Council to be in charge of
making an overall survey of where we stand in space.

1. Do we have a chance of beating the Soviets by
   putting a laboratory in space, or by a trip
   around the moon, or by a rocket to land on the
   moon, or by a rocket to go to the moon and
   back with a man. Is there any other space
   program which promises dramatic results in
   which we could win?

2. How much additional would it cost?

3. Are we working 24 hours a day on existing
   programs. If not, why not? If not, will you
   make recommendations to me as to how
   work can be speeded up.

4. In building large boosters should we put our
   emphasis on nuclear, chemical or liquid fuel,
   or a combination of these three?

5. Are we making maximum effort? Are we
   achieving necessary results?

I have asked Jim Webb, Dr. Weisner, Secretary
McNamara and other responsible officials to cooperate with
you fully. I would appreciate a report on this at the
earliest possible moment.

MEMO FROM PRESIDENT KENNEDY TO VICE PRESIDENT JOHNSON
REGARDING THE SPACE PROGRAM, APRIL 20, 1961

learn more. Now right now, all through our universities, some of the brilliant able scientists are recognizing this and beginning to get into this area, and you are generating here on a national basis an intellectual effort of the highest order of magnitude that I've seen develop in this country in the years I've been fooling around with national policy. Now, to them, there is a real question. The people that are going to furnish the brainwork, the real brainwork, on which the future space power of this nation for twenty-five or a hundred years are going be to made, have got some doubts about it and . . .

JFK: Doubts about what?

WEBB: As to whether the actual landing on the moon is what you call the highest priority.

JFK: What do they think is the highest priority?

WEBB: They think the highest priority is to understand the environment and . . . and the areas of the laws of nature that operate out there as they apply backwards into space. You can say it this way, I think. Jerry ought to talk on this rather than me, but the scientists in the nuclear field have penetrated right into the most minute areas of the nucleus and the subparticles of the nucleus. Now here, out in the universe, you've got the same general kind of a structure, but you can do it on a massive universal scale.

JFK: I agree that we're interested in this, but we can wait six months on all of it.

WEBB: But you have to use that information to do these things.

JFK: I see what you're saying, yeah, but only when that information directly applies to the program. Jim, I think we've got to have that.

WIESNER:[3] Mr. President, I don't think Jim understands some of the scientific problems that are associated with landing on the moon, and this is what Dave Bell was trying to say and what I'm trying to say. We don't know a damn thing about the surface of the moon, and we're making the wildest guesses about how we're going to land on the moon, and we could get a terrible disaster from putting something down on the surface of the moon that's very different than we think it is, and the scientific programs that find us that information have to have the highest priority. But they are associated with the lunar program. The

---

3. Jerome Wiesner (1915–1994) was the science advisor to Presidents Eisenhower, Kennedy, and Johnson, and president of the Massachusetts Institute of Technology (1971–1980).

scientific programs that aren't associated with the lunar program can have any priority we are pleased to give them.

UNKNOWN: That's consistent with what the President was saying.

SEAMANS: Yeah. Could I just say that I agree with what you say, Jerry, that we must gather a wide variety of scientific data in order to carry out the lunar mission. For example, we must know what conditions we'll find on the lunar surface. That's the reason that we are proceeding with Centaur in order to get the Surveyor unmanned spacecraft to the moon in time that it could affect the design of the Apollo.

JFK: Yeah. The only thing is I would certainly not favor spending six or seven billion dollars to find out about space. Why are we spending seven million dollars on getting fresh water from salt water, when we're spending seven billion dollars finding out about space? So obviously, you wouldn't put it on that priority because, except for the defense implications behind that, and the second point is the fact that the Soviet Union has made this a test of the system. So that's why we're doing it. So I think we've got to take the view that this is the key program, the rest of it we can find out about, but there's a lot of things we want to find out about, cancer and everything else.

WEBB: But you see, when you talk about this, it's very hard to draw a line with what, between what . . .

JFK: Everything that we do ought to really be tied in to getting onto the moon ahead of the Russians.

WEBB: Why can't it be tied to preeminence in space, which are your own words?

JFK: Because, by God, we've been telling everyone we're preeminent in space for five years, and nobody believes it because they have the booster and the satellite. We know all about the number of satellites we put up, two or three times the number of the Soviet Union . . . we're ahead scientifically. It's like that instrument you've got at Stanford which is costing us a hundred and twenty-five million dollars and everybody tells me that we're the number one in the world. And what is it? I can't think what it is.

MANY VOICES: The linear accelerator.

JFK: That's wonderful, but nobody knows anything about it!

WEBB: Let me say it slightly different. The advanced Saturn is eighty-five times as powerful as the Atlas. Now we are building a tremendous giant rocket with an index number of eighty-five if you give me Atlas one. Now, the Russians have had a booster that'll lift fourteen thousand pounds into orbit. They've been very efficient and capable in it. The kinds of things I'm talking about that give you preeminence in space are what permit you to make either that Russian booster or the advanced Saturn better than any other. A range of progress possible [unclear].

JFK: The only . . . We're not going to settle the four hundred million this morning. I want to take a look closely at what Dave Bell . . .

But I do think we ought to get it, you know, really clear that the policy ought to be that this is the top priority program of the agency and one of the two, except for defense, the top priority of the United States government. I think that that's the position we ought to take. Now, this may not change anything about that schedule, but at least we ought to be clear, otherwise we shouldn't be spending this kind of money, because I'm not that interested in space. I think it's good. I think we ought to know about it. We're ready to spend reasonable amounts of money, but we're talking about fantastic expenditures which wreck our budget and all these other domestic programs, and the only justification for it, in my opinion, is to do it in this time or fashion is because we hope to beat them and demonstrate that starting behind as we did, by a couple of years, by God, we passed them.

CALL TO MAJOR GORDON COOPER, MAY 16, 1963

Gordon Cooper (1927–2004) was one of the original Mercury astronauts and flew an important mission on May 15–16, 1963, orbiting the earth twenty-two times and guiding his craft back safely after several major navigation systems had failed. JFK called Cooper just after he was taken aboard the recovery ship. In 1965, Major Cooper commanded Gemini 5.

JFK: Hello, Major Cooper!

COOPER: Yes, sir.

OPERATOR: Can you hear the President?

COOPER: Yes, sir.

JFK: All right. Major, I just want to congratulate you. That was a great flight.

COOPER: Thank you very much, sir.

JFK: We talked to your wife, and she seemed to stand it very well.

COOPER: Oh, very good.

JFK: And we hope, we are looking forward to seeing you up here Monday, but we are very proud of you, Major.

COOPER: Thank you, sir. It was a good flight, and I enjoyed it.

JFK: Oh good, fine. Well, I look forward to seeing you Monday. Good luck.

COOPER: Thank you, sir.

JFK: Thanks, Major.

PRESIDENT KENNEDY INSPECTS ROCKET MODELS
AT CAPE CANAVERAL, FLORIDA, SEPTEMBER 11, 1962

MEETING WITH JAMES WEBB,
SEPTEMBER 18, 1963

This conversation, held a year later, shows considerable evolution from that of November 21, 1962; Kennedy shows more caution and Webb more boldness. Indeed, they have roughly switched roles in a dialogue that was moving very quickly.

JFK: If I get reelected, I'm not, we're not, go to the moon in my, in our period, are we?

WEBB: No, no. We'll have worked to fly by, though, while you're president, but it's going to take longer than that. This is a tough job, a real tough job. But I will tell you what will be accomplished while we're president, and it will be one of the most important things that's been done in this nation. A basic need to use technology for total national power. That's going to come out of the space program more than any single thing.

JFK: What's that again?

WEBB: A basic ability in this nation to use science and very advanced technologies to increase national power, our economy, all the way through.

JFK: Do you think the lunar, the manned landing on the moon is a good idea?

WEBB: Yes, sir, I do.

JFK: Why?

WEBB: Because . . .

JFK: Could you do the same with instruments much cheaper?

WEBB: No, sir, you can't do the same.

[break]

WEBB: While you're president, this is going to come true in this country. So you're going to have both science and technology appreciating your leadership in this field. Without a doubt in my mind. And the young, of course, see this much better than in my generation. The high school seniors and the college freshmen are 100 percent for man looking at three times what he's never looked at before. He's looking at the material of the earth, the characteristics of gravity and magnetism, and he's looked at life on Earth. And he understands the universe just looking at those three things. All right, maybe he's gonna have material from the moon and Mars, he's going to have already a measurement from Venus about its gravity and its magnetic fields. And if we find some life out beyond Earth, these are going to be finite things in terms of the development of the human intellect. And I predict you are not going to be sorry, no sir, that you did this.

PRESIDENT KENNEDY TOURS THE SATURN ROCKET LAUNCH PAD,
CAPE CANAVERAL, FLORIDA, NOVEMBER 16, 1963

VIETNAM

n *Profiles in Courage*, Kennedy wrote that politics is a field where "the choice constantly lies between two blunders." That aphorism must have felt increasingly true to him as he contemplated his bleak options in Southeast Asia. His interest in Vietnam went back surprisingly far; he had traveled there in 1951, as the French were beginning a quite inglorious exit from their former colony. An early dictated reflection indicates Kennedy's long-standing interest about the underdeveloped world in ways that did not fall into the dualistic framework of the Cold War.

In the early months of the Kennedy administration, Laos was far more in focus than Vietnam, and there the United States was able to engage in minor levels of support for sympathetic allies in a way that did not threaten large-scale conflict. But with Vietnam, a larger and more sophisticated country, it was very difficult to control the outcome of history, as meddling outsiders had discovered before. Under President Eisenhower, the United States had been a very interested observer as Vietnam tried to live under the 1954 Geneva Accords as an independent nation divided into two halves, one of which, South Vietnam, depended on American aid. In the summer of 1963, the options of the United States declined in both number and quality, as the administration of President Ngo Dinh Diem, South Vietnam's president, began to lose popular approval, brutally repress Buddhists, and threaten new alliances with the French and the North Vietnamese. Even if President Kennedy did not subscribe to the famous "domino theory," he was deeply troubled by the prospect of "losing" a once-reliable ally in this part of the world. Accordingly, he increased the number of U.S. military advisors in Vietnam. At the end of 1962, there were 11,500; at the end of 1963, more than 16,000.

But as the tapes indicate, Kennedy consistently resisted pressure to send American troops into combat, and privately expressed skepticism toward the military advisors who urged that he do so. As Diem's fortunes plummeted, Kennedy was unhappy with the increasingly drastic recommendations on the table in late 1963, including a plan to overthrow President Diem and his brother (Ngo Dinh Nhu), hatched by Vietnamese generals with the support of the CIA, the State Department, and his new ambassador to South Vietnam, Henry Cabot Lodge. That plan ultimately went forward, with the result that

Diem and Nhu were brutally executed on November 2, 1963, and a series of unpopular and incompetent governments installed, all of which failed, along with the United States, in the long tragedy of the Vietnam War. Kennedy's dictated memorandum of November 4 indicates how disturbed he was by that violent result, and the knowledge that the coup had resulted from faulty communications, incomplete instructions, and a process that had spun out of control. Since then, a cottage industry has sprung up speculating on how a second term for Kennedy might have altered the calculus in Vietnam.

DICTATED MEMORANDUM ON CONVERSATION WITH
RICHARD NIXON ABOUT VIETNAM, APRIL 1954

On the eve of the French disaster at Dien Bien Phu in 1954, then-Senator Kennedy enjoyed a spirited conversation with the vice president, Richard Nixon, his future adversary in 1960. Given that each would encounter considerable difficulty in Vietnam as president, this early fragment offers a surprisingly early and candid assessment of the problems that would embroil Democratic and Republican administrations in Indochina.

In conversation with Nixon last night, he felt that Reston's[1] article was, in this morning's paper about Dulles'[2] failure [unclear] was most unfair, and he added that he remembered when Reston was so wrong about Alger Hiss.[3] And second, he said that Dulles told him that, no, second, he said that the French had asked for air assistance, for an air strike on Dien Bien Phu,[4] that there were a lot of troops concentrated there, that it would have both the advantage of being of military assistance, and also would be a terrific morale factor. That the British, however, refused to join in the strike, and therefore nothing was done about it. The French have been digging us on it since then by saying they asked for help and we rejected them, and Nixon is very bitter against the British, saying they won't fight except if Hong Kong and Malaya[5] are involved. And they've been always trying to play a balance of power, and now, of course, there's no such balance, no such thing, because it's really 160 million Americans against 800 million Communists. He admits that the only, I asked him what united action

---

1. James "Scotty" Reston (1909–1995) was a columnist and reporter for the *New York Times*, reporting for many years from Washington.

2. John Foster Dulles (1888–1959), secretary of state under President Eisenhower.

3. Alger Hiss (1904–1996) was a prominent lawyer and State Department official who became embroiled in national controversy after he was denounced as a Communist in 1948, a cause that was taken up by Senator Joseph McCarthy. He was convicted of perjury in 1950.

4. Dien Bien Phu was the site of the climactic battle between the French and the Vietnamese fighters for independence led by Ho Chi Minh, fought between March and May 1954.

5. The former British colony of Malaya became independent in 1946, and was integrated into the new nation of Malaysia in 1963.

could be taken that would be effective, he admits that there wouldn't be any use in sending troops in there, as the Chinese would come in, and he finally admitted that the only thing that could be done would be to support the French and the Vietnamese and hope that they were going to be successful. He admits, however, he wonders sometimes [distorted] . . . they're really in bad shape over there, and the forces pushing for peace are increasingly strong. [distorted] He said he's been arguing with Republican colleagues . . . [distorted] Democrat now he would be attacking the [Eisenhower] administration not for doing too much, and for going too far into Indochina, but for not going [distorted]. He says neither partition nor coalitions, of course, would work. He says there's enough manpower and materiel, but he said that, of course, that pushing this independence thing is liable to push the French out and there's no solution there.

INDICATE: ☐ COLLECT
☐ CHARGE TO

~~TOP SECRET~~

Initial telegram cleared by persons listed below.
BK

M
Origin
SS

ACTION: AmEmbassy SAIGON - OPERATIONAL IMMEDIATE AUG 24 9 36 PM '63

243

EYES ONLY - AMBASSADOR LODGE
FOR CINCPAC/POLAD EXCLUSIVE FOR ADMIRAL FELT
NO FURTHER DISTRIBUTION

019

XXXXXXXXXXXXXXXXXXXXXXXX

Re CAS Saigon 0265 reporting General Don's views; Saigon

320, and Saigon 316, and Saigon 329.

It is now clear that whether military proposed martial

law or whether Nhu tricked them into it, Nhu took advantage of

its imposition to smash pagodas with police and Tung's Special

Forces loyal to him, thus placing onus on military in eyes of

world and Vietnamese people. Also clear that Nhu has maneuvered

himself into commanding position.

US Government cannot tolerate situation in which power

lies in Nhu's hands. Diem must be given chance to rid himself

of Nhu and his coterie and replace them with best military

and political personalities available.

If, in spite of all of your efforts, Diem remains obdurate

Drafted by:
FE:RHilsman:ml 8/24/63

Telegraphic transmission and classification approved by: M - W. Averell Harriman

Clearances:
FE - Mr. Hilsman
WH - Mr. Forrestal
U - Mr. Ball

S/S-O - Mr. XXXXXXXX Getsinger

~~TOP SECRET~~

REPRODUCTION FROM THIS
COPY IS PROHIBITED
UNLESS "UNCLASSIFIED".

FORM
DS-322

Committee Print

DECLASSIFIED
MFD   10/21/75

ABOVE AND NEXT PAGE:

U.S. DEPARTMENT OF STATE CABLE 243 DISPATCHED ON AUGUST 24, 1963,
TO U.S. AMBASSADOR TO VIETNAM HENRY CABOT LODGE, JR., CALLING FOR
PRESIDENT DIEM TO REMOVE HIS BROTHER NGO DINH NHU FROM A POSITION
OF POWER IN SOUTH VIETNAM

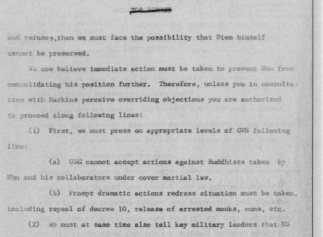

and refuses, then we must face the possibility that Diem himself cannot be preserved.

We now believe immediate action must be taken to prevent Nhu from consolidating his position further. Therefore, unless you in consultation with Harkins perceive overriding objections you are authorized to proceed along following lines:

(1) First, we must press on appropriate levels of GVN following line:

(a) USG cannot accept actions against Buddhists taken by Nhu and his collaborators under cover martial law.

(b) Prompt dramatic actions redress situation must be taken, including repeal of decree 10, release of arrested monks, nuns, etc.

(2) We must at same time also tell key military leaders that US would find it impossible to continue support GVN militarily and economically unless above steps are taken immediately which we recognize requires removal of the Nhus from the scene. We wish give Diem reasonable opportunity to remove Nhus, but if he remains obdurate, then we are prepared to accept the obvious implication that we can no longer support Diem. You may also tell appropriate military commanders we will give them direct support in any interim period of breakdown central government mechanism.

...of removing taint on military ...quarely on Nhu. You are authorized ...on as you consider desirable to ...to take same line here and ...ared/to have Voice of America make ...ext numbered telegram whenever you ...possible.

Concurrently with above, Ambassador and country team should urgently examine all possible alternative leadership and make detailed plans as to how we might bring about Diem's replacement if this should become necessary.

Assume you will consult with General Harkins re any precautions necessary protect American personnel during crisis period.

You will understand that we cannot from Washington give you detailed instructions as to how this operation should proceed, but you will also know we will back you to the hilt on actions you take to achieve our objectives.

Needless to say we have held knowledge of this telegram to minimum essential people and assume you will take similar precautions to prevent premature kxxxkxx leaks.

GP-2.

END.

BALL

MEETING WITH VIETNAM ADVISORS, AUGUST 28, 1963

On the same day as the March on Washington, Kennedy convened a long meeting on Vietnam and responded to the recommendations he was receiving to support a coup by Vietnamese generals against President Diem.

JFK: I don't think we ought to let the coup . . . maybe they know about it, maybe the generals are going to have to run out of the country, maybe we're going to have to help them get out. But still it's not a good enough reason to go ahead if we don't think the prospects are good enough. I don't think we're in that deep. I am not sure the generals are, they've been probably bellyaching for months. So I don't know whether they're, how many of them are really up to here. I don't see any reason to go ahead unless we think we have a good chance of success.

FRENCH GENERAL JEAN DE LATTRE DE TASSIGNY IN VIETNAM.
CONGRESSMAN JOHN F. KENNEDY (CIRCLED) APPEARS IN THE BACK ROW. 1951

MEETING WITH ADVISORS ON VIETNAM, OCTOBER 29, 1963

The planning of the coup continued into the fall and reached a terminal phase in late October. President Kennedy sought the counsel of his advisors, who included William Colby, chief of the CIA's Far East Division; Secretary of State Dean Rusk; Special Assistant for National Security Affairs McGeorge Bundy; Maxwell Taylor, military advisor to the President; Defense Secretary Robert S. McNamara; CIA Director John McCone; and Attorney General Robert F. Kennedy. Always quick to protect his brother, and eager to avoid the kind of ill-advised planning that had led to the Bay of Pigs, Robert Kennedy here spoke forcefully of his reservations about the timing and benefits of a coup. His criticism of the war would only deepen as the United States escalated its involvement under President Lyndon Johnson, and led to his own candidacy for the presidency in 1968.

RFK: Could I make a suggestion?

JFK: Yeah.

RFK: I, this may be a minority, but I just don't see that this makes any sense on the face of it, Mr. President. I mean, it's different from a coup in Iraq or a South American country. We are so intimately involved with this. What we are doing really is what we talked about when we were sitting around this table talking about almost the same thing we talked about four weeks ago. We're putting the whole future of the country, and really Southeast Asia, in the hands of somebody that we don't know very well, that one official of the United States government has had contact with him, and he in turn says he's lined up some others. It's clear from the map [math?] and from Diem,[6] he's a fighter. I mean, he's not somebody that's like Bosch,[7] who's just going to get out of there. He's a determined figure who's going to stick around and I should think go down fighting, that he's going to have some troops there that are going to fight, too. That if it's

---

6. Ngo Dinh Diem (1901–1963) was the first president of South Vietnam, which he led from 1955 to his assassination on November 2, 1963.

7. Juan Bosch (1909–2001), a longtime opposition figure in the Dominican Republic, became its president in February 1963, after the assassination of President Rafael Trujillo on May 30, 1961. After a mere seven months, he was overthrown in a coup on September 25, 1963.

172

THE WORD "VIETNAMESE"
APPEARS AT THE CENTER
OF THIS PAGE OF
PRESIDENTIAL DOODLES
FROM OCTOBER 25, 1963

Prospect		Coup plans	
8:00 P.M.	Coup	Coup	2:30
Press problem		Coup plans	
		Coup plans	2:30
Press problem		coup plans	2:30
			2:30

Vietnamese
Constitution   Constitution   Too significant
Algeria   V.P to
Algerians   Algerians

a failure, that we risk such a hell of a lot. Because the war, as I understood from Bob McNamara, was going reasonably well. And whether, just based on these rather flimsy reports, that a coup is going to take place in two or three days, to risk the whole future of the United States in that area on these kinds of reports, which are not extensive and which don't go into any detail, which don't list, I mean, the reports that come in from the ambassador don't really list our assets or throw out or give a plan as to what's going to occur or how it's going to take place. I would think we have some very large stakes to balance here.

I mean, we certainly, I think, should be entitled to know what's going to happen and how it's going to be effective, and not just hope that the coup is going to go through and they're going to be able to work it out satisfactorily. I would think unless we knew we were going to be involved—everybody's going to say we did it—then if we think that's the right thing, I think we should play a major role. I don't think we can go halfway on it, because we're going to get the blame for it. If it's a failure, I would think Diem's going to tell us to get the hell out of the country and, see, he's going to have enough with his intelligence to know that there's been these contacts and these conversations, and he's going to capture these people. They're going to say the United States is behind it. I would think then that we're just going down the road to disaster. Now maybe this is going to be successful, but I don't think that anybody, any reports that I've seen, indicate that anybody has a plan to show where this is going. And I think this cablegram, sent out like it is, indicates that we are willing to go ahead with the coup, but we think that we should have a little bit more information.

MEETING WITH VIETNAM ADVISORS,
SEPTEMBER 10, 1963

In the fall of 1963, President Kennedy continued to receive conflicting reports on Vietnam and whether U.S. efforts were succeeding or not. These contradictions were brought into unusual focus on September 10, when a group of top advisors gathered to hear reports from General Victor Krulak and State Department advisor Joseph Mendenhall. Krulak reported that the American military effort was proceeding well and that the growing war would be "won" if the United States remained committed. Mendenhall, reporting immediately afterward, warned of the "complete breakdown of the civil government of Saigon" and described a city riven with fear, with government agencies shuttered and a top economic minister reading detective novels in his office.

MENDENHALL: My conclusion is that, and this conclusion is shared, I might say, by Mr. Trueheart, our deputy chief of mission, who is the American with political experience who has been longer on the scene I think than anyone else, also shared by our consul [unclear], is that Mr. Nhu must go, or we will not be able to win the war in Vietnam if he stays. Trueheart commented, at a meeting in the ambassador's office, that he was very much afraid that the people were going to begin to move over toward the VC if the alternative was only between Nhu and the Vietcong. I found that on the part of other U.S. civilian officials in central Vietnam. That is my conclusion as well, Mr. President.

JFK: You both went to the same country? [nervous laughter]

MENDENHALL: Yes, sir.

KRULAK: One talked to military, one to civilians.

JFK: But I mean, how is it that we get this difference, this is not a new thing, this is what we've been dealing with for three weeks. On the one hand, you've got the military saying the war is going better, on the other hand you've got the political saying there's a deterioration that's affecting the military. Now, you gentlemen have a lot of experience, we've got a lot of confidence in both of you. What is the reason for the difference? You must have an explanation, what is the reason for the difference?

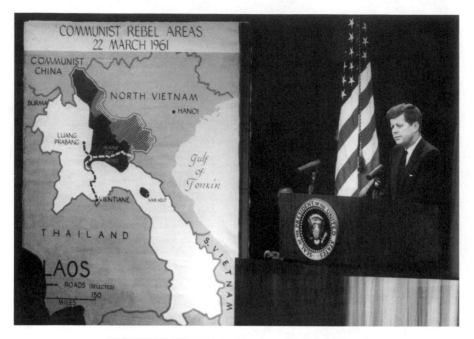

PRESIDENT KENNEDY AT A PRESS CONFERENCE
DISCUSSING SOUTHEAST ASIA, MARCH 23, 1961

KRULAK: I'll tell you the reason. It's metropolitan versus national. That's my judgment, sir. Mr. Mendenhall has expressed a metropolitan viewpoint, and I have expressed one that reflects more of the countryside. Now, this is not to say that my viewpoint should prevail, at all, but the city of Saigon is like the bull's-eye in a target, but there's a great big target around it, too. The attitudes in Saigon indeed are different, they are far more political, far less pragmatic, than are those in the countryside. With respect to Mr. Mendenhall's comments regarding degradation in the war effort in one of the northern provinces, I was there, and talked to our military advisors, whose view is the reverse, and I believe that their view is correct. It would seem difficult to make a synthesis between these two widely divergent views, until our attention is focused on our purpose in Vietnam, which is to win. And I believe in military terms, we are winning. And this wretched government that is there, much as we deplore it, and Mr. Nhu is certainly the figurehead of the things that we deplore, we can still [unclear] through and win the war if somehow we could be permitted to tolerate their conduct, I feel sure of it.

PRIVATE DICTATION, NOVEMBER 4, 1963

The mere fact that he recorded this dictation indicates that President Kennedy was upset by the events that had led to the overthrow of President Diem and his brother, and by the faulty planning process that had allowed the coup to move forward. As he had done during the Cuban Missile Crisis, Kennedy paused to outline how an event of unusual historic significance had germinated and how the members of his top staff had felt about it. Midway through taping, he was interrupted by his son, which deepened the personal tone of his remarks, and the shock he expressed into the Dictaphone.

JFK: Monday, November 4, 1963. The . . . Over the weekend, the coup in Saigon took place, culminated three months of conversation about a coup, conversation which divided the government here and in Saigon. Opposed to a coup was General Taylor; the attorney general; Secretary McNamara; to a somewhat lesser degree, John McCone,[8] partly because of an old hostility to Lodge, which causes him to lack confidence in Lodge's judgment, partly, too, as a result of a new hostility because Lodge shifted his station chief. In favor of the coup was State, led by Averell Harriman, George Ball, Roger Hilsman, supported by Mike Forrestal at the White House.[9] I feel that we must bear a good deal of responsibility for it, beginning with our cable of early August in which we suggested the coup. In my judgment, that wire was badly drafted, it should never have been sent on a Saturday, I should not have given my consent to it without a roundtable conference in which McNamara and Taylor could have presented their views. While we did redress that balance in later wires, that first wire encouraged Lodge along a course to which he was in any case inclined. Harkins[10] continued to oppose the coup on the grounds that the military effort was doing well. There was a sharp split between Saigon and the rest of the country. Politi-

---

8. John McCone (1902–1991) was director of Central Intelligence from September 1961 to April 1965.

9. Roger Hilsman (b. 1919) was assistant secretary of state for Far Eastern affairs; Michael Forrestal (1927–1989) was a National Security Council aide and the son of former defense secretary James Forrestal, who brought JFK to Europe in 1945.

10. General Paul D. Harkins (1904–1984) was a commander in Vietnam from 1962 to 1964.

cally the situation is deteriorating. Militarily they had not had its effect. There was a feeling however that it would for this reason, Secretary McNamara and General Taylor supported applying additional pressures to Diem and Nhu in order to move them . . .

[John F. Kennedy, Jr., enters room]

JFK: Do you want to say anything? Say hello.
JOHN: Hello.
JFK: Say it again.
JOHN: Naughty, naughty Daddy.
JFK: Why do the leaves fall?
JOHN: Because it's autumn.
JFK: Why does the snow come on the ground?
JOHN: Because it's winter.
JFK: Why do the leaves turn green?
JOHN: Because it's spring.
JFK: When do we go to the Cape? Hyannisport?
JOHN: Because it's summer.
JFK: It's summer.
JOHN: [laughter] Your horses.

[John F. Kennedy, Jr., exits room]

JFK: I was shocked by the death of Diem and Nhu.[11] I'd met Diem with Justice Douglas many years ago. He was a extraordinary character, and while he became increasingly difficult in the last months, nevertheless, over a ten-year period he held his country together to maintain its independence under very adverse conditions. The way he was killed made it particularly abhorrent. The question now, whether the generals can stay together and build a stable government, or whether Saigon will begin to turn on public opinion in Saigon. The

---

11. Ngo Dinh Nhu (1910–1963) was the younger brother of President Diem and served without portfolio as the chief defender of his brother's repressive policies.

PRESIDENT KENNEDY AND ATTORNEY GENERAL ROBERT
F. KENNEDY WITH JOHN F. KENNEDY, JR., AND
CAROLINE KENNEDY, THE WHITE HOUSE, OCTOBER 14, 1963

intellectuals, students, et cetera, will turn on this government as repressive and undemocratic in the not too distant future.

Also, we have another test on the Autobahn[12] today. This is serious, and not the result of any misunderstanding. It's obviously a determination by the Soviets to demonstrate that they determine the conditions under which we move on the Autobahn. We are attempting to determine that we have free access and that therefore are not subject to their artificial rules. This is a substantive matter, and we cannot tell how it will end.

Also concerned about the prospective annulment of all the American oil contracts. The Argentine. This will mean that the Hickenlooper Amendment[13] goes into effect, and we'll find it very difficult to give them assistance, and it will make our relations more bitter. We may have a similar situation in Peru. The use of the Hickenlooper Amendment in Ceylon has not been a happy augury for its use in other countries, particularly in Latin America, where nationalist passions run high.

Adenauer said that we should have pulled the wall down in 1961, that for sixty hours we were immobilized in spite of their fervent pleas. This is totally erroneous. I asked Bundy to get together a whole record on that period to show that no German party, no major paper, certainly not our military, nor that of France or England, advocated any actions such as that.

---

12. Because West Berlin was separated from West Germany, it was important for U.S. troops to be able to move freely along the Autobahn highway system. The Russians and their East German allies often tested American resolve by hindering access.

13. In 1962, Congress proposed an amendment to the Foreign Assistance Act of 1961 that restricted aid to Communist countries and to countries that nationalized the property of American corporations. Targeted primarily at Cuba, it was named after Senator Bourke B. Hickenlooper of Iowa. The Kennedy administration opposed the amendment, which undermined its hope to find a creative path forward in the developing world, and in Latin America in particular.

EIGHT

THE WORLD
AS IT IS

"We must deal with the world as it is," President Kennedy asserted in his speech at American University in June 1963.[1] But a world in flux made that a constant challenge. When he ran for president in 1960, one of Kennedy's many arguments was that the world was changing quickly and the United States was not doing enough to change with it. For eight years, Americans had heard of dominoes falling and chessboards divided into two colors. Kennedy wanted to describe the world with more nuance. As a senator he had nurtured this vision with speeches on Vietnam and Algeria, and as president, he went to considerable lengths to convey his interest in Africa, India, China, Indonesia, the Middle East, North Africa, and many other parts of the global community. There were nineteen new nations in 1960 alone, and as the former colonial powers continued their retreat from dominance, these new nations needed to be addressed with seriousness and respect. Kennedy understood this instinctively; he invited numerous African heads of state to appear at state ceremonies with him and spent surprising time with their ambassadors. Arthur M. Schlesinger, Jr., called him "the Secretary of State for the third world."

Sometimes this new diplomacy paid surprising dividends—as, for example, when African nations refused to allow Soviet aircraft to refuel on the way to Cuba during the Missile Crisis. At other times, it did not; Vietnam was a former colonial power whose wishes did not run especially parallel to those of the United States, no matter how much money and military aid was offered. But as the new decade dawned, these imperfect aspirations marked an important attempt to give new relevance to the core principles of self-reliance at the heart of American history.

---

1. President Obama repeated the phrase in his Nobel lecture of December 2009.

MEETING WITH AFRICA ADVISORS, OCTOBER 31, 1962

Throughout his career as a senator, and then as President, Kennedy displayed an interest in Africa that was unusual for the time, and for anyone schooled, as he surely was, in Cold War brinksmanship. He spoke up for Africa's relevance to the world, championed African student exchange programs, and referred to Africa 479 times during the 1960 campaign. An impressive number of state visits came from African leaders—eleven in 1961, ten in 1962, and seven in 1963. The Cuban Missile Crisis was barely over when the President's Africa advisors sat down with him to discuss matters relating to the Congo, where the cruel legacy of Belgian colonialism, combined with more recent acts of violence (particularly the assassination of the charismatic leader Patrice Lumumba, on January 17, 1961), had led to increasing volatility.

G. MENNEN WILLIAMS:[2] Mr. President, there's one other factor that we ought to have in mind, and that is, we needed the Africa vote in the Cuban situation . . .

JFK: Yeah.

WILLIAMS: . . . and we needed it in the ChiCom[3] situation. And they're not going to have much faith in us if we don't push through with the Congo, so I think we've got to keep this thing moving. Now, I think the plan that George has outlined will do it. But I just think we've got to show our determination.

JFK: Well, I think we've done a hell of a lot. I mean, I know that we haven't been successful, but no one can say that we've been less than any European country. My God, just look through the list! The English haven't done anything for us. The French, nothing for us. [unclear] The Germans and Italians can't even, so that there's no other Western power that's doing anything now, we haven't done enough to get the job done, but . . .

WILLIAMS: Now, sir, after Cuba you look ten feet tall to them, and they say, here's a man who can do it in Cuba, what's he doing for us here? So I think we can . . .

JFK: Well I think we ought to use whatever influence we've got very hard now, in the next couple of weeks with these people.

---

2. G. Mennen Williams (1911–1988), governor of Michigan (1948–1960), assistant secretary of state for African Affairs (1961–1966).

3. Chinese Communist.

PRESIDENT AND MRS.
KENNEDY WELCOME FELIX
HOUPHOUET-BOIGNY,
PRESIDENT OF THE
IVORY COAST, NATIONAL
AIRPORT, WASHINGTON, DC,
MAY 22, 1962

MEETING ABOUT DEFENSE BUDGET, DECEMBER 5, 1962

JFK often threw out arresting thoughts in his frequent meetings with military advisors, fighting against the conventional doctrine that was so easy to find in Washington. This conversation between Kennedy and his advisors took place shortly after the Cuban Missile Crisis and centered on U.S. policy toward Cuba, the military budget, and the value of nuclear weapons, both as a deterrent and as a practical weapon. At the meeting, Secretary of Defense Robert McNamara presented the President with a review of the Department of Defense's $54.4 billion budget for FY 1964. Recommendations on funding, programs, and forces for each of the service branches were also discussed in detail. McNamara was a helpful ally as he brought his formidable executive skills to bear on reforming the enormous bureaucracy he was charged to lead. In this meeting to review the Department of Defense budget, JFK questioned the military's nimbleness at planning for the years ahead.[4]

JFK: What I'm thinking about is, in Cuba where we'll be on a unilateral basis, in which we bear total responsibility, Southeast Asia, where you can see a crisis coming, either something in Laos, or something in South Vietnam, number 2 . . . number 3, where we'd be required to do a rather rushed job in India, in which we'd have to send a lot of equipment, planes. Those seem to me to be the most likely things to happen. What is rather unlikely is to have a long sustained conventional war in Europe, because I don't think that our allies are preparing for that.

MAXWELL TAYLOR: We are not prepared to fight that kind of war in Europe at the present time.

JFK: Well, then what's the use of having six divisions, plus two spares, plus

---

4. Identified participants at the December 5, 1962, meeting were: President John F. Kennedy; Robert McNamara, secretary of defense; General Maxwell Taylor, chairman of the Joint Chiefs; McGeorge Bundy, national security advisor; George Ball, undersecretary of state; and Jerome Wiesner, special assistant to the President.

enough equipment to carry on a conventional war there until we get our [unclear] reduced? I think it makes sense, I'm all for it if it gets the Europeans to do it, but if they're not going to do it, then that's what we'll decide at NATO, then it seems to me that we ought to say to them, this is what we're prepared to do, but it only makes sense if we've got somebody on our right and our left.

ROBERT MCNAMARA: This is exactly the theme of my statement, I have a draft of it ready now. [some chatter] What I propose to say is exactly this, it makes no sense for us to buy enough for the U.S. divisions, and have our flanks bare at the end of thirty days. And that's exactly the position we're in. But I fully agree that in fact, there are other situations in the world that would justify the major part of that, if not all.

JFK: Well, I'm thinking of . . . I'll give you three examples. Number one might be, if civil war in Brazil or someplace, and you'd want to send down a lot of equipment there, your airlift and so on, so I think as long as we don't sort of concentrate it on Europe, I'm all for it. I just don't think we ought to be thinking about it, except [unclear] in the rather unlikely contingency, when we're fighting a conventional war in Europe, until such a point where our [unclear] can sustain us.

CALL FROM SARGENT SHRIVER,
APRIL 2, 1963

In this brief call, Peace Corps Director and President Kennedy's brother-in-law R. Sargent Shriver voices his concern that one of the President's most idealistic proposals, the Peace Corps, is in danger of being subverted by the Central Intelligence Agency. Kennedy quickly understands the danger posed by this threat to one of his most valued forms of cultural diplomacy and promises to put a stop to it.

JFK: Hello.

SHRIVER: Hello, Jack?

JFK: Yeah, Sarge.

SHRIVER: Hi, how are you?

JFK: Good. Fine, fine.

SHRIVER: I'm sorry to bother you.

JFK: Not a bit.

SHRIVER: But I'm getting rather suspicious over here that, despite your instructions, that some of our friends over in the Central Intelligence Agency might think that they're smarter than anybody else, and that they are trying to stick fellows into the Peace Corps.

JFK: Yeah, yeah.

SHRIVER: And John McCone has told me on two or three occasions, and Dulles of course did, that they never would do that.

JFK: Right, right.

SHRIVER: They sent out messages and the rest of it.

JFK: Right.

SHRIVER: But we've got a group in training now that looks suspicious, and I'd like to follow whatever you recommend, but I sure in hell want those guys . . .

JFK: Well, would you call Dick Helms?[5]

SHRIVER: Dick Helms?

---

5. Richard Helms (1913–2002) was deputy director of plans at the Central Intelligence Agency in 1963; he would ultimately serve as director of Central Intelligence (1966–1973).

JFK: Yeah. He's the operations officer over there, and just say to him that you've talked to me and that I don't want anybody in there.

SHRIVER: OK.

JFK: And if they are there, let's get them out now, before we have it. And if there is any problem about it, that Dick Helms ought to call the President about it. That . . .

SHRIVER: OK.

JFK: This is very, we are very, very anxious that there be no, we don't want to discredit this whole idea.

SHRIVER: OK, fine.

JFK: And they, Christ, they're not gonna find out that much intelligence!

PRESIDENT KENNEDY AND PEACE CORPS DIRECTOR R. SARGENT SHRIVER,
THE WHITE HOUSE, WEST WING COLONNADE, AUGUST 28, 1961

SHRIVER: That's right.

JFK: Now, the other thing is, I notice with these people coming back, can we do anything about seeing if we can get some of them to go into the Foreign Service?

SHRIVER: Yes. The Foreign Service has already changed their examination schedules, and the kind of exams they give, and the places that they are going to be given, and done everything that they think they can this year to facilitate Peace Corps guys getting into the Foreign Service, and . . .

JFK: Yeah.

SHRIVER: USIA[6] has done the same thing, and AID[7] is trying to do something.

JFK: Yeah. Yeah.

SHRIVER: I think we'll have to find out by one trial run to see whether it's successful.

JFK: OK. Well, I just wanted to be sure. Let me know if there's anything we can do, but these are the guys I'd like to get into the Foreign Service.

SHRIVER: OK, fine.

JFK: OK.

SHRIVER: Thanks.

JFK: Bye, Sarge.

---

6. United States Information Agency.

7. U.S. Agency for International Development.

MEETING ON INDIA AND CHINA, MAY 9, 1963

Most Americans were trained to think of nuclear war in the traditional way, as a conflict between the United States and the Soviet Union. In this excerpt, JFK contemplates a range of other disturbing scenarios, including the unpredictable actions of the Chinese.

JFK: I gather we're coming to the defense of Israel, and Saudi Arabia. What I think we ought to think about is, [unclear] it's desirable (?) for us, to give India a guarantee which actually we would carry out. I don't think there's any doubt that this country is determined that we couldn't permit the Chinese to defeat the Indians. If we would, we might as well get out of South Korea and South Vietnam. So I think that's what we'll decide at the time. Now, therefore, I don't mind making, seeing us make some commitments. Now, if it is politically important . . .

MAXWELL TAYLOR: Mr. President, I would hope before we get too deeply in the India question, we take a broader look at where we're, the attitude we're going to maintain versus Red China, all the way from Manchuria to [unclear]. This is just one spectacular aspect of the overall problem of how to cope with Red China, politically and militarily, over the next decade.

JFK: It seems that India is the only place where they've got the manpower to really do it.

TAYLOR: I would hate to think we'd fight this on the ground in a non-nuclear war, if indeed Red China came in and matched us in any part of Asia.

JFK: That's right, I think the chance would be much less if they knew we were clearly committed. Maybe they know by our actions last fall that we are, and by our actions in South Vietnam. What I was thinking is, whatever restraint we impose on them, and whatever assistance it would give us politically, we should be prepared to go some distance to give a guarantee, because I think it'd be just like, an attack on India in force would be just as much a red flag as the North Korean attack on South Korea was in 1950.

ROBERT MCNAMARA: Mr. President, I think General Taylor is implying that before any substantial commitment to defend India against China is given, we should recognize that in order to carry out that commitment against any substantial Chinese attack, we would have to use nuclear weapons.

MEETING WITH SOVIET FOREIGN MINISTER ANDREI GROMYKO, OCTOBER 10, 1963

Following Kennedy's historic speech at American University on June 10, 1963, in which he proclaimed a desire to work toward peaceful cooperation with the Soviet Union, Russian-American relations took a notable turn for the better. In the fall of 1963, Soviet Foreign Minister Andrei Gromyko came to the White House for a high-level discussion of the relations between the two countries. Kennedy stated repeatedly his desire to move the relationship to a firmer footing based on reduced military spending and minimal frictions. In the course of his meeting with Gromyko, JFK's children interrupted, leading to a rare belly laugh from a Soviet bureaucrat normally known for his monotone. These excerpts are taken from a long conversation that shows how far the U.S.–Soviet relationship had evolved in a year, since the Cuban Missile Crisis.

JFK: I don't want you to get discouraged. You may not be conscious of much progress where you sit. But we've been [unclear] the United States for the last three months, and in several directions, and we think we've made some progress in our relations with the Soviet Union. We may not get the German question disposed of. We may not solve all the matters. But considering some of the difficulties that both our countries face, internally and externally, it seems to me we've done pretty well. So I'm rather encouraged, not discouraged. I don't want you to be discouraged.

GROMYKO: [unclear] Well, there is improvement . . .

JFK: . . . There's only a certain tempo that you can move in these matters. We went ahead with the test ban. We've made some progress, which for the United States is rather . . . Do you realize that in the summer of 1961 the Congress unanimously passed resolutions against trade with the Soviets? And now we're going ahead, we hope, with this very large trade arrangement. That represents, that's a change in American policy of some proportions. That's progress. We're talking about next week going ahead with this matter on the space, we're talking about getting the civil air agreement settled, we've got the communications. I agree, we haven't settled Berlin, but considering that we've got a lot of problems . . . you've got, you taking out some of your troops out of Cuba, so it's less of a problem for us here. That's some progress.

PRESIDENT KENNEDY AND CHAIRMAN KHRUSHCHEV AT THE SOVIET
EMBASSY IN VIENNA, JUNE 4, 1961. *LEFT TO RIGHT:* U.S. AMBASSADOR
LLEWELLYN THOMPSON, PRESIDENT KENNEDY, CHAIRMAN KHRUSHCHEV,
AND SOVIET FOREIGN MINISTER ANDREI GROMYKO

GROMYKO: You are right, Mr. President, there is change in the atmosphere, in the broad sense of this word, information atmosphere, and in more narrow but important one, that is our relations, relations between United States and Soviet Union, concerned. But the program . . . unsolved problems are unsolved problems.

[break]

GROMYKO: Now to formalize officially our understanding of this matter, [unclear] . . .

CHILDREN: Daddy!

JFK: Just open the door there, say hello to my daughter and son. Say hello. Come in a minute and say hello. Do you want to say hello to the minister?

GROMYKO: Hello, hello.

JFK: Do you want to say hello to John? Do you want to say hello to the ambassador?

GROMYKO: Well, well, well. They are very popular in our country. [laughter]

JFK: His chief is the one who sent you Pushinka.[8] You know that, the puppies?

GROMYKO: You do not [unclear] any secrets from them? [laughter] So, Mr. President, I mentioned aggression treaty . . .

---

8. In a response to a request by Jacqueline Kennedy during the height of the Cold War, Pushinka (Russian for "Fluffy") was a gift from Soviet leader Nikita Khrushchev to Caroline Kennedy. Pushinka was a puppy from Strelka, one of the first Soviet space dogs who returned to Earth. Pushinka and the Kennedys' Welsh Terrier Charlie had four puppies together.

CALL TO MARSHAL JOSIP BROZ TITO, OCTOBER 24, 1963

President Kennedy was always eager to work his charm on foreign leaders, particularly when those leaders had shown a disposition to thwart the will of the Soviet Union. When Yugoslavia's Marshal Josip Broz Tito came to the United States for a visit in the fall of 1963, President Kennedy reached out personally to convey his regards.

JFK: Hello?

OPERATOR: Yes, please.

JFK: Hello?

UNIDENTIFIED: 2192.

OPERATOR: Ready.

JFK: Mr. President?

TITO:[9] Yes, I am . . .

JFK: Oh, how are you? This is . . .

TITO: I am very good, Mr. President . . .

JFK: How are you feeling? Are you feeling better?

TITO: Yes. Much better.

JFK: I'm very sorry about some of your difficulties in New York.[10] And I'm very sorry you didn't get a chance to get to California and some other parts of the United States.

TITO: Thank you, thank you. It was not so bad.

JFK: Well, they always, they boo me in New York, too, sometimes. So, I hope that you have a good trip back, and we were very glad you came to the United States.

TITO: Thank you, thank you very much.

JFK: And give my best to Mrs. Tito.

---

9. Tito had led Yugoslavia's fierce partisan resistance to the Nazis in World War II, and conceived a unique path during the Cold War, as the head of a Communist nation capable of standing up to the Soviets and embracing certain values of the West.

10. In October 1961, Tito visited the United States. During a visit to the United Nations, he encountered protests from Croats and Serbs and was criticized by Senator Thomas Dodd of Connecticut.

TITO: Thank you.

JFK: And as I say, we've been glad you're here, and we want you to come back sometime.

TITO: Yes.

JFK: And to see California and Massachusetts and the rest of the United States.

TITO: Yes, thank you.

JFK: Good.

TITO: I hope, but I hope also that I will meet you in Yugoslavia. [laughs]

JFK: [laughs] All right, fine, good, thank you very much.

TITO: Bye.

JFK: Bye-bye.

MEETING WITH ASIA SPECIALISTS,
NOVEMBER 19, 1963

In early 2012, the John F. Kennedy Presidential Library released its final batch of tapes, including meetings from the last week of President Kennedy's life. In this meeting, held on November 19, he spent an hour talking with Asia specialists about a major trip to the region, with a particular focus on Indonesia and its charismatic but volatile leader, Sukarno. Kennedy displayed fascination with Sukarno and his troubled nation, full of resources and potential, yet held back by roiling internal conflicts. Throughout his life on the public stage, Kennedy had sought new ways to recast the Cold War and the binary logic of the 1950s. A major exchange of visits with Sukarno was designed to be a first step toward this end, and in this meeting Kennedy committed to a sixteen-day journey that would take him to, among other places, Malaysia, Thailand, the Philippines, Taiwan, Japan, Korea, and Indonesia. Kennedy was well aware that using the full prestige of a presidential visit and his particular popularity was "the most powerful lever we've got," in the words of one of his advisors, and he hoped to use the visit to improve political conditions in Indonesia. Also present at the meeting were the U.S. ambassador to Indonesia, Howard Jones; the secretary of state for Far Eastern affairs, Roger Hilsman; and Michael Forrestal from the National Security Council.

JFK: Why don't we proceed. I think we're pretty well in agreement as far as what we can do on all these matters we've discussed. I'd like to go up there, I don't know if I can go to all the places where Roger's got me going, I'd like to go, I don't know if politically . . .

JONES: How long would you be thinking of, sir?

JFK: I don't think I can be away more than sixteen days.

JONES: What month, sir?

JFK: Well, I want to go to Latin America twice, if I can, or at least once. [unclear]. Actually, politically, Latin America is going to be a big part of policy issues. Actually, politically, domestically, the only place that really makes a hell of a thing is Japan, because it's impressive to Americans. Eisenhower's difficulties, and so on. So going to Japan and having a successful visit would be very helpful. The Philippines are pretty old hat. But going to see Sukarno, who is not a political asset here, and we got a hell of a reception, and it was well done, and it would make an impression.

NINE

THE BURDEN
AND THE GLORY

A presidency is often defined by its most glorious ceremonial moments. That is certainly the hope of administration officials, in any administration, and an elaborate machinery of pomp and circumstance contributes to that stage-managed effect. Elevated speeches, triumphal processions, and state dinners are only a few of the cogs in that machinery, and remind us that our democracy still retains features from the monarchical system it displaced.

John F. Kennedy reveled in all of the above, and his charisma infused the ceremonial events with an unusual degree of excitement between 1961 and 1963. That excitement still colors his memory, and many of the most iconic images from that time show him outside, speaking to a huge throng and basking in their attention, in places ranging from the East Portico of the Capitol to Rudolph Wilde Platz in Berlin.

But the tapes restore some balance by offering a window into the hard work of a presidency—the long indoor meetings, the disagreements, and even worse, the constant agreements, arrived at too quickly, by underlings all too eager to please. "The Burden and the Glory" was a phrase he used in his 1962 State of the Union address, and that title was later given to a book of his speeches. In the excerpts that follow, a very human President Kennedy vents his occasional frustration at the burden that lies not far below the surface of the glory.

And as the private dictation of November 12 indicates, President Kennedy faced real worries as he headed into what promised to be a bruising campaign year. Reelection would validate the New Frontier and give him four more years to consolidate the progress of his first term. Indeed, it would allow him to complete his original campaign promise from 1960 and shape the entire decade along the lines he had first sketched out in his convention speech, creating a time of youthful activism, broader civil and economic rights, and a willingness to confront difficult problems with courage rather than complacency.

Rejection, on the other hand, would constitute a crippling setback, and place the United States on a very different trajectory. Personally, it would have been devastating as well; John F. Kennedy would have left the White House as a forty-seven-year old man, with no political office, a single term to mull over, and well-chronicled health problems. Writing a memoir based on these recordings might have been one of the few consolations available.

The events in Dallas removed all of those speculations and gave us a far different history that we are still coming to terms with. The New Frontier did not exactly end; indeed, it is likely that Kennedy's martyrdom advanced many of the causes he cared about, especially that of Civil Rights. President Lyndon Johnson cited his memory powerfully as he rounded up the votes needed for the great Civil Rights Act of 1964. But those achievements came at a cost, including the departure of much of the South from the Democratic coalition, the rise of a powerful right, and a stridency that has never left our politics since. A tragic entanglement in Vietnam, far deeper than it is likely John F. Kennedy would have permitted, was also pursued by President Johnson, sometimes with the explanation that Kennedy would have made the same decisions, although most of the evidence disputes that theory. Like most theories, it remains subject to interpretation.

A few fleeting moments from the tapes capture the effort that was building in the fall of 1963 to plan a successful Democratic convention, ward off challenges, and carry through to victory in November 1964. It was in pursuit of this plan that President Kennedy went to Texas, an essential battleground state.

In the 1960 speech that named the New Frontier, Kennedy cautioned Americans against seeking comfort in "the safe mediocrity of the past," and he certainly would not have wanted readers to attack the problems of the twenty-first century by repeating the well-worn catchphrases of an earlier generation. But perhaps by asking Americans to deepen their acquaintance with the issues, and to renew their commitment to talk with one another, as the participants in these conversations do so well, these tapes will serve a new purpose that he never intended. That would be a worthy final legacy of John F. Kennedy; not to romanticize his time, but to embrace and engage with our own.

CALL ABOUT U.S. HOCKEY TEAM,
MARCH 13, 1963

No theater of Cold War competition was too small for Kennedy to take an interest in—for example, the absorbing athletic rivalry that pitted the United States against the Soviet Union, and the many proxy contests in which they and their allies participated. At the very least, it was essential to perform to the utmost of one's ability; to win, if possible, but if not, to at least show well. Unfortunately, that presidential directive did not reach the U.S. men's hockey team, who suffered a series of ignominious defeats in the spring of 1963.

JFK: Dave?

DAVID HACKETT:[1] Yeah.

JFK: How are you?

HACKETT: How are you?

JFK: Dave, I noticed in the paper this morning where the Swedish team beat the American hockey team, 17 to 2.

HACKETT: Yeah, I saw that.

JFK: Christ, who are we sending over there? Girls?

HACKETT: They haven't won a game.

JFK: I know it. I mean, who got them up?

HACKETT: I don't know. I can check into it.

JFK: God, we've got some pretty good hockey players, haven't we?

HACKETT: Yeah. Well, I think. Yeah.

JFK: I suppose they are all playing on their college teams, are they, or something? I'd like to find out whether it was done . . . under what . . . who sort of sponsors it and what kind of players they've got, and I think it's a disgrace to have a team that's 17 to 2. That's about as bad as I've ever heard, isn't it?

---

1. David Hackett (1927–2011) was executive director of the President's Committee on Juvenile Delinquency and Youth Crime from 1961 to 1964. He was a close friend of Robert Kennedy since they had attended Milton Academy together, and a hockey standout who played for the U.S. Olympic team.

HACKETT: And they have been beaten by everybody by a score almost equal to that.

JFK: So obviously, we shouldn't send a team unless we send a good one. Will you find out about it and let me know?

HACKETT: I'll find out about it and let you know.

TWO CALLS ABOUT FURNITURE PURCHASE,
JULY 25, 1963

Ever sensitive to public opinion, Kennedy was horrified to open the paper one day and see a photograph of a navy aide standing next to an expensive new naval project—a hospital bedroom that had been built at a base on Cape Cod, to be ready in case Jacqueline Kennedy went into labor with their son, Patrick Bouvier Kennedy. Such an expenditure seems modest today, but Kennedy was irate at the cost and, even worse, the publicity involved.

JFK: . . . spent $5,000 for that! Let's cut their budget another hundred million.

ARTHUR SYLVESTER:[2] Precisely, Mr. President. The last word that they had from me yesterday after my talk to Pierre[3] was to keep the photographers out of there and sign 'em out of there.

JFK: OK.

SYLVESTER: They went ahead on their own. The funny part about this is, it's a sidelight which might lighten your day, is that the army, you know, we're saved from this sort of thing out at Walter Reed. When they saw this yesterday, they are unhappy, if you please.

JFK: Well then, that's why the goddamn service, they ought to cut them a billion dollars.

SYLVESTER: That's right, exactly.

JFK: When you think of the waste that goes on.

SYLVESTER: It is absolute nonsense.

JFK: Imagine what they'd do if you didn't just stay on their ass. They were gonna order me three planes instead of one.

SYLVESTER: Precisely.

JFK: They're gonna do all these, that's the way these guys spend money.

SYLVESTER: Absolutely.

JFK: They're shocked that we don't. Now the only thing is it would seem to me,

2. Arthur Sylvester was assistant secretary of defense for public affairs.

3. Pierre Salinger, President Kennedy's press secretary.

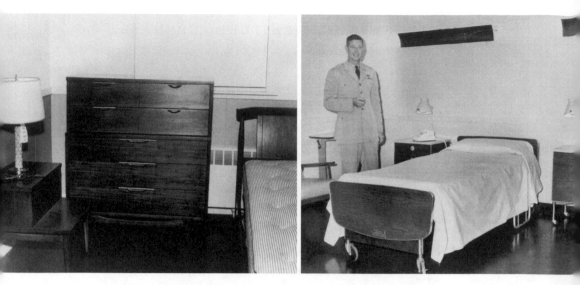

HOSPITAL ROOM PREPARED FOR JACQUELINE KENNEDY,
OTIS AIR FORCE BASE, JULY 1963

that I would like to turn that, I'd like to send that furniture back. Have they paid for it?

SYLVESTER: I'll find out, Mr. President.

JFK: Just on my own. I don't care what we owe on the store, I'd just like to send that goddamn furniture back. It's probably worth fifteen hundred, two thousand bucks.

SYLVESTER: When I asked them yesterday, "Where did the $5,000 go?" from the things they told me, I said it, well, you couldn't have possibly spent $5,000 on that. They lied about it. Now I've gone back to them this morning, said, get the facts, I'm sick of it.

JFK: Let's find out. Yeah.

SYLVESTER: Tell the President at the White House the wrong facts, and let's get the facts to begin with.

JFK: Let's find out how much they spent on this thing. I mean, let's find out what they spent, where the money came from also.

SYLVESTER: We'll get a rundown.

JFK: Where, if the bills have been paid, because a lot of this stuff we can just ship right back today.

SYLVESTER: Right, I'll get right on it.

JFK: I'd love to send it right back to Jordan Marsh[4] in an air force truck this afternoon with that captain on it.

SYLVESTER: [laughs]

JFK: [chuckles] Now, what about transferring his ass out of here in about a month? He doesn't have any sense.

SYLVESTER: Carlton.

JFK: For incompetence, not for screwing us.

SYLVESTER: Exactly. Well, I . . .

JFK: And that silly fellow who had his picture taken next to the bed, have him go up to Alaska too. Pierre will be talking to you about that.

SYLVESTER: Right.

[new call]

JFK: General?

GENERAL GODFREY MCHUGH:[5] Yes, sir.

JFK: That air force has caused itself more grief with that silly bastard. Did you see the *Post* this morning?

MCHUGH: Yes, sir, I'm . . .

JFK: See that fellow's picture by the bed?

MCHUGH: Yes, sir.

JFK: And did you see that furniture they bought from Jordan Marsh? What the hell did they let the reporters in there for? Are they crazy up there? Now you know what that's gonna do? Any congressman is going to get up and say, "Christ, if they can throw $5,000 away on this, let's cut 'em another billion dollars." You just sank the air force budget! You're crazy up there! Are they crazy? That silly bastard with his picture next to the bed?

MCHUGH: Sir, I'm appalled but . . .

JFK: Well, I'm appalled, too.

MCHUGH: Yes, sir.

---

4. Jordan Marsh was a department store in downtown Boston.

5. Godfrey McHugh (1911–1997) was a brigadier general in the U.S. Air Force and the air force aide to President Kennedy.

JFK: Now, the thing is, the thing of the matter is, I'm gonna get that furniture, and I just told Sylvester and you can talk to him. I want to find out if we paid for that furniture because I want it to go back to Jordan Marsh.

MCHUGH: All right, sir.

JFK: Then I want, that fellow's incompetent who had his picture taken next to Mrs. Kennedy's bed, if that's what it is. I mean, he's a silly bastard! I wouldn't have him running a cathouse! And that Colonel Carlson [sic], who let in Larry Newman and those reporters. Is he crazy, too? Christ, they're all incompetents! Is that the way they are throwing money around over there? You better look into it, and especially when you told me that they hadn't spent a cent.

MCHUGH: Why, sir, this is obviously . . .

JFK: Well, this is obviously a fuckup.

MCHUGH: That's right.

JFK: That's right.

CALL ABOUT FILMING OF *PT-109*, DATE UNKNOWN

The story of *PT-109* and JFK's heroics rescuing his crewmates had been integral to his rise as national political figure in the 1950s, and the campaign of 1960. When Hollywood decided to issue a film version of the story, JFK was interested to a highly personal degree, and even was given the right to choose the lead actor, Cliff Robertson (Peter Fonda and Warren Beatty were also considered). The film was released in 1963 and achieved only modest success. This conversation shows him following the course of the film's production, concerned that the film will be too long.

JFK: Yeah.

AL[6]: But the big miss that I made is Lawford[7] had already talked to Steve Trilling.

JFK: Yeah.

AL: So that when I got to Warner,[8] Warner said, "Well," he says, "you know where this is coming from?" And I said, "Well, I know the President and his family are very concerned about this." And he said, "Well," he says, "it's coming from Lawford because Lawford already talked to Trilling."

JFK: Who's Trilling?

AL: Trilling is Warner's number-one boy.

JFK: Yeah, yeah.

AL: So Peter had already talked to Trilling . . .

JFK: Yeah, well I told him not to.

AL: . . . and delayed some of the impact that, I got . . .

JFK: Yeah.

AL: . . . by putting your message in.

JFK: Yeah.

---

6. "Al" is unidentified.

7. Peter Lawford (1923–1984) was an English-American film actor married to President Kennedy's sister Patricia Kennedy (1924–2006). They divorced in 1966.

8. Jack L. Warner (1892–1978) was a Canadian-American film executive who was the president and driving force behind the Warner Bros. Studios in Hollywood, Los Angeles, California.

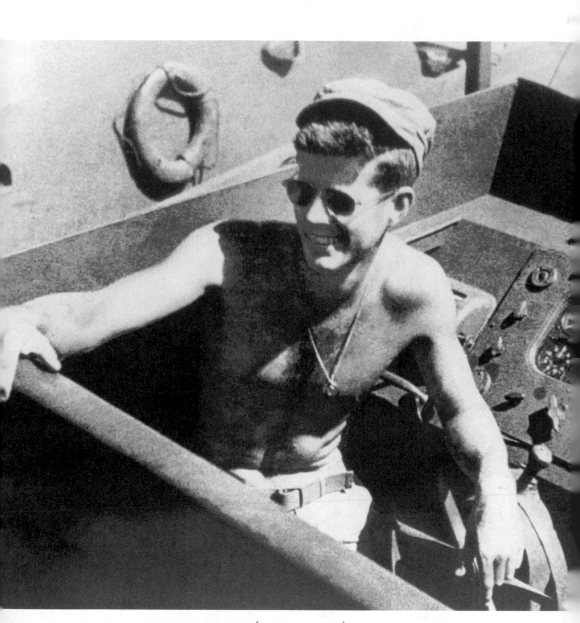

NAVY LIEUTENANT (JUNIOR GRADE) JOHN F. KENNEDY
AT THE HELM OF *PT 109*, SOLOMON ISLANDS, 1943

CREW OF *PT 109*, SOLOMON ISLANDS, 1943

PT 109, SOLOMON ISLANDS, 1943

AL: However, I will keep following them and, uh, keep you advised.

JFK: Well, they know what they're doing, but I do think, myself, that two minutes, two hours and twenty minutes for that kind of a picture is pretty long. Of course, they all get to think it's a work of art and they can't change anything.

AL: [laughs]

JFK: But that seems like a long night, and there's no doubt Pat felt it.

AL: [laughs] Right. Well, we'll keep chiseling away on him and I think we can get him to cut some of . . .

JFK: Can he get somebody out there to look at it that he's got confidence in?

AL: What?

JFK: Can he get somebody out there to look at it that he has confidence in?

AL: You mean some, an objective viewpoint?

JFK: Yeah, some fellow who just knows something about movies.

AL: Well, unfortunately, by this time he has shown it to enough people that have patted him on the back. You know, the old Hollywood yes men.

JFK: Yeah.

AL: And of course, some of his hardheaded distributor people have looked at it and they're usually pretty damn objective in their comments . . .

JFK: Yeah.

AL: . . . and they have said it was good and so he's kind of got his neck bowed right now.

JFK: Yeah.

AL: He feels that he's got a good product.

JFK: Yeah.

AL: But we'll . . .

JFK: Well, he has got a good product, it's just a question of whether there's too much of it. Well, in any case, that's his judgment finally.

AL: We'll keep working on it.

JFK: Okay, good, Al.

AL: Fine, bye.

MEETING WITH ECONOMIC ADVISORS, DECEMBER 12, 1962[9]

JFK: I'd like to make sure that, in that, I don't know, if we have a recession in '63, then we can assume we won't be having one in '64, but we can go through '63 and sort of a plateau, and it looks kind of tough in '64. I'd hate to see us go to the people in '64 . . . you know, the one that would ball break [garbled] me more would be to have people think we're in a recession . . . [garbled] I'd like to be in a position to have something in that economy, I think it ruined Nixon in '60, in the major industrial states. . . .

If you're running for reelection in 1964, what's the thing you worry most about? The recession? That's what I'm worried about. [several voices] Otherwise we're liable to get all the blame for the deficit, and none of the advantage of the stimulus for the economy.

MEETING WITH TREASURY SECRETARY DOUGLAS DILLON, SEPTEMBER 3, 1963

JFK: Well, the problem that I'm concerned about is, that we're all going to be judged, I'm going to be judged, if they're able to produce a crisis [unclear] in '64, that's going to say, because of, you know, all the problems we've had, here we've had price stability, and yet they keep mouthing the same old things. If I have to have happen to me what happened to the Eisenhower administration in the fall of '60 [unclear], it would have cost the election. So I hate to get myself as vulnerable as that, at the mercy of bankers who I know would like to probably screw us anyway.

---

9. This meeting included three advisors. Wilbur Mills (1909–1992) was a Democratic member of the United States House of Representatives from the state of Arkansas and chairman of the House Ways and Means Committee. Lawrence O'Brien (1917–1990) was special assistant to the President for congressional relations and personnel. O'Brien was also one of the Democratic Party's leading electoral strategists and served as the director of Kennedy's successful U.S. Senate election and reelection campaigns and nationally as the director of his presidential campaign. Ted Sorensen (1928–2010) was President John F. Kennedy's special counsel.

MEETING WITH POLITICAL ADVISORS
TO DISCUSS 1964 CONVENTION[10]

JFK: Steve,[11] on this question of the films and who's going to do them. I thought that film *Five Days* or *Cities in June* was—have you seen that film? The guy who wrote the music was called Vershon or something, but God it's good. Why don't you get it from George Stevens. *Five Cities in June.* Look at it. I think the guy's fantastic. I'd like to see what else he's done, whether that just happened to be lucky. . . . Should they be made in color? They'd come over the television in black-and-white. I don't know if maybe they'd come over the NBC one in color. Probably a million watching it in color and it would have an effect. I don't know how much more expensive it is. Be quite an effect on the convention. The color is so damn good. If you do it right. . . . You'd have a film the first night, ahead of the keynoter. . . .

I think you can get the real story told if it's a good speaker. That's why the film's gonna be—and you might lead off with the film, then the keynoter, because people are sick of it after half hour of watching anyway; if you lead off with the film, then the keynoter. . . . There's no doubt, I don't think there's anything wrong with a short one [film] on Franklin Roosevelt.

JOHN BAILEY: Well what you could do is on the Democratic Party is have the five Presidents of—that we've had since Cleveland, Wilson . . .

JFK: Well, this century. I think, I think Wilson, Roosevelt, Truman . . . but I think that Wilson's good if you can get a lot of good film. Roosevelt, Truman, I think that's a good idea—four Democratic Presidents—that's a good idea.

BAILEY: And that way you—can bring you in at the end. . . .

JFK: But what is it that we can make them decide they want to vote for us, Democrats and Kennedy? The Democrats [are] not as strong in appeal, obviously, as it was twenty years ago. The younger people, party label—what is it that's going

---

10. This meeting included Robert Kennedy, Lawrence O'Brien, DNC Chairman John Bailey, Kenneth O'Donnell, and Ted Sorensen.

11. Stephen E. Smith (1927–1990) was married to President Kennedy's sister Jean. He was expected to serve as the campaign manager for the 1964 election.

to make them go for us? What is it we have to sell them? We hope we have to sell them prosperity, but for the average guy, the prosperity is nil. He's not unprosperous, but he's not very prosperous; he's not going make out well off. And the people who really are well off hate our guts.

So that, what is it? There's a lot of Negroes, we're the ones that are shoving the Negroes down his throat. What is it he's got, though? We've got peace, you know what I mean, we say we hope the country's prosperous, I'm trying to think of what else. I think probably, we've got so mechanical an operation here in Washington that it doesn't have much identity where these people are concerned. And they don't feel particularly—I'm not, they really didn't have it with Truman, only in that retrospect they have Truman . . . hell of a time. Franklin Roosevelt had it, even Wilson had it, but I think it's tough for a Democrat with that press apparatus working. So I'm just trying to think what is it?—

[tape ends]

PRESIDENT KENNEDY AT THE HMS *RESOLUTE* DESK

"OUR LOT BECOMES MORE DIFFICULT," PRIVATE DICTATION, NOVEMBER 12, 1963

This dictated memorandum, never before published, was recorded privately, in the same format that Kennedy reserved for events of high significance. It reveals him to be in a state of some apprehension and perhaps even low morale as he contemplated a bleaker than expected political picture in November 1963. The progress of the Civil Rights Movement had created major problems in the South, where reliable Democrats were becoming Republicans, and required considerable attention as he turned his thoughts to the hard campaign he would face in 1964. The exasperation with which he says the date, "Tuesday, November 12," is quite out of character with the driving confidence so clearly on display in the vast majority of the recordings.

JFK: Politically, the news is somewhat disturbing, looking toward 1964. The election in Texas on the poll tax. The Republican meeting in Charleston, South Carolina, which, the Republicans were more optimistic than usual about the South. The slowness of the Congress, which is giving it a bad name, and therefore the administration, which is also Democratic. The hatchet job on the foreign aid bill, which has gone on more than two weeks, led by the liberals, supported by the Southerners and conservative Republicans.

All these make the situation politically not as good as it might be. In addition, the cattle growers are angry because of the increase in imports and the depression of their prices, which, while it comes about from their overproduction, is blamed upon us.

Tuesday, November 12, having difficulties in Latin America or the Alliance for Progress.[12] The Argentines threatening to expropriate our oil. The Brazilians, the Brazilian [João] Goulart,[13] ignoring the Alliance for Progress. Obviously, both playing a very nationalist game. And then the rumor that the Dominican

---

12. The Alliance for Progress was a Kennedy administration initiative to improve relations with Latin America, emphasizing trade and development, and announced in 1961.

13. João Goulart (1919–1976) was president of Brazil from 1961 to 1964; his progressive policies often put him at odds with the United States at the time.

Republic may break relations with us. They're irritated with the United States for not recognizing, and making their lot more difficult. All this is, indicates a rising tide of nationalism and a lessening of their dependence upon the United States. In addition, they have a radical left who [unclear] at home, so that our lot becomes more difficult.

KENNEDY CAMPAIGN SONG, 1960

Kennedy, Kennedy, Kennedy, Kennedy, Kennedy, Kennedy,
Ken-ne-dy for me!
Kennedy, Kennedy, Kennedy, Kennedy, Kennedy!

Do you want a man for president,
Who's seasoned through and through?
But not so doggone seasoned,
That he won't try something new.
A man who's old enough to know,
And young enough to do.
Well, it's up to you, it's up to you,
It's strictly up to you.

Do you like a man who answers straight,
A man who's always fair?
We'll measure him against the others,
And when you compare,
You cast your vote for Kennedy,
And the change that's overdue,
So, it's up to you, it's up to you,
It's strictly up to you.

And it's Kennedy, Kennedy, Kennedy, Kennedy, Kennedy, Kennedy,
Ken-ne-dy for me!
Kennedy, Kennedy, Kennedy, Kennedy, Kennedy, Kennedy, Kennedy!
Kennedy!

CAROLINE KENNEDY WITH HER FATHER
IN THE OVAL OFFICE, OCTOBER 10, 1962

ACKNOWLEDGMENTS

This book would not have been possible without the help of the extraordinarily talented and devoted team at the John F. Kennedy Presidential Library and Museum, who work tirelessly to preserve history and make my father's legacy accessible to new generations of Americans.

I am especially grateful to Tom Putnam, the Library's outstanding director, who gave this project his full support; Chief Archivist Karen Adler Abramson, who made her exceptional staff available to assist with the research and compilation of materials; Maura Porter, who has been overseeing the declassification of the White House recordings since 2001, and whose encyclopedic knowledge of their content was invaluable; Maryrose Grossman, Laurie Austin, and Bill Bjelf of the Audiovisual Archives, who helped find, compile, and duplicate the key recordings and photographs; Audiovisual interns Hannah Weddle and Sara Ludovissy for their help with the sound recordings and scanning of images; and to Stephen Plotkin and Stacey Chandler of the Research Room, who went out of their way to find the best documents and memoranda to give historical context to the recordings.

I am also grateful to Tom McNaught, executive director of the Kennedy Library Foundation, who oversaw every aspect of this project with his customary commitment to excellence, and to Karen Mullen for her help and assistance.

I am particularly indebted to Cliff Sloan for his judgment and legal expertise, and to Rachel Day Flor and Debra Deshong Reed for their expert assistance in promoting and publicizing these historical records.

I always give thanks for Lauren Lipani, whose keen intelligence, good humor, and skillful organization is indispensable in keeping everything on track.

Listening In is the third book that the Library has done in partnership with Hyperion, and I am grateful to all those who have made these projects successful—most of all to Gretchen Young, who has been a dedicated champion, gifted editor, and wonderful friend.

She was assisted once again by the talented team of Shubhani Sarkar, who brings an inspired sense of design to all her books, and Laura Klynstra, whose cover captures the spirit of this project. The hard production work behind the scenes was so capably done by Navorn Johnson, David Lott, Allyson Rudolph, and Linda Prather. Once again, Jill Sansone did a wonderful job on the audio, and Joan Lee, Maha Khalil, SallyAnne McCartin, and Mike Rotondo made sure this important history was available to the widest possible audience.

—CAROLINE KENNEDY

SELECTED BIBLIOGRAPHY

Bradlee, Benjamin C. *Conversations with Kennedy*. New York: Norton, 1975.

Branch, Taylor. *Parting the Waters: America in the King Years, 1954–1963*. New York: Simon and Schuster, 1988.

Caro, Robert A. *The Passage of Power: The Years of Lyndon Johnson*. New York: Alfred A. Knopf, 2012.

Dallek, Robert. *An Unfinished Life: John F. Kennedy, 1917–1963*. Boston: Little, Brown and Co., 2003.

Dobbs, Michael. *One Minute to Midnight: Kennedy, Khrushchev and Castro on the Brink of Nuclear War*. New York: Alfred A. Knopf, 2008.

Freedman, Lawrence. *Kennedy's Wars: Berlin, Cuba, Laos and Vietnam*. New York: Oxford University Press, 2000.

Fursenko, Aleksandr, and Timothy Naftali. *"One Hell of a Gamble": Khrushchev, Castro and Kennedy, 1958–1964*. New York: W.W. Norton, 1997.

Kennedy, Caroline, and Michael Beschloss. *Jacqueline Kennedy: Historic Conversations On Life with John F. Kennedy*. New York: Hyperion, 2011.

Kennedy, Robert F. *Thirteen Days: A Memoir of the Cuban Missile Crisis*. New York: W.W. Norton, 1969.

Lincoln, Evelyn. *My Twelve Years with John F. Kennedy*. New York: D. McKay, 1965.

Mackenzie, G. Calvin, and Robert Weisbrot. *The Liberal Hour: Washington and the Politics of Change in the 1960s*. New York: Penguin, 2008.

May, Ernest R., and Philip D. Zelikow, eds. *The Kennedy Tapes: Inside the White House During the Cuban Missile Crisis*. Cambridge: Belknap Press of Harvard University Press, 1997.

Naftali, Timothy, ed. *The Presidential Recordings: John F. Kennedy: The Great Crises* (3 vols). New York: W.W. Norton, 2001.

Prados, John, ed. *The White House Tapes: Eavesdropping on the President*. New York: New Press, 2003.

Public Papers of the Presidents: John F. Kennedy (1961–1963). Washington: U.S. Govt. Printing Office, 1962–1964.

Reeves, Richard. *President Kennedy: Profile of Power*. New York: Simon and Schuster, 1993.

Rosenberg, Jonathan, and Zachary Karabell, eds. *Kennedy, Johnson, and the Quest for Justice: The Civil Rights Tapes.* New York: W.W. Norton, 2003.

Schlesinger, Arthur M., Jr. *A Thousand Days: John F. Kennedy in the White House.* Boston: Houghton, Mifflin and Co., 1965.

Sorensen, Ted. *Counselor: A Life at the Edge of History.* New York: HarperCollins, 2008.

Sorensen, Theodore C. *Kennedy.* New York: Harper and Row, 1965.

Stern, Sheldon M. *Averting "The Final Failure": John F. Kennedy and the Secret Cuban Missile Crisis Meetings.* Stanford: Stanford University Press, 2003.

PHOTOGRAPHIC CREDITS

AP Images: 132

> Bettmann/Corbis/AP Images: 102–103

> Bill Hudson/AP Photo: 111

Bettmann/Corbis: 274 (*right*)

Elliot Erwitt/Magnum Photos: 284

John F. Kennedy Presidential Library and Museum, Boston: iii, v, vi, vii, 19, 20, 21–22, 45, 59, 63 (photographer unknown), 148, 149, 162, 190, 191, 192, 193, 222, 231, 237, 238 (*top and bottom*), 239, 241, 249, 261, 274 (*left*), 278, 279 (*top and bottom*)

> Jacqueline Kennedy/John F. Kennedy Presidential Library and Museum: 139

> Robert Knudsen, White House/John F. Kennedy Presidential Library and Museum, Boston: ii, xix, 15, 25, 58–59, 97, 184–185, 199, 211, 227, 253, 267

> Abbie Rowe, White House/John F. Kennedy Presidential Library and Museum, Boston: 52, 56, 61, 66, 109, 130–131, 169, 177, 195, 221, 244, 257

> Cecil Stoughton, White House/John F. Kennedy Presidential Library and Museum, Boston: xvii, 7, 29, 74, 75, 85, 100, 160–161, 168–169, 204–205, 217, 229, 288

> U.S. Department of Defense/John F. Kennedy Presidential Library and Museum, Boston: 135, 142–143, 187

Library of Congress, Washington, DC: 170, 171, 172, 173

Jacques Lowe: i

Rolls Press/Popperfoto/Getty Images: 197

Stanley Tretick/*Look* magazine: 247

INDEX

NOTE: Page numbers in italics refer to illustrations. The letter *n* indicates footnotes.